Thinking about the Future:
Guidelines for Strategic Foresight

Edited by Andy Hines and Peter Bishop

Social Technologies, LLC
1776 Massachusetts Avenue, NW
Suite 815
Washington, DC 20036
www.socialtechnologies.com

ISBN-13: 978-0-9789317-0-4
ISBN-10: 0-9789317-0-X

Brief Contents

Preface

It is a rare pleasure to welcome this book of guidelines for excellence in strategic foresight. Something like this has long been needed. As part of the run-up to creating the Australian Foresight Institute (AFI) I tried my hand at some possible definitions. One was that:

Strategic foresight is the ability to create and sustain a variety of high quality forward views and to apply the emerging insights in organisationally useful ways; for example, to detect adverse conditions, guide policy, shape strategy; to explore new markets, products and services.[1]

This is not a perfect definition. It doesn't mention social foresight, which later became a primary focus as we saw how, properly understood, this modality can rise up from its relatively humble human origins and become a social principle of remarkable power. What we also grappled with was how to access and distill widely scattered professional knowledge and capability in a way that would be broadly useful both to our students and, possibly, to others. That goal has finally been achieved by Andy Hines and Peter Bishop.

There are several other reasons why I am delighted to welcome this book. First, it is, in part, a marvelous response to a challenge I attempted to set out in a paper for futures on "professional standards in futures work" published in 1999.[2] There I drew on some of the earlier work of futurists such as Eleonora Masini, Yehezkel Dror, and Wendell Bell, to propose a broad framework for approaching the topic, but it fell a long way short of providing the kind of detailed practical recommendations set out here.

Second, the editors have synthesized some of the best applied thinking available and, in the process, have created one of the first, if not THE first, truly "broad church" and "ecumenical" futures texts. What makes it distinctive is that it moves lightly and with ease across so many of the fruitless lines of difference and paradigm conflicts that have divided our field and, in so doing, draws upon any and all who have something useful to contribute.

Third, they do this in a way that's both critically and integrally informed throughout. This is a real achievement in its own right. Critical and integral futures perspectives bring into play "interior individual" and "interior collective" factors that have a great deal to offer but have often been misunderstood or set aside. Practitioners have not been universally willing to accept these gifts, to take on the challenges they imply, or to explore their implications—not only for background theorizing but also for day-to-day practice across the board. The book clearly demonstrates some of the payoffs of accessing and applying these powerful new perspectives.

Fourth, it addresses the concerns of practitioners in a clear and accessible manner. I imagine that virtually everyone engaged in applied foresight work will want to read it through in its entirety and then return, over and over again, to key sections. Equally, those who ignore it, believing that their own toolkit is already complete and needs no further improvement, will discover over time that they produce inferior results. In other words, this book helps move the field towards a new stage of practical competence and capability.

Finally, it reads very well. There are few signs of the extensive editing, the cutting, pasting, and liaison necessarily involved in a project of this kind. Overall we must be profoundly grateful to Andy Hines and Peter Bishop for their time, effort and—most of all—their vision. The book will be of enormous and enduring value to practitioners everywhere. It will also help propel the field into a future where work of the quality suggested here is not merely available to the few but eagerly sought and promoted by organizations of all kinds.

This is a future in which the foresight profession thrives and, in so doing, illuminates new options for an ever more hard-pressed world.

Richard A Slaughter
Foresight International, Brisbane, February 2006

Notes

1. Australian Foresight Institute, publicity flyer, Melbourne, December 1999.
2. Slaughter, R. Professional Standards in Futures Work, *Futures*, 31, 1999, 835 - 51. Revised and updated as Chapter 3 of Slaughter, R. (2004). *Futures beyond Dystopia: Creating Social Foresight*. London: Routledge.

Contributors

This book rests upon a firm foundation provided by its contributors. The guidelines presented here represent the collective wisdom of a select group of leading foresight practitioners and academics. These foresight professionals were enthusiastic about the theme, and assured us that practitioners need a clear compilation of the best guidelines for strategic foresight. Their confidence and willingness to help inspired us throughout this project.

Our charge to contributors was to share what they know about long-term thinking and foresight with a broader business audience. Additionally, we wanted them to organize and synthesize what we know to be good foresight practice.

Contributors participated in two phases. The first was a brainstorm of potential guidelines. We cast a wide net and asked for what was known and agreed upon as established best practice in strategic foresight. In the second phase, many wrote in more depth about at least one guideline by responding to questions we devised; these contributors have asterisks beside their names in the list below. They and their institutions represent a veritable Who's Who of the foresight field. It goes without saying that we are even more grateful to them for their extended commitment to the project—but we're going to say it anyway: thank you very much!

The rich diversity of contributors has enabled this volume to showcase a range of views that would be simply impossible for two authors to come up with on their on. At the same time, it presents a challenge in terms of providing a consistent "voice." This challenge is particularly exacerbated since a significant portion of the contributors outside the US have English as a second language. In our multiple rewrites and edits of the book, the editors have done our best to provide a consistent voice. Any potential injustice to the contributors is our responsibility, but we believe that ultimately the readers are best served by this attempt to present a consistent voice.

Tom Abeles*	*On the Horizon*
Enrique Bas*	Université d'Alacant
Michele Bowman*	Global Foresight Associates
Lynn Burton*	Simon Fraser University
Joseph Coates	Joseph Coates Consulting Futurist, Inc.
Tom Conger	Social Technologies, LLC
Cornelia Daheim	Z Punkt: The Foresight Company
Peter de Jager*	de Jager and Company, Ltd.
Kate Delaney*	Delaney and Associates
Jay Forrest*	JayForrest.com
Jim Gelatt*	University of Maryland University College
Jerry Glenn	The Millennium Project
Michel Godet	Conservatoire National des Arts et Métiers
Jack Gottsman	The Clarity Group

Ken Hamik	LipidViro Tech, Inc.
Peter Hayward*	Swinburne University
Jennifer Jarratt	Leading Futurists
David Jarvis*	IBM Business Consulting Services
Trudi Lang*	Curtin Business School
Richard Lum*	Vision Foresight Strategy LLC
John Mahaffie*	Leading Futurists
Mika Mannermaa*	Futures Studies Mannermaa Ltd.
Eleonora Masini*	Gregorian University
Pero Micic*	Future Management Group AG
Danny Miller*	École des Hautes Études Commerciales
Stephen Millett	Battelle Columbus
Mary Jane Naquin	Informed Futures
Erszebet Novaky*	Corvinus University of Budapest
Ian Pearson*	BTexact
John Petersen	The Arlington Institute
Alan Porter	Georgia Institute of Technology
Dominique Purcell*	Visioware
Wendy Schultz	Infinite Futures
Charles Snow	Pennsylvania State University
Rohit Talwar	Fast Future
Ruud Vanderhelm*	ENGREF

Acknowledgements

This book is the work of roughly three dozen foresight professionals who strove to convey their knowledge and experience through a simple, usable set of guidelines to improve—or in some cases introduce—the practice of strategic foresight. We are particularly indebted to our many colleagues at the Association of Professional Futurists (APF) who provided inspiration, support, and, of course, many of the guidelines. We also owe thanks to students and alumni of the Futures Studies Master's program at the University of Houston, which has provided a steady stream of both providers and consumers of the knowledge and wisdom contained in this book. And let us not forget the many clients who spent their hard-earned dollars learning about and applying strategic foresight, and providing us the opportunity to learn while we earned. Finally, we thank Gary Hamel, David Learned, and Will Lidwell of the Applied Management Sciences Institute for having the foresight and courage to conceive and help launch this project.

To synthesize the diverse inputs provided by these groups has been the job of the editors. After reviewing all of the guidelines and reviewer feedback, we made the final decisions about which guidelines to include and exclude. Additionally, we edited the submissions with an eye to presenting readers with guidelines that are consistent in both style and substance. Any errors of omission or commission in this process are ours and ours alone.

We hope this book meets with the approval of all these participants. Without their hard work and dedication, it would not have been possible.

Andy Hines

Peter Bishop

Introduction

There has perhaps never been a time in human history where strategic foresight is more needed. Whether for business, government, education, nonprofits, or even individuals, the ability to—as Richard Slaughter suggests in the preface—"create and sustain a variety of high-quality forward views and to apply the emerging insights in useful ways" is at a premium. Yet precious little guidance is available on the best ways to do this. This book is not an explicit methodology text, but rather suggests what executives and analysts should be thinking about and doing when contemplating or performing activities involving strategic foresight. It aims at communicating the collective wisdom of three dozen expert contributors for attaining excellence in strategic foresight. Thus, its primary goal is to provide readers with clear and useful guidance regarding how best to practice strategic foresight.

This guidance is presented in the form of guidelines that represent a distillation of best practice. The presentation style is brief and to the point—designed to provide essential, need-to-know information that can be immediately put into practice. We believe that analysts and organizations that follow these guidelines will be more effective than those that do not.

Many practicing analysts today have little experience or formal training in strategic foresight. This work addresses that gap by cataloging the best guidelines for successfully applying strategic foresight, offered by professionals in the field today. It is intended both for those new to strategic foresight who would benefit from a reference guide, and for more experienced practitioners who will be able to pick out ideas to refine and improve their practices. As organizations become more efficient, payrolls are shrinking and more analysts are being tasked with activities that require strategic foresight. At the same time, analysts find themselves with few places to turn for readily available and applicable guides on how to do it. Providing that guidance is the primary aim of this book.

How the book is organized

The book is organized by the six groups or steps of activities identified by Association of Professional Futurists' Professional Development team over the course of 2004 and 2005 as fundamental to a comprehensive strategic foresight activity. The guidelines submitted by our contributors fit easily into this framework—which the editors have also adopted as part of the curriculum for the University of Houston's Master's degree program in Futures Studies. The six steps are: *Framing*, *Scanning*, *Forecasting*, *Visioning*, *Planning*, and *Acting*. Some strategic foresight activities, of course, are not and need not be comprehensive. If, for example, all that is required is Forecasting, then that chapter of the book can be referred to.

This framework focuses on those aspects of strategic foresight our contributors deemed most critical for success. *Framing* contains guidelines regarding attitude, audience, work environment, rationale and purpose, objectives, and teams. *Scanning* contains guidelines concerning the system, history, and context of the issue and how to scan for information regarding the future of the issue. *Forecasting* uses the information from Scanning and outlines guidelines regarding drivers and uncertainties, tools, diverging and converging approaches, and alternatives. *Visioning* contains guidelines focused on thinking through the implications of the forecast and envisioning designed outcomes for the organization. *Planning* contains guidelines that develop the strategy and options for carrying out the vision. Lastly, *Acting* contains guidelines communicating the results, developing action agendas, and institutionalizing strategic thinking and intelligence systems.

The format

The guidelines are numbered within each section for convenient reference. The format for each guideline is consistent:

- Statement of the guideline
- Description in a paragraph or two
- Key steps: how to follow the guideline
- Benefits: expected outcomes of following the guideline
- Example: how the guideline has been employed in practice
- Further reading: for follow-up investigation

The six sections are arranged in a step-wise fashion; that is, in most business applications one would typically undertake the Framing guidelines (section one) first and the Acting guidelines (section six) last. But these sections and the guidelines within them are not intended to be followed in a rigorous chronological order. Rather, they are presented in the order judged to be most commonly encountered in performing a strategic foresight activity. One activity in particular, Visioning, is sometimes done immediately after Framing rather than after Forecasting, although the latter is more common.

The guidelines are "best practices," distilled from the experiences of contributors across business, government, and nonprofit sectors in a myriad of organizational settings. They are not like laws of physics or mathematics—true in all cases, all of the time. On the other hand, they are true in most cases, most of the time—and for that reason alone, valuable to know.

How executives and analysts can use this book

This book provides guidelines for executives and analysts tasked with carrying out a strategic foresight activity or at least being involved with one. It assumes they will be carrying out the activity for a client organization, whether as a member of the organization or as an external consultant. It is a reference guide clearly aimed along the lines of "here are the things one should try to do." It further recognizes that, in practice, it will rarely be possible to do everything exactly as it should be. Here, executives and analysts must know when to push and when to back off. Comparing these guidelines with an organization's current practice will provide valuable insights and opportunities for improvement. A few specific suggestions on how this book can be used by analysts:

- *Design strategic foresight projects*
  Executives and practitioners who find themselves tasked with projects or issues requiring strategic foresight can use the book to scope and design the activity.

- *Provide how-to answers to specific tasks*
  The book focuses on specific tasks that need to be accomplished. It suggests how to accomplish them in a concise, straightforward manner designed to translate into immediate action.

- *Use as a reference guide*
  Executives and analysts engaged in a strategic foresight activity, or an activity requiring strategic foresight, can use the book as a credible reference guide to get up to speed quickly on what leading practitioners recommend.

- *Provide a refresher for experienced practitioners*
  The book will be a handy reference for even the most advanced foresight practitioner in need of a quick refresher or of

help exploring an unfamiliar facet of strategic foresight. Analysts can review these guidelines to gain insight into different ways of approaching strategic foresight problems, and for self-evaluation and coaching on their existing practice.

- *Adopt guidelines for excellence as an organization*
Consider adopting the guidelines in this book at the organizational level, adapting them as needed to best fit the needs of the organization.

These suggestions are intended to directly impact the performance of executives, analysts, and their organizations. The outcome should be observable improvements in the performance of analysts and in the results of the strategic foresight activities they help their organizations perform.

How educators can use this book

The guidelines in this book can also be used to help students learn the effective practice of strategic foresight. Practicing and critiquing the guidelines in a classroom setting coupled with observing and testing them in real contexts will provide valuable learning experience. A few specific suggestions on how this book can be used by educators:

- *Examine theory and research*
Assign individuals or groups to examine the evidence behind different guidelines and report on their findings.

- *Corroborate or falsify guidelines*
As individuals or teams, present evidence and argue the case for or against selected guidelines, showing the tradeoffs in pursuing one guideline over another.

- *Role play*
Develop role-play scenarios in which students apply and act out guidelines. The class can critique the role play and discuss the abilities and skills that participants should strengthen.

- *Interview analysts*
Assign the class to interview practitioners about a specific guideline or set of guidelines. Does the analyst use the guidelines or something similar? How? Why? When? Prepare and present a report on the findings to the class.

- *Develop additional guidelines*
Establish teams to work on the development of additional guidelines using the same architecture and standards found in this book. The group's additions can be rated and graded on the following criteria: strength of evidence, relevance, practicality, and ethics/legality.

These suggestions are intended to improve learning through in-class or external exercises and interactions. The outcome will be more knowledge about guidelines of good practice, as well as the evaluative skills that govern their use.

The Guidelines

1.0 Framing

1.1 Adjust attitudes

    1.1.1 Have positive expectations about the future

    1.1.2 Know your biases

    1.1.3 Recognize that self-delusion and wishful thinking are barriers to strategic foresight

    1.1.4 Use whole-brain processes

    1.1.5 Embrace complexity in addition to linear thinking

    1.1.6 Recognize that different changes occur at different rates with different impacts at different times

1.2 Know the audience

    1.2.1 Learn as much as possible about the organization

    1.2.2 Find out what the organization is trying to get done, and what's keeping its people awake at night

    1.2.3 Don't try to make clients into foresight professionals

1.3 Understand the rationale and purpose

    1.3.1 Explore the future to influence the present

    1.3.2 Seek to improve the mental model of decision-makers

    1.3.3 Balance exploration and exploitation

    1.3.4 Evaluate whether the problem as presented is really the problem to be solved

1.4 Set objectives

    1.4.1 Define objective in terms that can be measured

    1.4.2 Focus on outcomes, not outputs

    1.4.3 Work in multiple time horizons

    1.4.4 Weave "outside and then" with "inside and now"

1.5 Select your team

    1.5.1 Recognize that strategic foresight is a team sport

    1.5.2 Make strategic foresight as immersive and interactive as possible

    1.5.3 Include people who do not agree

1.6 Create a strategic work environment

    1.6.1 Create an environment conducive to open and uninhibited thinking

    1.6.2 Encourage experiments and prototypes

2.0 Scanning

2.1 Map the system

    2.1.1 Adopt a global perspective

    2.1.2 Map the system under consideration

    2.1.3 Take an integral view of the issue

    2.1.4 Conduct a stakeholder analysis

2.2 Study history

    2.2.1 Start by looking backwards

    2.2.2 Don't reinvent the wheel

    2.2.3 Be wary of past success that leads to thinking in a rut

2.3 Scan the environment

    2.3.1 Scan the environment for awareness of how the context is changing

    2.3.2 Integrate the external and internal

    2.3.3 Explore unfamiliar and "uninteresting" areas

    2.3.4 Don't try to win with research—not all the data exists

2.4 Involve colleagues and outsiders

    2.4.1 Consult "remarkable people"

    2.4.2 Consult unusual sources, people and places—including outliers, complainers, and troublemakers

    2.4.3 Design workshops so learning can be integrated in a group setting

3.0 Forecasting

3.1 Identify drivers and uncertainties

    3.1.1 Uncover the underlying drivers

    3.1.2 Use a layered approach to get below the surface and see the different types and levels of change

    3.1.3 Assess fundamental shifts that could impact business-as-usual

    3.1.4 Look for colliding change trajectories

    3.1.5 Look for turning points

    3.1.6 Improve decision-making by reducing uncertainty

3.2 Choose forecasting tool(s)

    3.2.1 Use the right approach and tool(s)

    3.2.2 Use at least one formal method

    3.2.3 Adapt existing methods and models to the situation

4.2 Challenge assumptions

    4.2.1 Uncover and clarify assumptions

    4.2.2 Challenge conventional wisdom

    4.2.3 Assume nothing; question everything

    4.2.4 Identify and tear down taboos ghosting the organization

    4.2.5 Validate assumptions by cross–checking them

4.3 Think visionary

    4.3.1 Develop a strategic vision

    4.3.2 Put the strategic vision in a time continuum

    4.3.3 Set strategic goals as stretch goals

    4.3.4 You get what you think—leverage the positive

    4.3.5 Remember Dator's Law: any useful statement about the future should appear to be ridiculous

    4.3.6 Ask the "What if" questions

    4.3.7 Sense and enable the emerging future

5.0 Planning

5.1 Think strategically

    5.1.1 Enable emergence

    5.1.2 Make the sociocultural context central

    5.1.3 Crafting strategy is about stimulating strategic conversation

    5.1.4 Know what to change and what not to change

    5.1.5 Spot areas of strategic choice by identifying critical branching points

5.2 Develop strategic options

    5.2.1 Base strategic recommendations on the organization's distinctive attributes

    5.2.2 Evaluate proposed strategy along multiple dimensions

    5.2.3 Include the "no-go," the "most plausible" and the "preferred" when recommending options

    5.2.4 Have contingency plans for surprises

6.0 Acting

6.1 Communicate results

    6.1.1 Design results for communicability

    6.1.2 Tailor the message to the thinking styles of the audience

6.1.3 Immerse stakeholders and decision-makers in the alternatives to increase buy-in

6.1.4 Be provocative

6.1.5 Modularize outcomes—keep the good and deal with the bad

6.1.6 Build awareness of change through experience, insight, and reframing

6.2 Create an action agenda

6.2.1 Create a sense of urgency

6.2.2 Reinforce what the organization is already doing and build from there

6.2.3 Aim the activity at helping to make better decisions

6.2.4 Make decisions without all the desired data

6.2.5 Create milestones along the path to the preferred future, and celebrate small successes along the way

6.2.6 Recommend investing in at least one unlikely idea

6.3 Create an intelligence system

6.3.1 Create an intelligence system aligned by strategic foresight and linked to the planning process

6.3.2 Establish an early warning system to detect weak signals

6.3.3 Look for sources of turbulence in the system

6.3.4 Look for indicators that suggest a crisis may be pending

6.3.5 Choose indicators that are easy to understand and easy to collect

6.4 Institutionalize strategic thinking

6.4.1 Choose, design and make explicit a conceptual framework

6.4.2 Develop future cadence

6.4.3 Repeat strategic activities on a regular basis

6.4.4 Develop training programs to institutionalize strategic foresight

6.4.5 Reinforce that learning is the best approach for organizations in complex and unpredictable environments

6.4.6 Shift attitudes towards receptiveness to change

1 ▶ Framing

1.0 Framing

"If you don't know where you are going, you may end up somewhere else." —Yogi Berra

Framing enables analysts to define the scope and focus of problems requiring strategic foresight. The premise of Framing is that taking time at the outset of a project to clarify the objective and how best to address it will pay big dividends in the later phases. Most of all, Framing prevents misunderstandings that generate confusion and wasted work. Far too many strategic foresight activities—and business analyses in general—end up addressing and "solving" the wrong problem, or discovering the real issue halfway through the project, after investing significant time and resources. The organization then faces the prospect of starting over—with less confidence in the activity overall—or simply abandoning it altogether.

Strategic foresight activities are unique among business practices because they deal with the long-term future. For this reason, they naturally introduce fuzziness and expose uncertainty. For example, take the question "What will a particular technology mean for the world of business in ten years?" Framing issues that arise immediately are 1) defining the boundaries of the technology and what is meant by "world of business"; 2) understanding the depth and scope of research required and assessing available resources to accomplish it; and 3) considering the number of alternative scenarios or images likely to be required and what outcomes the client is likely to want. And these are only the beginning. Yet pressure to "get on with it" often leads both clients and practitioners to skim over Framing, or skip it altogether.

The six groups of guidelines in this section highlight why Framing is so important for solving organizational issues and how an practitioner can best accomplish it. The first set of guidelines, *1.1 Adjust Attitudes*, emphasizes the importance of making it clear upfront to those involved that strategic foresight is different from typical management approaches. Most organizations are more comfortable with straightforward challenges that can be answered "correctly" if the right skills and knowledge are applied. Strategic foresight, on the other hand, does not deliver cut-and-dried, right-and-wrong answers. Answers do not emerge immediately, and whether the organization is on the right path is not always clear as the activity proceeds. Dealing with the ambiguity inherent in strategic foresight requires an attitude different from simply finding the right data or information.

The second set of guidelines, *1.2 Know the Audience*, advises practitioners to understand the client or client organization well enough to customize and tailor the process and the results for the best chance of success. These guidelines suggest there is no cookie-cutter approach that works with everyone, and that the practitioner needs to understand in particular how the organization views the future.

The third set, *1.3 Understand the Rationale and Purpose*, gets to the heart of strategic foresight. It suggests a razor-sharp focus at the outset of the activity on its desired outcomes. Unlike many business challenges, where the form of answer is obvious—e.g., a spreadsheet with financial calculations—strategic foresight often aims at more subtle goals, such as informing the mental models of decision-makers. Analysts therefore need to stay focused and not get side-tracked into producing just data and spreadsheets.

The fourth set, *1.4 Set Objectives*, suggests the analyst translate the rationale and purpose into tangible outcomes. It is tempting, given the fuzzy nature of strategic foresight, to allow for fuzzy outcomes. Fuzzy approaches, however, will not succeed in today's bottom-line organizations. So the practitioner must be precise about what he or she can—and cannot—deliver.

The fifth set, *1.5 Select the Team*, reinforces the point that strategic foresight is a team sport. While the guidelines are written as if an individual is using them, it is assumed that practitioners will also have a small analysis team, and in practically all cases be working with a larger client team within the organization.

The last set, *1.6 Create a Strategic Work Environment*, reflects in the work environment itself how strategic foresight differs from other kinds of management activities. The open-endedness of strategic foresight requires a mindset that encourages imagination and creativity—along with logic and rigor—a synthesis that is beyond the norm for many organizations. The work environment can be a strong cue to team members, suggesting "something different is being asked for here."

These guidelines need not require a huge time investment. Certainly some can be incorporated more quickly than others. Nevertheless, the practitioner must be alert to any resistance that emerges within the activity team. While in some cases a step may simply be seen as redundant or unnecessary, in others it may be that one of the organization's core issues has been touched and the response is to avoid rather than confront it. At the end of the process, too, the outcomes of applying a guideline may engender resistance. Participants may disagree with the conclusions or expect another type of outcome, e.g., "I thought we were going to do X." This is when the analyst needs to slow down, be more careful, and resolve disagreements—as such disputes will invariably come back to undermine the process and its ultimate results.

1.1 Adjust Attitudes

1.1.1 Have Positive Expectations about the Future

It is important to construct positive images of the future—not just avoid negative ones. Foresight is often employed in crises, leading to an avoidance bias. Also, executives often use foresight to anticipate potential negative outcomes of their decisions. Thus, negative images of the future tend to be overemphasized. But overlooking positive images misses the power they have to create a pull towards a positive future.

Consciously develop positive expectations from the very beginning of a foresight activity. Deal with any cynicism and criticality right away. A common mistake of teams in a foresight activity is to look only for negative signs and miss the positive ones. Thus, an ethos of collecting positive signals should be established and maintained throughout the activity.

Key steps

Simply recognizing the tendency to emphasize the negative can help avoid it. There is no tried-and-true process to generate positive expectations. A couple of practical suggestions:

- Create a "positive" checklist. During a strategic foresight activity, pay special attention to signs indicating a positive outcome and create a list of them. This list can be used later to define more precisely the positive directions that could emerge.
- Before finishing the activity, check the final output to see if the positive signs or outcomes have been highlighted appropriately and if the general message being put forth incorporates those signs. Look for a constructive strategy option that can be built into a positive future.

Benefits

Having positive expectations imparts a certain confidence to actions and decisions. It is impossible to recognize one's ability to shape the future without developing a certain level of positive attitude. Moreover, a truly plausible picture of the future is enabled only by exploring positive as well as negative trends and indicators, or both the advantages and disadvantages of a proposed strategy.

Note that a positive attitude does not imply a naïve belief that "we will get lucky." Failing to take responsibility for the decisions and actions that result from a strategic foresight activity would be imprudent. Instead, the point is that a negative attitude towards the future can limit one's capacity to change the course of events. Toffler (1970) popularized this concept as "future shock"—a phenomenon in which people feel so stunned by the complexity of the future and the possible negative outcomes that they become paralyzed for problem-solving.

Example

The history of a small Hungarian company illustrates the importance of having positive expectations. Graphisoft (www.graphisoft.com) was founded in 1982 as an architecture company in Budapest. At the time of its founding, IT support for architects was not oriented to PC users, as most architectural software required powerful IT backup.

Graphisoft strongly believed in a positive future for PCs and in the future success of its software for PC users—even though the spread of the PC was not a given in the 1980s. The company decided to focus on its capacity for innovation and, in 1984, released the first 3D architectural CAD software, called ArchiCAD, in cooperation with Apple Computer. This established Graphisoft as an international player. Today the company is firmly established in three major markets—Germany, Japan, and the US.

Sources

Seligman, M.E.P. (1998). *Learned Optimism: How to Change Your Mind and Your Life*. New York: Free Press.

Toffler, A. (1970). *Future Shock*. London and Sydney: Pan Books.

1.1.2 Know Your Biases

Analysts inevitably bring personal biases to their strategic foresight work. Thus they need to pay particular attention to their own *thinking content* and *thinking style*.

Thinking content encompasses one's worldview—what one believes to be true about how the world works. Even among analysts, who strive to remain objective and neutral, worldview can color which trends and supporting data are sought out and accepted, and may lead to ignoring or rejecting trends or information at odds with this worldview.

Thinking style influences how one approaches the work at hand, interacts with teammates and stakeholders, and communicates learnings to the organization. It can mean recommending certain approaches or tools to deal with issues that might be better addressed with another tool less favored by the practitioner. Thinking style can also be a source of friction among the stakeholders, which may hinder the activity. And an analyst may fail to influence the organization if his or her favored style does not fit well with the organization's preferences.

Key steps

When working with an analysis team, it is best to start with a team-building activity that includes an assessment of the participants' styles, thus providing clues to potential biases. At the outset of team-building, practitioners should ideally perform at least one thinking content assessment and one thinking style assessment. Not only will this help break the ice for the team, it will provide useful information about biases the practitioner may need to account for during the course of the activity.

Myriad assessment instruments are available for exploring biases. These typically measure a person's preferred style or approach—they are not intended to imply that an individual is only capable of one style or another. One popular new approach for assessing thinking content is Spiral Dynamics. While this tool does not measure participants' particular views, it does measure the kinds of views they will be predisposed towards. The Spiral Dynamics tool is a relatively simple questionnaire, scored by a certified practitioner. It indicates one's place on a "spiral" of eight worldviews (called "value memes" in the system's parlance) that have been identified over the course of decades of surveys and research. It describes the ideas and values a person holding a particular worldview tends to have and suggests how a person with that view will tend to interact with information and with people of different worldviews.

Many other assessment tools are available for evaluating thinking style. The Kirton Adaptor-Innovator Assessment (KAI), the Myers-Briggs Type Indicator (MBTI), and the Hermann Brain Dominance Inventory (HBDI) (see *Guideline 1.1.4: Use Whole-brain Processes*) are three popular and useful ones. The KAI measures one's preferences towards problem solving along a continuum from Adaptor to Innovator. People closer to the Adaptor pole favor solving problems by working within established rules and frameworks and adapting existing solutions. Those tending towards the Innovator pole prefer to invent new rules.

Meyers-Briggs measures four types of personality characteristics, using letters to indicate one of two preferences for each of the four characteristics. An individual will tend to be an introvert (I) or extrovert (E), intuitive (N) or sensing (S), thinker (T) or feeler (F), and perceiver (P) or judger (J).

Whichever assessments are used, the team shares and discusses the results and their implications.

Benefits

Teams may do a solid analysis based on their styles only to find when they present their results that they have overlooked important information or ignored important people because these didn't mesh with the team's style and biases. It is a rare activity indeed that does not involve confronting some uncomfortable information or people. Teams that are aware of their own biases from the outset will recognize their tendency to reject certain information, and be able to "hang in there" and take away the required learning. They will also seek out those with differing viewpoints in order to balance the activity.

Ideally, the team is a mix of contrasting styles, thus insuring a wide range of perspectives. Practically speaking, most teams will end up with a bias towards particular styles. Once the bias is identified, the team can take remedial steps. For example, a team with a heavy representation of Innovators (on the KAI scale) could periodically invite in Adaptors to meetings as a check on their biases.

Example

A classic example of biases leading an activity astray comes from the Bay of Pigs debacle during the Kennedy administration in the United States in the 1960s. Kennedy's team of brilliant analysts—later dubbed the "best and the brightest" by journalist David Halberstam—fell victim to their biases. In April 1961, under the direction of the Kennedy administration, 1,500 Cuban exiles landed on the southern coast of Cuba with the intention of sparking a popular uprising against Fidel Castro. However, the expected insurrection failed to materialize, thus allowing the invasion to be easily repelled by Castro's troops. Over a thousand of the invading exiles were captured by Cuban forces, requiring the US government to provide $53 million in food and medicine to Cuba to secure their release. The incident also served to heighten Castro's sense of paranoia, and led directly to the Cuban Missile Crisis shortly thereafter.

This story illustrates a textbook case of groupthink, in which the group rejected evidence contrary to its preferred worldview and sought out only confirmatory evidence. As a result, the team presented a distorted and flawed analysis to President Kennedy, with unfortunate results.

Further reading

Beck, D. and Cowan, C. (1996). *Spiral Dynamics: Mastering Values, Leadership, and Change*. Oxford: Blackwell.

The Error of Unison. (2005, May 26). *Total Information Awareness*. Viewed July 2005, http://tianews.blogspot.com/2005/05/error-of-unison.html.

Halberstam, D. (1993). *The Best and the Brightest*. Danvers, MA: Ballantine.

Hermann, N. (1989). *The Creative Brain*. Lake Lurie, NC: Brain Books.

Janis, I. (1982). *Groupthink*. (2nd ed.). Boston: Houghton-Mifflin.

Keirsey, D. and Bates, M. (1978). *Please Understand Me: Character and Temperament Types*. Del Mar, CA: Prometheus Nemesis.

Kirton, M. (1994, revised). *Adaptors and Innovators: Styles of Creativity and Problem Solving*. London: Routledge.

1.1.3 Recognize that Self-delusion and Wishful Thinking Are Barriers to Strategic Foresight

The easy way out of a quandary is to blame "them" for problems. "Them" is typically vaguely defined as the power structure that "doesn't get it." Blaming someone else enables analysts to avoid responsibility for their own role in creating or perpetuating difficulties during an activity, or for the activity's ultimate failure. Analysts need to look squarely at their own behavior and check to be sure that self-delusion and wishful thinking are not getting in the way—rather than condemning "them" or the institutional barriers "they" represent, which may include corporate culture, operational norms, large capital investments, or high overhead, including operational expenses and debt service.

The tendency to externalize blame in a strategic foresight activity should not be underestimated. Foresight work can be at odds with or different from traditional organizational work, and is often viewed with some skepticism. A common complaint about strategic foresight coming from inside an organization is that it is not sufficiently directed to the bottom line. Throughout the activity, analysts need to maintain a posture of understanding and openness to these types of criticisms and avoid defensiveness and the urge to counterattack. The complaints can suggest ways to tailor the activity to win greater internal credibility, such as being sure the activity links to the bottom line as much as possible.

Key steps

Self-diagnosis itself need not be overly complex. It is simply a matter of developing a mechanism that shifts the focus away from the institutional barriers and back onto oneself. It could be as simple as having a mirror in one's office (or in the project's dedicated space or war room; see *Guideline 1.5.2 Make Strategic Foresight as Immersive and Interactive as Possible*) that focuses attention back on the practitioner and team. Or it may be a quick reality check at the beginning of each team meeting.

Benefits

This guideline is not intended to suggest that institutional barriers do not exist. They undoubtedly do. Nevertheless, relying on these barriers as a crutch deflects focus on the practitioner's own responsibility when difficulties arise—as they inevitably will. Adhering to this guideline will keep the analyst action-oriented and avoid the tendency to feel defeated by the system. Analysts will find themselves emphasizing the search for solutions rather than trying to defend themselves.

It will also engender goodwill in the organization. No organization likes to hear that it is the source of problems. It will appreciate analysts that emphasize personal responsibility.

Example

Take an example in which a team finds itself blaming an organization's failure to provide sufficient capital. It may be that the organization simply lacks the financial wherewithal, and that the analysis team's hope that capital would become available was a case of wishful thinking. Rather than lamenting the organization's shortcomings, the team could reexamine its own approach and look for alternative ways to obtain capital, such as forming a strategic alliance with a partner who is able to provide it as part of an alliance agreement.

Further reading

Linkow, P. (1999, July 1). What Gifted Strategic Thinkers Do. *Training & Development*.

Ogilvy, J. (2004, February). What Strategists Can Learn from Sartre. *Strategy+Business*.

1.1.4 Use Whole-brain Processes

The concept of whole-brain thinking, popularized by Ned Hermann (1989) at General Electric in the 1970s, suggests there are multiple thinking styles which are centered in different parts of the brain. Whole-brain thinking involves tapping these different styles. Today the concept is most commonly heard in terms of left-brain and right-brain thinking. The left brain involves linear, rational, and logical modes of thinking, while the right brain involves holistic, emotional, and intuitive styles.

Hermann developed the concept as part of a diagnostic tool to assess the innovation capabilities of managers at GE. His initial research suggested four different thinking styles, centered in four different quadrants of the brain. Subsequent research has shown that the physical correlation is not true, but Hermann kept the metaphor of four different thinking styles located in four different parts of the brain.

Creativity consultant Gerald Haman of Solutionpeople (www.solutionpeople.com) has adapted Hermann's model, dubbing the left-brain styles as "investigator"—the function of thoroughly investigating needs—and "evaluator"—the function of evaluating which solutions are best. The right-brain styles are dubbed "creator"—generating ideas for the problem at hand—and "activator"—developing action plans.

Key steps

One approach is to administer the formal survey instrument developed by Ned Hermann, the Hermann Brain Dominance Inventory (HBDI). The drawback of the HBDI is that it needs to be mailed to a certified expert for scoring. In another approach, Haman and other creativity consultants adapted the assessment instrument into a game called the *Know Your Brain Game*. The game is a quick and fun way to assess people's preferred thinking styles, which the developers claim is 80% to 90% accurate. It is important to note that the instrument measures a person's preferences: individuals can access all the different thinking styles but tend to have a preference and strength in one or two.

Hermann and other advocates of whole-brain thinking suggest that teams be formed according to whole-brain thinking principles. During a strategic foresight activity, there will be certain points where particular thinking styles will be more appropriate. During Framing, for example, the investigative style will be most prevalent. The creator approach is best used early in the Forecasting phase, when generating ideas for the forecast. Later in the Forecasting phase and in Visioning, the evaluator style will be at the forefront. The activator style will be most prevalent during Acting.

Benefits

Ideally, team members should have a diverse mix of thinking-style preferences so the group as a whole can achieve whole-brain thinking. If the team is already set, it is still valuable to know members' preferred thinking styles as a way to avoid the traps of relying excessively on one or more styles. It is also helpful to look for ways to bring individuals with different thinking styles into the activity where possible.

The strengths and weaknesses associated with each of the styles include:

- *Investigators* are great at research, but prone to "paralysis by analysis."
- *Creators* are great at coming up with lots of ideas but typically don't show a lot of concern for their practicality or for following up on them.
- *Evaluators* are great at organizing, planning, and seeing the flaws of an idea, but often lose sight of the big picture by excessive focus on the details.
- *Activators* are great at networking and knowing how to get things done, but are often seen as overly emotional or more concerned with feelings than the bottom line.

Hermann believed that whole-brain thinking that taps all four thinking styles tends to produce better results than thinking that relies on one or two styles.

Example

A case example from Hermann International (www.hbdi.com) involves a $4 million, long-term client of a printing company that had experienced quality problems over a six-month period. The printing company had repeatedly attempted to resolve the problems with no success and was unable to figure out what was causing them. The consultants profiled the thinking preferences of the team working on the issue, and discovered they all shared similar thinking. So they expanded the team, inviting in others with different thinking styles.

The new team took another look at the problem, and from this expanded perspective discovered the problems were clearly occurring on a specific day, and consistently with one of the company's best people. Further interviews and research revealed that this employee was involved in a weekly poker game the evening before every quality issue occurred. A person on the following shift had been covering for this individual, and consequently was incorrectly blamed for part of the problems. The shift schedule was revised, the immediate quality issues were resolved, the client was retained, and the department became totally error-free within three months.

Further reading

Herrmann-Nehdi, A. A Whole-Brain Approach to Solving a Customer Problem. Retrieved July 13, 2005 from www.hbdi.com/download/casestudies/wb-appro.pdf.

Hermann, N. (1989). *The Creative Brain*. Lake Lurie, NC: Brain Books.

Edwards, B. (1999). *The New Drawing on the Right Side of the Brain*. East Rutherford, NJ: Putnam.

1.1.5 Embrace Complexity in Addition to Linear Thinking

Foresight requires the ability to recognize patterns, in order to explain how things work or what causes what. Most patterns involve relationships and systems that are nonlinear and complex. Most people, however, tend to see patterns in linear and simple terms. Simple explanations are easier to understand and deal with, even when they are wrong. Jay Forrester (1971), a noted systems researcher, expressed it this way:

The human mind is not adapted to interpreting how social systems behave. Social systems belong to the class called multi-loop nonlinear feedback systems. In the long history of evolution it has not been necessary until very recent historical times for people to understand complex feedback systems. Evolutionary processes have not given us the mental ability to interpret properly the dynamic behavior of those complex systems in which we are now imbedded.

Every explanation in a foresight activity should be tested for the right level of complexity. Explanations tend to be simplified in two ways: too few causal factors or too many straight-line relationships among causes and effects. On the first point, one simple cause would be nice if it were true, but it is rarely so. When a company's product is losing sales, some want to blame the sales force, some the competition, some the product's quality, some market saturation. While causes should not be multiplied unnecessarily, it should not be assumed that every effect can be explained by just one cause either.

On the second point, there is the tendency to see everything in straight, linear patterns. Double the cause, you double the effect. Increase your effort to get more output. But very few, if any, relationships follow a linear pattern. Take the example of a lily pond: the number of lilies in a pond may double every day for a month, but hardly any lilies are visible for the first 25 days until—boom, it's full!

Key steps

The analyst needs to learn to recognize common nonlinear relationships, such as:

- exponential decline or growth (a population becoming extinct or exploding)
- logarithms or asymptotes (product sales approaching saturation, which invokes the law of diminishing returns)
- cycles (politics moving from liberal to conservative and back again)

One of the most useful approaches to characterizing nonlinear relationships is the *S-curve*. The S-curve starts out slowly, accelerates for a short time and then levels off. It is used to plot technology diffusion, product life cycle, population growth into a new habitat—almost anything that moves rapidly from one steady-state to another. Malcolm Gladwell made the S-curve famous in his bestseller, *The Tipping Point: How Little Things Can Make a Big Difference*, in which he described how phenomena can spread rapidly following an S-curve path.

Another nonlinear relationship to look for is *"the fix that fails,"* which is a short-term solution that increases the long-term problem. For instance, US auto manufacturers have been losing ground to Japanese manufacturers for a long time. A typical response has been to offer discounts and incentives that increase sales for a short time—but this approach also depresses profits, making it harder for the companies to invest in the technology and training to produce better cars. The result is that incentives to increase sales in the short run decrease sales in the long run.

Analysts can also take advantage of insights from *systems thinking* and the study of complex adaptive systems, in which a pattern emerges from the interaction among the "agents" or actors in the system. In a commodity market, for example, the price for any commodity is not set by anyone; it arises from the interaction of millions of buyers and sellers over time. Complex adaptive systems are being used to model ant colonies, markets, supply chains, voters—any system in which independent agents interact to form emergent patterns. This form of complexity reminds us that many important systems, notably organizations, communities, and whole societies, do not act like machines with simple cause-effect relationships, but are more akin to natural ecosystems.

Benefits

The following quotes suggest the benefits of embracing complexity:

- "For every problem there is one solution which is simple, neat, and wrong." —H. L. Mencken
- "Seek simplicity, and distrust it." —Alfred North Whitehead
- "Everything should be made as simple as possible, but not simpler." —Albert Einstein

Embracing complexity also avoids the problems arising from quickly accepting the explanation that comes first—which is also usually the simplest. Simple solutions tend to be incomplete, and working off an incomplete explanation leaves one open to enormous risk that the part of the explanation left out will be the one that comes to shape the future.

Example

The US tried many strategies for solving the problem of poverty in the 1960s. One was to build low-cost housing for the poor, which became commonly known as "projects." That strategy was clearly recognized as a failure ten years later, but Jay Forrester (1971) made the point much earlier using a more complex explanation than was favored at the time. The mainstream explanation held that people were poor because they could not afford decent housing, and the solution was for the government to build housing and rent it to the poor at a cost they could afford. Their standard of living would rise, and they would not be poor anymore.

Forrester turned that explanation on its head. He argued that, far from there being too little low-cost housing, there was too much! The excess attracted more poor people with lower levels of skills than the urban job market could handle. As more poor people came in, unemployment increased, urban areas become more dangerous, businesses left, and the plight of the poor became that much worse. Therefore, Forrester's solution was to *reduce* the amount of low-cost housing in urban areas and replace it with industry that would employ the people in the area so they could afford decent housing themselves.

Further reading

Forrester, J.W. (1971). Counterintuitive Behavior of Social Systems. *Technology Review.*

Gladwell, M. (2002). *The Tipping Point: How Little Things Can Make a Big Difference.* Boston, MA: Back Bay Books.

1.1.6 Recognize that Different Changes Occur at Different Rates and Will Have Different Impacts at Different Times

Much is said about change in business: how to anticipate it, manage it, or even create it. Yet there is usually a high level of anxiety around the idea of change because for the most part, the general consensus is that "change happens fast." In fact, change occurs at different rates and degrees throughout society. The effects of environmental and demographic change, for instance, can take years or decades to be felt, while the impacts of a technological change can be felt in just months.

The misperception about all change being fast was nicely captured by Chakravorti (2003) in his aptly titled *The Slow Pace of Fast Change*. He argues that change—in his case business innovations—is embedded in a system. Breakthroughs are slowed down by the complexity of the actors and connections in the system. For example, a potential innovative breakthrough in automobile propulsion, such as fuel cells, must deal with long lead times in design, the need for a fueling infrastructure, and other systemic aspects that slow down what at first seemed to portend a fast change.

Key steps

The practitioner needs to be aware of the time dimensions of change throughout the activity. When analyzing the impacts of a particular trend, for example, first consider current assumptions about where the trend is now and where it's likely to go. Next, determine the perceived rate of change, by consulting both conventional wisdom in the marketplace and expert opinion and quantitative evidence. The degree of consensus about the trajectory of the trend may also reveal the depth of certainty or uncertainty about its potential impacts. Ask questions such as: How fast is this trend moving? Is the growth moderate or exponential?

Next consider the timeframe of impact: When is this likely to impact the organization? Many organizations use "short, medium, and long term" as the qualifying metric of change. Be as specific as possible.

Finally, create a timeline or other visual representation that displays the perceived point of impact of all of the trends being analyzed. This step is critical because it allows decision-makers to consider relationships between trends and their potential influence on the organization. A useful technique here is to have participants in a group setting each draw a curve depicting their view of change over time. The differences in the curves lead to interesting discussions about the underlying assumptions.

Benefits

Considering the different rates of change opens the organization to short-, medium-, and long-term risks and opportunities. It places the concept of change in a manageable context, illustrating that it's not all happening at once. This in turn helps shift the mental model of the organization away from seeing change as threatening. It also allows people time to gain support and/or resources necessary to deal with a particular trend or issue, and helps them distinguish between urgent and important trends.

Example

The Executive Council for a County Commissioner's office was tasked with incorporating an environmental scan into the county's strategic plan. In previous years the Council had produced a "top trends" report that briefly described a wide variety of trends and issues—from the aging of the baby boomers to the impact of the state's newly instituted sales tax. Previous reports had organized the trends into broad categories (generally under the headings social, technological, economic, environmental, and political) and used statistics and anecdotes to illustrate why the trend was important to the county. While the report was informative, it failed to consider the timeframes in which the various trends might impact the county, thus limiting its usefulness from a strategic planning perspective.

The Council then reanalyzed each of the trends, considering a timeframe for impact. An additional section included a "strategic roadmap," essentially placing each of the issues on a timeline of three to twenty years. This allowed the

Council to reprioritize the strategic issues and reallocate resources accordingly. In addition, the Council funded a series of white papers to consider the potential impacts of issues beyond the ten-year range—thus putting these issues on the county's radar screen for the future.

Further reading

Chakravorti, B. (2003). *The Slow Pace of Fast Change: Bringing Innovations to Market in a Connected World*. Cambridge, MA: Harvard Business School Press.

Dator, J. (1999, February). From Tsunamis to Long Waves and Back. *Futures, 31*(1).

Schultz, W. (2003, February 15). Identifying and Monitoring Change. Retrieved July 7, 2005, from www.infinitefutures.com/essays/ff/ch5b.shtml.

1.2 Know the Audience

1.2.1 Learn as Much as Possible about the Organization

No two organizations are alike. Approaches that work well with one organization may turn off another. Each brings its own set of assumptions, culture, and situation to the table. It behooves the analyst to learn as much as possible about the client, including assumptions, culture, customers, competitors, audiences, markets, history, issues, etc. Most of this learning will take place in the early phases of an activity. Much of it may occur while negotiating about whether or how to do an activity, just as good sales practice involves knowing the customer.

Key steps

Begin with what the organization says publicly about itself. This may be in the form of annual reports, press releases, speeches, white papers, etc. After gathering this information, the next step is to gather what is being said by others about the organization. Information is readily available about larger, high-profile organizations, but understanding smaller ones, or small units within a larger organization, may take some digging.

Interviewing is usually a good place to start. The Framing phase of an activity and the more specific task of data gathering both provide opportunities for interviewing internal clients about the activity—opportunities that can also be used to gather information about the organization. Project updates provide another means of learning about the organization. Monitor reactions as indicators of what works and what doesn't. Reactions can also signal the ability and/or willingness to challenge the status quo. The organization might bristle at provocations or yawn at incremental suggestions. These reactions provide clues that can be useful for positioning upcoming interactions.

At the same time, knowledge of the organization should not lead the analyst to alter fundamental conclusions. In other words, avoid the temptation to tell the organization what it wants to hear. The goal here is to put the message in the most favorable light so that results are evaluated on their merits—not to alter the message itself. But there will be times when the organization simply will not like the results. The advice here is to take the heat and stand by the analysis. While this may cause short-term pain, in the long run, most organizations will value integrity. Organizations are increasingly sensitive to their own tendencies to hear what they want to, and value analysts who will tell them the bad news. For more on this, see *Guideline 6.1 Communicate Results*.

Benefits

Knowing the client can help direct the analyst to areas to emphasize and avoid. It can help discriminate what's important from what isn't. It can also provide valuable clues to communication strategy that will give the results the best chance of receiving a fair hearing.

Example

A familiar complaint regarding foresight work is that the organization "didn't get it." It is an all-too-common topic among practitioners when discussing difficulty or failed activities. There is no need to rehash a specific case. This guideline suggests, however, that this outcome actually reflects a failure of the analyst to understand the organization and communicate with it effectively.

Further reading

Block, P. (1999). *Flawless Consulting: A Guide to Getting Your Expertise Used*. (2nd ed.). Hoboken, NJ: Pfeiffer.

Maister, D.H. (2000). *The Trusted Advisor*. New York: Touchstone.

Weiss, A. (1997). *Million Dollar Consulting: The Professional's Guide to Growing a Practice*. (2nd ed.). New York: McGraw–Hill.

1.2.2 Find Out What the Organization Is Trying to Get Done, and What's Keeping Its People Awake at Night

Meet the organization on its own terms. Unless a message about the need for change or a strategic shift is made clear and relevant, the organization will not be able to understand and act on it. The analyst will typically have a different perspective or style from the norm of the organization. Even when the goal is to stir up new thinking—to provoke with fresh ideas—the analyst needs to frame insights and build arguments in such a way that the organization can find meaning in them.

Key steps

Begin by learning what the core issues, mental models, hopes, and fears of the organization are. Meeting the organization on its own terms means connecting with the people. At the same time, it does not necessarily mean agreeing with their views. In fact, the purpose of an activity may be to change them.

Next, analyze the trends, forces, and issues at play from the perspective of the organization. Let this perspective shape the discussion, but continue to push the stakeholders to broaden their thinking as well. That means stating or restating conclusions and implications from the activity in terms that hold meaning for them. As they expand their thinking, reframe the discussion in familiar terms and a familiar point-of-view.

Finally, ask whether the organization is finding the discussion and its outcomes meaningful and satisfying. Do the stakeholders know what to do next? Can they see how to move to action? Too often, an organization will know something important is passing in front of it, but fail to make the essential connections that lead to action. The analyst needs to help the organization connect the discussion with action.

Benefits

Messages about change and the future cannot break through to most audiences if they are simply sprung on people without some background and preparation. Too often, messages about change and the future are delivered in such a way that people throw their hands up in confusion, fear, or helplessness. This may be the fault of the messenger carrying a "here's the future, take it or leave it" attitude. Analysts must think of themselves as translators who help the organization understand and prepare for the heady challenge of confronting and dealing with change.

Example

An analyst led two multi-sponsor research programs on the future of packaging. Packaging executives are by habit focused narrowly on their sector and its operations and issues. The analyst and his colleagues—who had often served clients who were in-house strategists and planners for their organizations—faced groups of able and thoughtful executives who were very operationally focused. The analysts found it valuable to immerse themselves in the interests of the packaging sector, learn the language, and discover the hopes and fears behind what packaging executives do.

Then, by engaging these executives in developing scenarios for the future of packaging, they discovered the issues and concerns most on the minds of the sector. The different futures messages and divergent views on the possibilities took those sectoral worldviews into account. The activities were successful because they didn't just open up a gee-whiz future view for the sector, but used the language and perspectives of the sector itself to broaden the executives' thinking, and ultimately to show ways that operations executives could empower themselves to forge new, more strategic future roles.

Further reading

Slaughter, R. (1998). Transcending Flatland: Some Implications of Ken Wilber's Meta-Narrative for Futures Studies. *Futures, 30* (10), 993 - 1002. (available at www.foresightinternational.com.au)

Wilber, K. (1997). An Integral Theory of Consciousness. *Journal of Consciousness Studies, 4* (1), 71 - 92.

1.2.3 Don't Try to Make Clients into Foresight Professionals

Don't argue with the focus of clients: accommodate it. It is not necessary to make clients into foresight professionals. Too many analysts promoting strategic foresight want to reform or transform the clients they are working with. It won't work. Most clients in organizations have a dedicated focus on their issues and areas of expertise for good reason—they are paid for it—and they stray from it at their peril.

Key steps

Rather than trying to convert clients to futures approaches, a more effective tactic is to raise awareness of the different perspectives present, with the analyst seeking to stretch the participants' thinking. While accommodating the client's perspective is the typical approach, some cases call for shaking up the status quo. In these cases, it is best to be upfront about the goal of trying to change perspectives, and acknowledge everyone involved.

Define roles and expectations clearly, e.g., "I see my job here as to bring in new ideas that may challenge our thinking and at least briefly shift our focus to new possibilities. I know your job is to keep an eye on your product line and your bottom line. But bear with me for a little while so we can explore some new ideas and check our assumptions about the next few years." It may make sense to repeat this message from time to time and let clients express their views about it—or vent their frustrations, since this approach may be seen as too high-level or theoretical.

Conversely, sometimes the organization, or some members participating in the activity, will be very enthusiastic about using foresight and will push to take on roles that are best performed by the analyst. It can be difficult to maintain focus and distinguish clearly what the analyst brings to the activity and what the best interests of the organization are. The best suggestion is to acknowledge and applaud this enthusiasm. Suggest training opportunities that can be explored after the current activity is completed.

Benefits

Following this advice could help prevent a rebellion or shutdown by the clients. It is nearly certain that the analyst will be working with organizations that have a much narrower or shorter-term mindset. The analyst will be viewed as an outsider trying to disrupt norms. If the analyst can provide a sense of comfort and openness to different perspectives, the clients will, in turn, be more willing to participate and share.

Example

In working with a client in an international organization, it became clear that the very idea of foresight and exploring change was alien. Nearly everyone had a program-focused way of thinking. They needed to understand if a proposed program was a good idea or not, and to envision not so much its future, but its success.

One approach might have been to try to get them to explicitly explore the future of the programs in the countries they were targeting. But the client organization's norms and culture just wouldn't tolerate that. The consultant was literally told not to use the "F" word—future. The solution was to get the clients to explore change and future possibilities with the techniques that foresight practitioners use, including scenarios and cross-impact analysis, but to explain them as tools for broadening thinking—for better brainstorming. Feeling safe and with their norms kept intact, the organization had a powerful foresight experience.

Further reading

Coates, J. (2001, October 23). Future and Technology Assessment Research for Business Clients. Retrieved July 13, 2005 from www.josephcoates.com/pdf_files/263_Future_Research_for_Biz.pdf.

Hines, A. (1999, April). The Simple Facts of Business Life. *foresight: the journal of futures studies, strategic thinking, and policy, 1* (2).

1.3 Understand the Rationale and Purpose

1.3.1 Explore the Future to Influence the Present

The purpose of looking to the future is to understand the possibilities ahead in order to make more informed decisions in the present. Good futures work reduces the risk of being surprised or blindsided. It can build momentum towards more favorable pathways and away from unfavorable ones.

In some cases a specific decision will clearly be the endpoint: should we invest in a new plant in a new geography? In others the exploration will be more open-ended and geared towards learning: is this rising market a potential new area of business for us? Even in the latter case, however, the learning must ultimately tie to a decision or action if it is to be useful. Failing to tie future insights to the present—whether for actual decisions or for learning that will eventually inform decisions—renders the activity an interesting intellectual exercise, without practical value.

Key steps

Every strategic foresight activity should begin by clarifying the decisions or learning objectives the activity is supporting. This is not always as straightforward as it sounds. Many times, organizations are unclear about what decisions they need to make or what they need to learn. Investing time upfront in clarifying a focal issue will pay dividends in keeping the activity focused and relevant.

Begin by looking at how the exploration will provide information that leads to better decisions or supports the learning objectives. If it is not clear how the expected information outcomes will help, reassess the activity's design—or whether it should be done in the first place. Unless the outputs are actionable, it may fall into the sin of providing information for information's sake—a time-waster in today's lean, downsized organizations.

Throughout the activity, continually calibrate whether the futures exploration continues to yield a different set of possibilities, or richer fodder for learning, as new decisions and actions are taken.

Benefits

Linking futures exploration to the decisions and learning objectives at hand ensures relevance. It also keeps the activity focused, reducing the chance that it will drift into arenas that don't matter to the stakeholders, and maximizes the productivity of the time spent. Failing to make this link will detract from the credibility of the present activity and damage the prospects for future activities.

Example

An example of how not following this guideline led to trouble involved a major oil company that merged three divisions into one. The new management team wanted to get an idea of the future of the new merged entity, so they chartered a group to develop scenarios for their future business environment in twenty years. The group began by collecting published materials on the future of the industry. They interviewed futurists and other experts and collected their responses into long reports. But then they were stuck. "We know a lot about the future, but what do we do with all this stuff? How do we turn all this information into scenarios?"

The group engaged a futures consultant to help them get over the hump and develop the scenarios. The consultant's questions included, "What does the management want from these scenarios? What are they concerned about? What decisions do they need to make?" The group didn't know so they asked the managers those questions. The answer came back that the managers didn't know either; they just wanted to look at the scenarios.

Despite this lack of clarity, the group moved ahead and developed five excellent scenarios with an imaginative and interesting presentation for each one. They presented these to the management team in an all-day offsite meeting. The management team commended them on the quality of the scenarios. They had done a great job on what they had been asked to do. The only problem was that the managers didn't know what to do with the scenarios. And to the consultants' knowledge, no mention of the scenarios ever surfaced again.

Further reading

Schwartz, P. (1997). *The Art of the Long View*. New York: Wiley.

Van der Heijden, K. (n.d.) Scenarios, Strategy, and the Strategy Process. *Presearch: Provoking Strategic Conversation*. Emeryville, CA: Global Business Network.

1.3.2 Seek to Improve the Mental Model of Decision-Makers

Mental models are the deeply ingrained assumptions, generalizations, or images that influence how one makes sense of and responds to the world. They are usually biased towards the past, and are often vague or based on faulty assumptions about the future. The mental models of key decision-makers should be assessed as early as possible in a strategic foresight activity—and continually reassessed. The aim, according to Wack (1984), "is to change the decision maker's assumptions about how the world works and compel him to change his image of reality."

Key steps

A first step is to identify the key decision-makers. There is the client or client team that either requested a study or is the target of the initiative. There are also influential stakeholders who are "not in the room" but whose views of a study can make or break it.

Once the key decision-makers are identified, the next step is to uncover their mental models. There are several ways to go about this. Ideally, but not always practically, the decision-makers should be interviewed directly. Analysts may also leverage any contacts they may have among the people who know or work for the decision-makers, to uncover clues about how they think and behave.

Without direct access, the decision-makers' thinking will have to be deduced from publicly available information. Look through public pronouncements, articles, or speeches. Other places to look for clues are case histories of decisions, decision criteria used to evaluate projects, announcements, project terminations, performance assessment and recognition rewards, profiles of new hires, etc.

"Pre-selling" to the decision-makers can provide valuable insights. Pre-selling is when the essence of the findings to date are discussed with decision-makers and their feedback is sought. The risk here is discovering too late that the findings run counter to the decision-makers' mental model and may predispose him or her against the actual pitch. On balance, It is better to find this out sooner rather than later.

Provocations are a useful technique to engage mental models. Provocation requires some subtlety, however, since decision-makers vary in how well they respond to challenge. Some may find it engaging, while others may become defensive and be put off. This needs to be handled on a case-by-case basis. It may also be useful to consider designing experiences beyond the cognitive, such as visioning.

Benefits

Influencing the mental models of decision-makers provides three Important benefits.

First, it leads to changed behavior that in turn leads to action and results. Put differently, failure to influence mental models likely means the failure of the activity. There are far too many well-designed strategic foresight activities sitting on shelves collecting dust because they failed to engage the mental models of the decision-makers. As Wack (1984) says, "the planner will succeed only if he can securely link the outside world, the business environment he scans, to the microcosm of the decision maker."

Second, influencing mental models gives the organization a chance to respond to information before crisis hits. Mental models are amenable to change during a crisis, but by then, flexibility and the range of options are usually more limited. Thus, influence mental models before a crisis.

Third, influencing the mental model is central to learning. Challenging existing mental models about the future provides the opening through which a new and enhanced picture of the future emerges.

Example

Shell's first four scenarios in 1971 were dubbed "first-generation" (Wack, 1984). They were well-designed, covered a wide span of possible futures, and were internally consistent. But when presented to Shell top management, they didn't inspire strategic thinking or action. They were effectively "useless for decision-making."

So in 1972, two sets of scenarios were presented based on the major discontinuity of the coming scarcity of oil and ensuing sharp increases in price. One scenario set highlighted the most likely outcomes from the team's analysis. The second set showed how the hoped-for, "business-as-usual" future of the managers was based on certain highly questionable assumptions. These new scenarios effectively preempted a counterattack, by addressing the mental models upon which the top management relied.

When the oil embargo hit in 1973, Shell's preparations enabled it to improve its position from the seventh to the second leading oil company in the world.

Further reading

Brown, J.S. (2004). Rethinking the Innovator's Dilemma with Modern Tools. *PDMA/IIR Best Practices, Tools, and Techniques for Managing the Front End of Innovation*. May 25, Boston, MA.

Prahalad, C.K. and Bettis, R.A. (1986). The Dominant Logic: A New Linkage between Diversity and Performance. *Strategic Management Journal, 7*, 485 - 501.

Senge, P., Kleiner, A., Roberts, C., Ross, R., and Smith, B. (1994). *The Fifth Discipline Fieldbook*. New York: Currency Doubleday.

Wack, P. (1984). Scenarios: The Gentle Art of Reperceiving. Reprinted by Global Business Network from *President and Fellows of Harvard College, Working Paper 9-785-042*.

1.3.3 Balance Exploration and Exploitation

Analysts need to help organizations account for both the near-term and longer-term effects of a decision. It is tempting for organizations to spend a lot of time strategizing, hypothesizing, and engaging in the "blue-sky" thinking of exploration. Alternatively, it is easy for organizations to get mired in day-to-day crisis management. Exploration is associated with the longer term; exploitation with the now. Balancing exploration and exploitation is essential for the analyst, since the two kinds of thinking feed one another and impact each other's success.

Key steps

There are a number of ways to incorporate balanced thinking into day-to-day activities. First, use distinct time horizons. Thinking along multiple time horizons balances exploration and exploitation. A proposal or investment might give great short-term results, but prove deficient in the long term. A competing idea could be adequate in the short term but provide better longer-term results and lead to the discovery of new possibilities. Simple techniques like charting the interactions of trends, ideas, and opportunities along a timescale is one way to balance the two kinds of results.

Second, create time and space for the incubation of ideas. Every company should have a place where new ideas can be generated and nurtured. It is important to have permission to explore and to fail. Exploring creates ideas that are available when the landscape is right for them.

Third, make the most of old ideas. What can be done with what the organization already has? Are there novel ways to use products that have already been developed? For example, the very successful Swiffer dusting product made by Procter & Gamble had its origins in an old and stagnant product—the dryer sheet.

Several pitfalls threaten to destabilize the balance between exploration and exploitation. The key is to know when to explore and when to exploit. When an organization enjoys surplus talent and other resources, or when the market is relatively stable, it is usually a good time for exploration. Clay Christensen (2003), who popularized the *Innovator's Dilemma*, suggests that the best time to meet a potential disruptive challenge is when the organization is doing well, before crisis strikes. Exploitation, on the other hand, is usually best conducted during lean times when resources are constrained.

Benefits

One problem analysts face when helping organizations think about the future is that the client generally wants to know how this thinking is going to help them in the short run. Very rarely can leaders accept a short-term downturn in performance with the promise of better future results. Without short-term successes, programs that have merit and promise can fall by the wayside. The analyst must strike a balance between exploring new ideas, technologies, and unproven strategies with exploiting things that have worked in the past, in order to survive in a rapidly changing landscape.

Example

An example of how to balance exploration and exploitation is taken from Axelrod and Cohen (1999). It applies a complexity perspective to military personnel management. In the military promotion process, individuals who are now junior officers will be senior officers in a decade or so. By that time, the geopolitical landscape will have probably changed dramatically and new technologies will have become reality. As junior officers move up the ranks, they often develop an attachment to a new idea which they believe has merit. The junior officers and their ideas will most likely be protected by senior officers, and as they advance in rank, they will be given the opportunity to develop them further.

The issue is that it is hard to recognize which of today's young officers have those vital new ideas to address the surprises of the future. In a period of relative peace, it is important to emphasize exploration for these junior officers. By exposing them early to new technologies and the backgrounds of previous military innovators, they can be better prepared to envision new technological capabilities and tactics. In this exploration mode, their assignments should include a wide variety of experiences that provide them with exposure to lots of different people.

Further reading

Axelrod, R. and Cohen, M.D. (1999). *Harnessing Complexity: Organizational Implications of a Scientific Frontier*. New York: The Free Press.

Christensen, Clay. (2003). *The Innovator's Solution: Creating and Sustaining Successful Growth*. Cambridge, MA: Harvard Business School.

Courtney, H. (2001). *20/20 Foresight: Crafting Strategy in an Uncertain World*. Boston: Harvard Business School Press.

1.3.4 Evaluate Whether the Problem as Presented Is Really the Problem to Be Solved

Be skeptical of the diagnosis the organization provides. Executives often feel they need to speak with certainty about issues on which they may not truly be authorities.

Furthermore, the organization's own diagnosis can be a hindrance to defining the focal issue because the "presented" problem may be more acceptable to the organization than the real problem. For example, it may be more politically palatable to blame onerous regulations for a problem than the ineffectiveness of the management team.

Key steps

The first step is to question reality as perceived. The reality that counts is that of the decision-maker who can turn thumbs up or thumbs down on the results of the activity. Questioning this person's perceived reality may suggest a different problem statement.

The true nature of the problem needs to be negotiated between the analyst and the organization. A useful approach can be borrowed from the new-product development chartering process. Here the work team and its sponsors negotiate the nature of the problem, the objective of the activity, the boundaries and resources involved, and the nature of an acceptable solution.

Benefits

Taking time to understand the true problem improves the chances of having an effective solution. Far too many foresight activities discover the "real problem" only after traveling far down the road. While the old adage "better late than never" applies, it is still preferable to ascertain the problem as early as possible and minimize wasted time.

Example

Normann (2001) describes how the Swedish furniture company Ikea began with a strong sense that there had to be a better way for middle- and lower-income families to afford quality living environments at home. Ikea initially focused on inefficiencies in the furniture supply system. Due to the strength of its competition at the time, the company was forced to turn to subcontractors and allocate activity to low-cost production centers. As legend has it, when the company opened the doors of its first warehouse, the line outside was so long that customers stormed the warehouse and began shopping for themselves. The organization was savvy enough to understand that the shift to having customers assume a share of the labor was a way to keep costs low.

Further reading

Boisot, M. (1998). *Knowledge Assets: Securing Competitive Advantage in the Information Economy*. London: Oxford University Press.

Christensen, C. (2004). *Seeing What's Next: Using Theories of Innovation to Predict Industry Change*. Boston: Harvard Business School Press.

Normann, R. (2001). *Reframing Business: When the Map Changes the Landscape*. New York: Wiley.

Rosenau, M.D., Griffin, A., Castellion, G.A., and Anschuetz, N.F., eds. (2002). *The PDMA Handbook of New Product Development* (1st edition). New York: Wiley.

1.4 Set Objectives

1.4.1 Define Objectives in Terms That Can Be Measured

Seek the greatest precision possible in defining the objectives of a strategic foresight activity. Strategic objectives entail bringing a greater understanding of the future to bear on current decisions. Often, they can turn into something of a fishing expedition, looking for possibilities, opportunities, or threats. Even in cases where the objectives are very broad, however, it is possible to set criteria that can be used to guide decisions and evaluate success. An activity that looks to identify opportunities, for example, could include a criterion that at least twenty-five opportunities will be identified.

The objectives and criteria should be defined during the initial chartering process with sponsors. Since defining objectives and criteria can be a complex process, it is not always possible to accomplish it in one meeting. It usually takes some back-and-forth discussion. Even after the objectives and criteria are agreed upon, the team should remain open to adjusting them during the process based on what they learn. Any proposed changes should be brought to the attention of the sponsors and negotiated with them.

Key steps

The objectives of a foresight activity can be defined in several ways. Hines (2003) suggests that, to choose the best approach, analysts need to first understand that there are three different kinds of foresight activities. Each has its own set of appropriate foresight tools—and its own set of traps.

- *Strategic activities*—A strategic activity may be aimed at helping the organization answer a known question or address a known issue. For instance, the issue could be whether or not to buy company XYZ. These types of activities typically have management buy-in and resources at their disposal. Tools useful for defining objectives in strategic activities include trend forecasting, technology assessment, scenarios, strategic planning, and the like. Typically, the big management-consulting firms handle this kind of analysis with different tools and a machine-like approach that may be too narrow in some cases. Conversely, when foresight analysts take on this kind of issue, they can get lost in generating endless alternatives, new questions, and new issues.

- *Creative activities*—These entail bringing fresh thinking to organizations stuck in their self-constructed "boxes." This kind of objective involves generating new ideas, such as identifying new practices or searching for new business opportunities. For these types of activities, analysts use environmental scanning, trend analysis, mind maps, cross-impact matrixes, and a host of creative thinking tools. Creative activities are essentially about helping the organization think differently—and it is up to the organization to decide what to do with this thinking. The analyst's trap here is in trying to prescribe solutions, when it is options that are really called for.

- *Educational activities*—Educational activities typically are broken out separately—but they are really a means for improving either the strategic objectives or the creative objectives. The educational challenge is to plant seeds of foresight which will take root in the organization and eventually flower. Education involves primarily a "push" approach—perhaps a newsletter, lecture, trip report, or workshop—in which the analyst is delivering a futures message that the organization has not necessarily asked for. The goal is to get some people in the organization excited about foresight and others at least exposed to it, so that it will seem less foreign when it comes time to carry out a foresight activity.

Once the type of activity is determined and the specific objectives can be set, metrics can be developed. While there is, and ought to be, overlap between the strategic and the creative objectives, a key delivery problem is to unintentionally mix the two, or to deliver on one when the other is really what was asked for. Keep in mind that it is not always going to be crystal-clear whether the activity is one type or the other. It may start one way and veer another.

Benefits

A good foresight activity will often uncover the real problem—which may be quite different than the officially stated one. When it is, the analyst may need to check in with the client throughout the project to make sure both sides stay on the same page regarding the nature of the problem. Too often, activities change after they are underway but some participants never make the transition.

Understanding the nature of the problem also allows the analyst to deliver what is truly needed, which in turn boosts his or her credibility. When a decision is called for, the analyst produces a decision; when options are called for, the analyst produces options.

The educational role is one with which many analysts feel deeply engaged—it is why many enter strategic foresight work in the first place. However, analysts need to be very thoughtful, and often quite subtle, in pursuing their educational objectives if they are to avoid turning clients off or being labeled a crusader or preacher. Rather, they should strive to be seen first and foremost as useful. Idealism need not be abandoned, but it should be tempered in a way that makes the analyst most effective.

Occasionally, analysts will meet the objectives as promised yet still find a hostile reception. This often occurs when they must deliver bad news. In the long run, clients will respect a team that delivers solid, reputable analysis and is willing to stand for what it believes in.

Example

Myriad cases exist of analysis teams either skipping or skimping on setting objectives with measurable criteria. Often there is a desire to "get on with it." In other cases, analysts set objectives without sufficient input from the organization. Or, they may set objectives but fail to identify measurable criteria. In all cases, trouble will emerge down the road, even if the activity is well done. Analysts may be surprised in such cases when the organization "doesn't understand" or "doesn't get it," and may resort to blaming the client. Following this guideline—to define objectives in measurable terms—will go a long way towards avoiding these hypothetical but all-too-familiar scenarios.

Further reading

Hines, A. (2003). An Audit for Organizational Futurists: Ten Questions Every Organizational Futurist Should Be Able to Answer. *Foresight, 5*(1), 20 - 33.

Rosenau, M.D., Griffin, A., Castellion, G.A., and Anschuetz, N.F., eds. (2002). *The PDMA Handbook of New Product Development* (1st edition). New York: Wiley.

1.4.2 Focus on Outcomes, Not Outputs

Every organization has a mission to reach certain outcomes—for which society, through its external stakeholders, provides resources and holds it accountable. In fulfilling its mission, the organization engages in activities that produce outputs or results.

Outcomes can be clearly and obviously good in themselves. In the case of schools, this would be student learning. With such outcomes, no one has to ask, "What is that good for?" These are the ultimate purpose of the organization.

Outputs, on the other hand, are the tangible results of the organization's activities, but they require justification in terms of a higher purpose (the outcomes). They are not intrinsically understood as goals in themselves. An output for schools would be the number of students graduated. While graduation is clearly good, it is a result of the students having learned enough to earn the graduation and be prepared for the next step in their lives.

Analysts need to keep the higher purpose—the outcomes—firmly in mind throughout the activity, to ensure relevant and actionable outputs that truly benefit the client.

Key steps

One approach to focusing on outcomes is to take a step back and question the very existence of the organization. Most people take the value of their organization for granted; for them, it is such an obviously good thing that no one can question it. But question it they should: "Just why are we here?"

The analyst should ask the organization to look in the mirror and ask several questions of itself. First, who are its customers? A customer is the individual or organization directly served. Businesses obviously have customers, but so do government agencies, nonprofits, and schools.

Second, what do those customers need? On the face of it, most organizations answer that the customer needs what the organization produces. So schools will often say that students need teachers. But what students really need are the knowledge and skills to be successful in life.

Third, what products or services does—or should—the organization produce to satisfy its customers' need(s)? The more an organization can correctly identify the needs, the more it realizes that there are many ways of satisfying those needs, not just the ones the organization happens to provide.

Fourth, what benefits does the organization receive for meeting these customer needs? An organization's relationship with its customers is always quid pro quo, even for a public or nonprofit organization. Every organization needs legitimacy and resources if it is to continue to fulfill its mission.

Finally, who are the stakeholders? Customers are not the only ones affected by how well an organization accomplishes its mission. Stakeholders are those individuals or groups whose wellbeing is affected by how well the organization serves its customers, yet who—unlike customers—do not receive a product or service directly from the organization.

Benefits

Over time, many organizations lose sight of their outcomes and focus more and more on their outputs. The outcomes are general, abstract, and even vague; it is hard to continue to focus on something so general. Outputs, however, tend to be tangible, measurable, and therefore much easier to focus on. Thus individuals and units within the organization tend to focus ever more narrowly on their job rather than on their and the organization's ultimate purpose.

The ultimate benefit of this guideline—*focus on outcomes, not outputs*—is to avoid spending lots of time and effort on activities that are unnecessary. Conversely, the most important outputs are those that support the ultimate purpose of the organization.

Example

Jim Collins (2001) takes on the issue of outcomes by questioning whether profitability or shareholder value is the ultimate purpose of commercial organizations. He cites Merck as an example: In 1950, George Merck II set forth his company's philosophy: "We try to remember that medicine is for the patient... It is not for the profits. The profits follow, and if we have remembered that, they have never failed to appear. The better we have remembered it, the larger they have been." Applying that philosophy, Merck earned profits ten times better than the market average from 1946 to 2000.

Further reading

Collins, J. (2001). *Good to Great*. New York: HarperBusiness.

Department of Finance and Administration. (2003a). Structured Agency Model. Canberra, Australia: Australian Government. Viewed June 2005, www.finance.gov.au/budgetgroup/Commonwealth_Budget_-_Overview/structured_agency_model.html.

Department of Finance and Administration. (2003b). The Outcomes and Outputs Framework. Canberra, Australia: Australian Government. Viewed June 2005, www.finance.gov.au/budgetgroup/commonwealth_budget_-_overview/the_outcomes___outputs_framewo.html.

"FAQs." (2002). Publishers Weekly. Viewed June 2005, www.publishersweekly.com/index.asp?layout=contentinfodetail&articleID=CA260302&channel=AboutUS&display=wildcard#trade.

1.4.3 Work in Multiple Time Horizons

Opportunities or challenges in strategic foresight are typically complex. They need to be studied from different perspectives and viewpoints, including their evolution over time. Thinking through the time perspective will bring richness and depth to the activity and could lead to insights that would escape a more traditional "snapshot" approach.

The timeframe should be negotiated with sponsors as part of the initial chartering in order to properly manage expectations. In most cases, analysts will want to look further into the future than the organization does. Analysts are usually more comfortable with a longer timeframe, and more skilled at identifying the longer-term possibilities and their implications for decision-making today. The organization, however, will often be skeptical of the long view and seek to shorten the timeframe.

Key steps

One way to allay concerns about the long-term timeframe is to talk about the time ecology of the issue: how issues change over time. Effective strategic foresight is not simply a matter of studying the present and/ or the long-term future; it also means studying the issue at points along the way. Different issues are embedded in different systems, which in turn have different relevant timeframes. The computer chip industry, for example, operates on a far more compressed timeframe than the automobile industry. See *Guideline 1.1.6 Recognize that Different Changes Occur at Different Rates*.

During the course of an activity, analysts are likely to uncover future points in time at which key changes are likely to occur. These points along the pathway are excellent fulcra around which to structure a useful pathway to the future. For instance, in analyzing the evolution of global management of global issues, the expected implementation of a global treaty in the years ahead might be identified as an important point on the pathway.

Identifying these critical leverage or trigger points can help the client appreciate the value of extending the activity into the future, by creating a picture of how this evolution (or revolution) may look over time. While the trigger points should become clear during the course of the activity, once the end state has been forecast, the analyst should also take a step back and consider whether any additional leverage or trigger events may have been missed. This can be as simple as asking, "How might we get there from here?" Thinking through these transition points or milestones will help the client appreciate time ecology.

Benefits

Appreciating time ecology adds depth and insight to strategic foresight activities. The longer the timeframe, the greater the range of strategic options that can be considered. It opens up the consideration set and may enable the analyst to see possibilities that would be missed in a shorter time horizon.

At the same time, looking at multiple points in time helps bring the activity to life. The organization will appreciate seeing how events might unfold and evolve over time. Constructing a plausible pathway with milestones into the future will lend credibility to the extended timeframe. The analyst can then tie the look to the future back to the present, and show how decisions made today might either lead to a preferable future or avoid an undesirable one.

Example

A multiclient project exploring the future of science and technology involved extensive negotiations between the analysts and clients as to the proper timeframe. The analyst team saw value in looking a generation ahead in the hopes of enabling the clients to see beyond current short-term concerns. They felt the clients would benefit by anticipating the breakthroughs of the next generation—the seeds of which could be planted in long-term R&D efforts in the present. The team's belief was that a generational approach was the right time ecology for long-term, breakthrough R&D. The timeframe settled on was thirty years ahead.

The clients were generally enthusiastic, but were concerned that their staff colleagues might not appreciate the value of a thirty-year outlook. Two mechanisms were adopted to allay the concerns. The first was an historical look at forecasts made in the past for various science and technology areas. This analysis brought to light the various strengths and weaknesses of previous looks to the future. It provided much-needed context for the forecasts the analysis team itself put together in the second phase of the project.

This second phase included a "critical events" timeline that summarized key potential developments along the pathway from the present to the longer-term future, in each of the topical areas forecast. These pathways provided credibility for the longer-term forecast by demonstrating a plausible series of events.

Further reading

Boulding, E. (2003). Visioning and Futures Studies. Interview by Julian Portilla. Viewed July 2005, www.beyondintractability.org/iweb/audio/boulding-e-3-future-studies1.html.

Coates, J.F., Mahaffie, J.B., and Hines, A. (1996). *2025: Scenarios of US and Global Society as Reshaped by Science and Technology*. Greensboro, NC: Oakhill Press.

Groff, L. and Smoker, P. (n.d.). Time Periods for Studying the Future. *Introduction to Futures Studies*. Viewed July 2005, www.csudh.edu/global_options/IntroFS.HTML#FSTimePrds.

1.4.4 Weave "Outside and Then" with "Inside And Now"

Systems theorist Stafford Beer pointed out that organizations tend to focus on *"inside and now"*—results and improvements in the present and near future. Strategic foresight, by contrast, focuses on *"outside and then"*—on what could be happening outside the organization and in the longer-term future. The analyst should seek to weave "inside and now" with "outside and then."

Key steps

Strategic foresight mediates two types of relationships, which might be termed *translation* and *transformation*.

- Translation involves translating "outside and then" so that it can be used to improve the organization's existing policies, strategies, and plans—its "inside and now."
- Transformation involves transforming the identity of the organization by reshaping its purpose, niche, or identity, using what's learned from "outside and then" to transform "inside and now."

Each relationship favors certain methods and carries unique responsibilities. The analyst should ask which of these relationships is being invoked. If the brief is clear, then it is easy to know whether the organization is seeking translation or transformation.

Translation is the more straightforward of the two. The "outside and then" perspective seeks opportunities for exploitation, improvements to existing strategies, environmental monitoring, and competitor evaluation. The stated aims often include improving responsiveness, reducing inputs, freeing up capacity, and raising strategic agility. It is about giving the organization what it wants. This work is less threatening since the messages are framed to fit within existing worldviews of decision-makers.

Transformation, however, is a greater challenge for all parties concerned. It is not about giving the organization what it wants; it's about framing a new organization. It is not about steering the ship (translation); it's about transforming the ship into a submarine or aircraft. The most important question for the analyst to ask here is, "Does the organization have the capacity to transform?" To try and transform without capacity is organizational bungee-jumping without a rope attached. The simplest way to assess the capacity for transformation is to ask the six questions set out by Beck and Cowan in *Spiral Dynamics* (1996):

1. Does the potential exist for people to think differently?
2. Do solutions exist for unresolved problems?
3. Is there sufficient dissonance about the present?
4. Is there insight about alternatives?
5. Are the barriers to transformation identified and addressable?
6. Is support available during transformation?

If all six are not present, then don't try transformation.

Benefits

Understanding the effects of foresight on organizational cybernetics—organizational design and systems thinking—is fundamental to satisfying the organization and winning return work. Translating the "outside and then" to the "inside and now" sounds easy. It may sound like compromising the integrity of the outside to make it more palatable to the inside, but it is really about respecting where an organization currently is and what capacities it has. It avoids bringing in too much variety and thereby compromising the organizational control systems.

Transformation is exciting and interesting stuff, but it also carries great responsibility. Attempting transformation involves a leap of faith. If the attempt fails, people will get hurt. If the attempt succeeds, magic happens.

The value of this guideline is in helping analysts help organizations and themselves. It prevents the "parachute" practitioner who drops into an organization and floods the system with variety that compromises its existing control systems, or who takes the organization partway down a transformational path only to discover that the capacity for transformation was not there.

Example

Beck (1996) describes how spiral dynamics was used as a tool for transformational thinking during South Africa's emergence from apartheid. He made dozens of trips to South Africa during this period, using spiral dynamics to illustrate the differences in worldviews among the parties and to demonstrate an acceptable alternative. The chief challenge was that the psychological center of gravity at the time was blue-orange (a mix of reliance on traditional authority and searching for a better way), and the question was where it would go next. Beck held that the black majority would see a shift back to red-blue, with more reliance on raw power to redress grievances from the past, while the European/Afrikaner-dominated status quo would move towards an all-out orange position focused on the material success of the ruling class. The resolution came when Beck was able to persuade the South African leadership to adopt a yellow thinking strategy, which emphasizes taking advantage of multiple worldviews according to the specific situation. This strategy created a synergistic rather than mutually exclusive approach which was instrumental in the ultimately successful transition.

Further reading

Beck, D. and Cowan, C. (1996). *Spiral Dynamics*. Oxford: Blackwell.

Beer, S. (1984). *Diagnosing the System for Organizations*. New York: Wiley.

Hayward, P. (2004). Facilitating Foresight: Where the Foresight Function Is Placed in the Organization. *foresight: the journal of futures studies, strategic thinking, and policy, 6*(1), 19 - 30.

1.5 Select Your Team

1.5.1 Recognize that Strategic Foresight Is a Team Sport

A strategic foresight activity will benefit more if it gathers input from a team than from individuals. An interacting team provides diverse perspectives and enriches both the quality and quantity of the ideas considered.

A typical strategic foresight activity involves, from the very beginning, a core team that remains together throughout. The core team should include representatives from key stakeholder groups where practical, and can be enhanced by adding temporary members depending on the activity's status and what kinds of expertise are needed. Thus, the size and composition of the team will likely fluctuate as the activity progresses, with the core members keeping the key learning intact.

Key steps

An initial consideration in putting together a team is the right size. Research by Richard Hackman (2002) suggests that for a core team, no more than six members is optimal. Once it grows beyond six, the productivity of the group begins to decline. Large groups are not well-suited to reaching closure and delivering an end product. Moreover, since individual contributions are usually less well-recognized in a large group, many people will not see the value of investing their time and effort in the activity if the group is too large. It is best to add and subtract people on an ad-hoc basis.

Assign core members to remain with the team for the duration of the activity. It is preferable to have 100% dedicated core team members wherever possible, as fractional commitments often lead to unfocused activity in which much time is spent simply updating team members about what has happened.

A second important consideration is that the core group should be directly involved in chartering the activity with sponsors. Additionally, although an analyst may rely on staff for some operational work, the core group should not become an advisory board. The members of this group should have the explicit charge to take a lead role in carrying out the work. A decision-maker should be among the participants, since neither the organizer nor the facilitator can step into this role. Participation enables the decision-maker to identify with both the process and the outputs.

Identify prospective ad-hoc members as early as possible. It is often difficult to get key experts or stakeholders to contribute their time, so the earlier the better. Others can always be added as more is learned and additional expertise or perspectives are required. At the same time, the analyst needs to avoid the perception that the process is elitist. This should be kept in mind while designing both the core group and the wider ad-hoc participation.

It is also advisable to include people with diverse thinking styles and perspectives. Some conflict within a team is actually healthy over the long run. Teams that share the same backgrounds and perspectives often fall into groupthink. At the same time, teams that are constantly at war are not productive either. Seek a balance of diversity such that conflicting views are put forward and heard, but participants are capable of coming to resolution and moving ahead.

Benefits

Involving a team in strategic foresight improves the quality of the solutions. In his popular book *The Wisdom of Crowds* (2004), journalist James Surowiecki outlines how the mathematics of probability favor the ability of a group, over that of an individual, to pick the best solution. While the process may at times seem laborious and time-consuming, the collective judgment of a group improves the odds of devising the best solutions.

Example

Hackman (2002) describes the birth of Brooks' Law: "Adding manpower to a late software project makes it later." Frederick Brooks managed the OS/360 systems programming project at IBM in the 1960s, then the largest such project ever undertaken. As the work fell behind schedule, the organization fell victim to the temptation to add staff to help catch up. Brooks, however, suggested that adding a dozen people to make up for being a dozen person-months behind was like assigning nine women to be pregnant for one month each to produce a baby quicker. As he predicted, rather than speeding up the project the extra people slowed it down—leading to the emergence of Brooks' Law.

Further reading

Hackman, J.R. (2002). *Leading Teams: Setting the Stage for Great Performances*. Cambridge, MA: Harvard Business Press.

Hines, A. (1999, August). The Foresight Amphibian in the Corporate World. *foresight: the journal of futures studies, strategic thinking, and policy, 1*(4).

Janis, I. (1989). *Crucial Decisions*. New York: The Free Press.

Nutt, P.C. (2002). *Why Decisions Fail: Avoiding the Blunders and Traps That Lead to Debacles*. San Francisco: Berrett-Koehler.

Stevens, G. and Burley, J. (May - June 1997). 3,000 Raw Ideas = One Commercial Success. *Research Technology Management, 40*(3), 16 - 27.

Surowiecki, J. (2004). *The Wisdom of Crowds: Why the Many Are Smarter than the Few and How Collective Wisdom Shapes Business, Economies, Societies, and Nations*. New York: Random House.

1.5.2 Make Strategic Foresight as Immersive and Interactive as Possible

Strategic foresight can tend to be esoteric or intellectual. It involves a lot of conceptual and strategic thinking. It emphasizes future possibilities and what they mean for the present. If the analyst is not careful, it can remain abstract and impractical. A solution is to make the activity *immersive and interactive*. In other words, make the conceptual and abstract as tangible and concrete as possible. Have participants "get their hands dirty" in order to get to concrete possibilities.

Key steps

Once the team is set, the choices made early about how to conduct the activity will set the tone for the rest of the activity. A team-building activity early on, for example, sets the tone of participation. Frequent updates and communication sessions will also build in the wide variety of perspectives essential to strategic foresight. Setting a regular communications schedule and keeping to it is a way of keeping participants updated and involved, which in turn increases the likelihood they will be fully engaged.

Another mechanism to help with immersion is a *war room*—a dedicated space where team members work on the activity. It should be away from the daily hubbub to minimize distractions and maximize focus on the activity. It can also serve as a showcase for work-in-progress, with visual displays of what the team is doing as a way to interest and involve others.

Workshops are an effective means for getting the organization immersed in the activity. Offsite workshops are particularly effective, as they remove participants from the daily distractions of phone, email, etc. A "no communications" rule, that is, no cell phones, PDAs, or email, can also help deepen engagement in the workshop.

Interaction and immersion are critical when presenting results, too. The decision-makers will be more engaged by participating in exploring the options and implications than by passively listening to a presentation or reading a report. The specific approach will depend on the results and on the makeup of the decision-makers, with options ranging from simple Q&A to a more exotic role-playing activity in which mock situations are used to dramatize the possibilities.

Benefits

The value of this guideline can be seen in the evolution of scenario planning over the years. There has been a clear trend away from carefully crafted and well-written scenario narratives as the key deliverable, in favor of participatory scenario workshops. Most practitioners now spend less time writing the narratives and more time designing interview protocols and workshops. Too many narratives were ending up unused on the shelves because the organization was unclear about how to use them; thus the shift towards immersion and interaction, in a workshop format, to engage the organization with the materials.

Example

A large multinational food company tasked an analysis team with developing an entirely new product line in the emerging arena of nutriceuticals or functional foods. The team asked for and was given a separate building to get some distance from the existing business units, which were somewhat skeptical of the venture. The team customized this new space and created an atmosphere and espirit de corps that enabled it to keep focus and launch a full range of products on schedule, despite significant turmoil in the rest of the organization, which was going through a restructuring. Although the product line was ultimately taken off the market—owing in part to being too far ahead of its time—the speed of the launch and the lessons learned will be valuable to the larger company when it inevitably explores this arena again in the future.

Further reading

Hines. A. (2000, August). The Facilitator versus the Expert, or Process versus Content. *foresight: the journal of futures studies, strategic thinking, and policy,* 2(4).

Shaker, S.M. and Gembicki, M.P. (1999). *The War Room Guide to Competitive Intelligence*. New York: McGraw-Hill.

1.5.3 Include People Who Do Not Agree

Disagreements arise from two sources—differences in information and knowledge and differences over fundamental assumptions or values. Both are important sources of new learning. Including people with access to different information expands the pool of ideas to draw upon. Including people with different assumptions or values expands the range of perspectives that can be accessed. Including both lessens the chances of overlooking a key piece of information or making an assumption that will be at odds with the organization's value system.

Key steps

The purpose of involving people who disagree is to enable the best possible decision-making. Therefore, include people who can express dissenting views yet work towards a common objective. The first step is to establish an atmosphere in which legitimate disagreements are allowed to flourish, as long as they are confined to the objective at hand. Make it clear that the disagreement is being carried on within the context of a specific objective and timeframe, in order to make the ultimate decision more robust.

The way to be sure the assembled team shares a common objective is to select people who agree about the ultimate objective and are prepared to surrender their individual or group objectives if the decision goes against their views. (Bradford, 2000:12 - 20) On the other hand, it is just as important to select people who might disagree, and to listen to them when they do.

Jim Collins (2001:73 - 80) suggests four guidelines for creating "a climate where the truth is heard" once the objective is established and everyone agrees to work for it:

1. Lead with questions, not answers.
2. Engage in dialogue and debate, not coercion.
3. Conduct autopsies, without blame.
4. Build "red flag" mechanisms (i.e., ways for people to raise objections without penalty).

The creativity consultant Edward de Bono (1985) suggests another mechanism for allowing disagreement to surface. He maintains that group discussion involves six different roles, one of which is to disagree. He characterizes each role with a different color hat: white for objective information, green for process remarks, black for disagreement, etc. Once the group learns this language, a person can begin an objection with "I'm going to put on the black hat for awhile and..." That remark alerts the group that a disagreement is coming. By identifying disagreements as such, they become acceptable and even welcome.

Benefits

A narrow technical topic can be handled by technical experts, but a broad scope of inquiry will benefit from diverse perspectives. Inferences and decisions on broader topics involve large amounts of data and rely heavily on the choice of assumptions and values. A larger and more diverse group therefore increases the likelihood that critical information will be included and critical assumptions and values given due consideration.

Disagreements do sometimes get out of hand. "Are we talking about that again?" However, disagreements that go on forever are really not disagreements; they are differences of another kind. They are about politics or personality.

So in the end, disagreement is healthy, even necessary, as long as people engage in it for the higher purpose of achieving the best result from the assembled group. "Contrary to the common belief that conflict is limited to a disruptive effect, a number of researchers acknowledge the substantial benefits of conflict to team processes." (McDaniel et al., 1998)

Example

In *Good to Great* (2001, pp. 65 - 69), Jim Collins relays how A&P and Kroger had different responses to the decline of the traditional supermarket in the 1970s and the rise of the superstore. In the 1950s, A&P was the largest retailer in the world and Kroger was an unspectacular chain less than half its size. By 1973 the companies were about even in size, and, over the next 25 years, Kroger generated returns eight times better than A&P's. Collins suggests that Kroger was able to confront the "brutal facts" of change in the world and describes A&P as "the Hermit Kingdom"—run like an absolute monarchy, an environment hardly conducive to disagreement. Collins notes, "By 1970, the Kroger executive team came to an inescapable conclusion: The old model grocery store was going to become extinct." Kroger conducted a series of experiments that led it to the superstore concept, then altered all of its stores to fit the new realities of what consumers wanted.

Further reading

Bradford, R.W. and Duncan, J.P. (2000). *Simplified Strategic Planning*. Worcester, MA: Chandler House Press.

Collins, Jim. (2001). *Good to Great*. New York: HarperCollins.

De Bono, E. (1985). *Six Thinking Hats*. New York: Little, Brown & Co.

McDaniel, G., Littlejohn, S., and Domenici, K. (1998). A Team Conflict Mediation Process That Really Works! In M. Bullock, C. Friday, K. Belcher, B. Bisset, S. Hurley, C. Foote, and D. Thai, eds. *The International Conference on Work Teams— Proceedings: 1998* (67 - 74). Denton: University of North Texas, Center for the Study of Work Teams.

1.6 Create a Strategic Work Environment

1.6.1 Create an Environment Conducive to Open and Uninhibited Thinking

Strategic foresight requires creative and innovative thinking, which is best stimulated in an environment of openness. The ideal physical space is open, comfortable, and full of stimulus, encouraging the free flow of ideas, risk-taking, and out-of-the-box thinking.

Key steps

Choosing a physical space can be straightforward. In the best case, creativity-inducing spaces will be widely available. Some organizations set up dedicated creativity or ideation spaces. Others have *futures rooms*, e.g., General Motors and Alticor. Some hire outside experts in creative-space design to customize a venue. In the more usual case, analysts will either have to search for or create the space they need. A space that is a bit isolated, away from the daily hubbub, is advisable. Often, some unused, less-desirable space can be claimed and revamped.

One optimal solution is a *war room*—a dedicated space where team members can congregate and work together for the duration of an activity. They can customize the room to the needs of the activity. Most end up covering the walls with relevant charts, graphs, diagrams, or useful stimuli.

Another option to consider is *offsite space*. Even when a team has a workable onsite space, it may be a good idea to arrange periodic offsite work sessions. Offsites can refresh the team as well as encourage participation by non-members. Many firms provide these kinds of spaces for hire. The value of getting away from the daily grind of emails and meetings can be an invaluable stimulus to strategic thinking.

A caution about the use of creative spaces—onsite or offsite: they are vulnerable to swings in organizational fortunes and priorities. Many initiatives to encourage innovation are reversed when an organization's fortunes dip, for example because its stock price drops or new management takes over. Do not invest too much political capital or credibility in these spaces. Some basic recommendations are:

- Make sure the room has windows, for daylight and fresh air.
- Arrange the room in a way that enables people to move and change places. Physical freedom helps free the mind (ideas need space and freedom).
- Avoid noisy areas. The center of attention should be inside, not outside.
- Make sure that everything required is available, such as Internet access.

- Make sure the physical concerns of participants are accounted for.
- Visit the place beforehand to see it yourself.

Benefits

As former IDEO head Thomas Kelley remarked in a segment on the ABC show *Nightline*, profiling IDEO's innovative work culture and physical space: "It's about ambience." Kelley was explaining why he was willing to invest $4,000 in a DC9 aircraft wing for one of IDEO's design studios. This example is not intended as an endorsement of extravagance for strategic foresight; rather, it makes the point that environment can be key to creativity.

Creating the right physical setting and atmosphere are as important as having the right participants in the room. Studies have shown that mood and performance during a meeting are highly influenced by the meeting room setup, including the food and drink (participants always remember the quality of the food). Thus it is important to ensure that mood is not dampened by the physical atmosphere. Also keep in mind that strategic foresight, in particular, demands a rather abstract level of thinking. The wrong setting can hinder participants from reaching the needed level of abstraction, since they will be continuously preoccupied by physical concerns.

Example

A leading materials company sought to launch an initiative to stimulate ideas for new business growth in the company. The company's culture was rather conservative and favored "in-the-box" thinking. In planning the initiative, the team discovered a great deal of skepticism in the company about doing things differently. Thus, the analysis team felt obliged to demonstrate the commitment to a new culture by organizing an offsite workshop at Gerald Haman's "Thinkubator" creativity space in downtown Chicago. The investment in the workshop clearly signaled the seriousness of senior management's commitment to doing things differently. It also provided an excellent forum to kick off the team's work. This success led the team to hire Haman to bring a portable version of his creativity room back to the home organization when the team had its regular monthly meetings. Several ideas begun in that forum lived on in a different form into the future.

Further reading

Kelley, T. (2001). *The Art of Innovation*. New York: Currency Doubleday.

Haman, G. (1999). *The Six Ingredients of Creative Thinking*. Chicago, IL: SolutionPeople.

Sittenfeld, C. (1999, April). What's the Big Idea? *Fast Company*.

1.6.2 Encourage Experiments and Prototypes

There is no single best approach to preparing organizations for the future. Choosing the right approach requires getting a sense of all the options—which in turn can be generated by *experiments and prototypes*.

Key steps

Ways to encourage experimentation and prototyping are legion. Creativity guru Edward de Bono (1996) recommends first acknowledging that the way things are currently done in the organization is just one way. The current approach may have been the best at the time it was implemented, but circumstances change with time. There is always the opportunity to rethink how things could be done better.

Innovation writer Andrew Hargadon (2003) recommends encouraging staff to work across different areas within and outside the organization. His research indicates that innovation is essentially a synthesis of ideas from different domains, brought together in novel ways. Therefore, encouraging staff to work in cross-sector teams and to visit external groups is one key to sparking new ideas.

Strategy expert Gary Hamel (2003) suggests creating a "marketplace for ideas" within the organization—essentially, bringing the concept of venture capitalism inside. For example, managers could be given the opportunity to spend a small percentage of their budgets each year on any in-house project of interest to them, anywhere in the organization. Often, says Hamel, one of the deterrents to ideas being further developed is lack of funding, so this idea of internal seed capital could give life to innovations that otherwise would have died on the vine.

Benefits

There are two major benefits from encouraging experiments and prototypes. First, if organizations are to evolve successfully into the future, they need to be seeding the next generation of products, services, or business models today. The odds of success are greater if there is a range of experiments from which to choose. As Hamel and Valikangas state (2003:59), "Most companies would be better off if they made fewer billion-dollar bets and a whole lot more $10,000 or $20,000 bets—some of which will, in time, justify more substantial commitments. They should steer clear of grand, imperial strategies and devote themselves instead to launching a swarm of low-risk experiments..."

Second, de Bono (1996) argues that the usual Western approach to problem-solving or improvement is to attack and criticize, then look for an alternative. This analytical approach does not always lead to creative or fruitful solutions. The alternative—often non-Western—perspective, he says, is to acknowledge what already exists, then look for and develop alternatives. Then, compare the alternatives and their results with what exists. This creative and free-flowing activity allows for a more diverse range of options, leading to a wider variety of potential solutions. As Buckminster Fuller once said, "You never change something by fighting the existing reality. To change something, build a new model that makes the existing model obsolete."

Example

Hamel and Valikangas (2003) describe the case of Whirlpool. Between 1999 and 2003 the company involved 10,000 of its employees in a range of workshops and training sessions to search for breakthrough ideas. The result was 7,000 ideas, which led to 300 small-scale experiments. The company went on to manage this innovation process through a set of measures that enable senior executives to track how many new ideas are being generated, where they are in terms of development, and their potential financial impact.

Further reading

de Bono, E. (1996). *Serious Creativity: Using the Power of Lateral Thinking to Create New Ideas*. Hammersmith, UK: Harper-Collins Business.

Hamel, G. (2003, Winter). Innovation as a Deep Capability. In *Leader to Leader*, viewed July 2005, www.pfdf.org/leaderbooks/L2L/winter2003/hamel.html.

Hamel, G. and Valikangas, L. (2003). The Quest for Resilience. *Harvard Business Review*.

Hargadon, A. (2003). *How Breakthroughs Happen: The Surprising Truth about How Companies Innovate*. Boston: Harvard Business School Press.

Maxwell, J. (2004, August). Whose Beautiful Mind? As Business Focuses on Creativity, There's a Fresh—But Not Surprising—Spin Emerging about How to Judge Those Big New Ideas. *Australian Financial Review BOSS*, 34 - 38.

2 ▶ Scanning

2.0 SCANNING

"Breadth + Depth = Foresight with Insight." —Andy Hines

Once the team is clear about the boundaries and scope of an activity, it begins to *scan* the internal and external environments for information and trends relating to the issue at hand. Internally, the team wants to learn the organization's experience with the issue. Externally, the team immerses itself in what's going on regarding the issue. The goal is to come up with a mix of basic driving forces that suggest the most likely future, and some insight into potential change-drivers that may lead to alternative future outcomes. In scanning parlance, this involves identifying the *macro-trends* that will form the basis of the baseline forecast (or "most likely future") and the *weak signals* that may portend discontinuities that drive alternative futures.

Recent advances in the art of environmental scanning have emphasized the need to go beyond the strictly empirical and incorporate more intuitive sources of information. Related to this is an emphasis on expanding the breadth and depth of the scanning activity to include a wider range of sources and to probe more deeply into their potential implications for the activity. It's less about finding a piece of information that no one else can find—since information is so freely available—and more about understanding and acting upon that information more quickly and creatively than competitors.

The first set of guidelines in this section, *2.1 Map the System*, sets the context by outlining forces, factors, and stakeholders and their relationships in light of the issue being studied. They suggest taking the widest and deepest possible view—one that considers elements beyond the typical narrow organizational interest. Insight will often come from thinking about things the organization does not typically consider and discovering relationships or impacts that would otherwise have escaped notice. A system map is often a key reference piece, and in many cases analysts will blow one up to wall-size and place it in either a dedicated war room or an area where those involved in the activity can routinely see it. An effective visual can be very helpful in stimulating interest and thinking.

The second set of guidelines, *2.2 Study History*, explains the importance of knowing how the organization got to where it is. This can provide valuable information, with insights into the organization's assumptions and its view of the "official future." This section also cautions the analyst not to be blindsided by organizational landmines, such as "We tried that before and..."—and helps the analyst anticipate trouble spots that may emerge.

The third set, *2.3 Scan the Environment*, is fundamental to any strategic foresight activity. Organizations tend to view the world "outside" only as it relates directly to their business concerns. Automotive companies, for example, may fall into monitoring only vehicle and transportation trends, ignoring or downplaying developments outside these two areas. It is the job of the analyst to engage the organization in the value of seeing the bigger picture. A trend towards portable foods, for example, may suggest possibilities for "dashboard dining."

The fourth set, *2.4 Involve Colleagues and Outsiders*, guards against the organizational tendency to "talk to ourselves." It can be very easy to fall into a pattern of talking only to trusted colleagues and seeing those outside the organization or industry as lacking the necessary expertise. This set of guidelines promotes the complementary value of bringing in fresh perspectives, as a means of triggering creative thinking.

2.1 Map the System

2.1.1 Adopt a Global Perspective

Strategic foresight needs to consider what is happening in other parts of the world. No situation or system is immune to events and forces elsewhere. Consider changes around the world and how they relate to the client's overall business as well as to the issue under study. Thinking about the rest of the world should be prominent in research, analysis, or discussion—literally in all aspects of an activity. Modeling this thinking approach will influence colleagues and collaborators to think this way as well.

Key steps

There is no single way to embrace a global perspective. But it is critical to build one into processes specific both to the work and to the larger organizational culture. Ways to do this include:

- Keep a world map or a globe nearby so events can quickly be placed in global context.
- Read international news daily and subscribe to news sources (print, email, RSS, etc.) that cover new developments from around the world.
- It practically goes without saying to travel as much as possible and see as much as possible firsthand.
- Borrow time from people in the organization who come from other countries. Make their views part of a reality check about the environment surrounding the activity. It is astonishing how many organizations neglect to take advantage of their own staff's "ground-level" observations.
- Keep in touch with people outside the organization who have different perspectives and knowledge—ideally people from around the world—and help incorporate their views into the organization's thinking.
- Make global regions and global forces part of an analytical checklist. For example, some people use the *STEEP framework* (social, technological, economic, environmental, and political) to ensure they think broadly enough about what they are studying. Also build in a way to consider important changes by region, by economic or political categories, or by using example countries.

Benefits

Strategic work that fails to consider the wider system is limited and vulnerable. Nevertheless, organizations will sometimes say they are only interested in a certain region or country, or their own industry. They may also consider it easier and less costly to just research and analyze trends in a narrow, familiar context.

These are traps. Work that considers the global context is more likely to be both accurate and useful. Many of the changes that can blindside an organization come from elsewhere—either directly, as for example with a newly competitive player in an emerging business sector in China or India, or indirectly, as with changing use of telecommunications technology in a bellwether society such as Japan or South Korea.

Example

An example of the value of global perspective comes from a weeklong foresight workshop held for a group of corporate executives envisioning their company in fifteen years. The company was a multinational that produces a wide array of instruments, sensors, and controls for air conditioning and heating equipment. The executives came from all over the organization, including Australia, China, Europe, and Latin America. But the dominant group was American, with American experience and American market responsibilities.

The participants began the week excited to explore a gee-whiz, highly optimistic future for their company's products. The handful of executives from outside the United States did their best to assert the interests of non-US markets and consumers. The outside futurist who was present also pressed this perspective, with remarks about emerging markets and rising incomes and aspirations around the world. He also explored with them wide-ranging environment and sustainability issues faced by different world regions. He insisted that the scenarios created by the group include images of the future beyond the United States.

A breakthrough moment came when a China-based executive pointed out that far from being interested in programmable smart thermostats, many in his region would like first to have home heating. Ultimately, the American executives got it. They broke through to new thinking about where their company's growth might come from. They discovered a whole world of potential opportunity for their company when they adopted a global perspective.

Further reading

Masini, E.B. (1994). *The Futures of Cultures*. Paris: UNESCO.

Tough, A. (1991). *Critical Questions about the Future*. Lanham, MD: University Press of America.

2.1.2 Map the System Under Consideration

Effective problem-solving requires understanding the context of the issue at hand. The best way to do this is to map the issue in a simple *systems map*—identifying the key stakeholders and driving forces influencing the issue, then exploring the relationships among them.

Mapping an issue in its systemic context is done at the very beginning of a strategic activity. The systems map lays out a framework for the activity. It points to important stakeholders to interview, trend areas to investigate, and assumptions that need to be checked. The map will evolve as the study proceeds and more is learned about the system. Also, new issues and stakeholders will likely emerge as the activity proceeds.

Key steps

Creating a systems map is straightforward, involving several steps. First, define the issue crisply. Studying the future of communications, for example, is likely to be overbroad. Studying the future of keypad size on mobile phones might be overly narrow. An appropriate scope might be the future of mobile-phone handsets.

Once your issue is crisply defined, identify the forces, trends, and actors relevant to it. Brainstorm a list of these forces, trends, and actors; then prioritize according to how important each item is to the future of the issue. Select two that portend the greatest impact on the issue and whether it will continue along its expected path. These two criteria can be placed on X and Y axes. The diagram can then be turned into a matrix so that the other items can be added to it, sorted into their respective "bins."

Next, stakeholders can be identified and prioritized using a similar process. Here the goal is to identify who currently and potentially has an important stake in, or influence on, the issue. Then sort the prioritized forces and stakeholders according to their relationships to the issue and to one another. Simply use arrows to indicate relationships among the factors and to the issue itself, and proximity to the issue as a way to indicate the strength of the relationship—with those closer to the issue indicating a strong relationship, those further away indicating a weaker one.

Lastly, check the systems map against a STEEP framework: social, technological, economic, environmental, and political forces, plus any additional categories of forces deemed relevant, e.g., educational trends. Run the issue through these categories to see if any influential forces or stakeholders were missed during the ideation.

A challenge in systems mapping is to get the level of complexity right. If too many forces and stakeholders are included, the map loses its utility as a navigational tool for dealing with complexity. If too few are identified, the activity risks being undermined by an unidentified force or stakeholder down the road. A similar challenge involves mapping the relationships. The purpose here is to provide a rough model or framework for thinking, not a scientifically defensible one. So don't get carried away with too much detail around the model—knowledge about the system will grow as the activity proceeds.

Once the system is mapped, the activity is on solid footing.

Benefits

A systems map is a tool for understanding the context of an activity. Placing the issue in context deepens understanding of it, and identifies ways the issue might be influenced and changed in the future by key forces or stakeholders.

Another benefit of systems maps is that they identify external factors that organizations might otherwise miss. Organizations are sometimes undone by failing to grasp the importance and influence of an external factor. They may take detailed account of issues within their industry, but miss relevant issues outside the industry that end up having a big influence.

A systems map also provides a visual framework for the activity. If the activity has its own physical space, create a poster- or wall-sized systems map. It will provide stimulus for thinking and a helpful backdrop for discussion, and can also be used to explain the activity to others in the organization. Of course, the wall map can also be adapted into a virtual format and housed on the Web.

Example

Consulting futurist Joseph Coates (1999) gives an example of how organizations run into difficulty when considering the broader system they are a part of. Coates was engaged by the US Environmental Protection Agency (EPA) to explore emerging environmental issues. His team pointed out the possibility of noise, particularly from loud radios, leading to hearing loss. Another issue identified was the possibility of environmental factors leading to declining sperm counts. EPA, however, was structured around its major concerns—air, water, solid waste, etc. No unit within EPA could fit these two emerging problems into its mission. Hence, nothing was done. Subsequently, of course, both issues have emerged as important threats to health.

Further reading

Coates, J.F. (1999, Fall). Technology Forecasting for Business Clients. *Futures Research Quarterly, 15* (3).

Coates, J.F. (2001, Fall). The Future as a Factor in Business Planning and Management. *Futures Research Quarterly, 17* (3).

Lovins, H. (1990, Spring). The Parachuting Cats. *InContext*. Viewed February 2005, www.context.org/ICLIB/IC25/Lovins.htm.

Senge, P., Kleiner, A., Roberts, C., Ross, R., and Smith, B. (1994). *The Fifth Discipline Fieldbook*. New York: Currency Doubleday.

2.1.3 Take an Integral View of the Issue

An integral view enables the analyst to identify and explore the broader context and connections in which the issue is embedded. It involves coming to the activity from different perspectives and exploring the issue from different angles.

Integral philosopher Ken Wilber (2000) has proposed a scheme for an integral view, which has been adapted to foresight by futurist Richard Slaughter and colleagues. Wilber suggests that many issues or problems are not properly analyzed because they are considered from a single perspective that neglects others. He has constructed a four-quadrant matrix that provides a framework for bringing multiple perspectives to bear. The ends of the horizontal axis are the "inner" and "outer" perspectives, and the ends of the vertical axis are the "individual" and "social" perspectives. Therefore, the four perspectives of an integral analysis are:

- The Intentional, or individual-interior "inner world of identity and meaning" (focus on psychology)
- The Cultural, or social-interior "world of cultures and shared meaning" (focus on culture)
- The Behavioral, or individual-exterior "world of individual capability and behavior" (focus on behavior)
- The Social, or social-exterior "physical world" (focus on systems)

Key steps

Wilber's four-quadrant matrix provides a useful check or reference throughout a strategic foresight activity. While it has the greatest utility within Scanning, it can be used in any of the six major steps outlined in this book. For example, during Framing, it is useful to adopt the integral perspective to consider aspects of the issue involving individual psychology or motivation, cultural trends, and supporting systems or infrastructure.

During Scanning and Forecasting, the integral perspective helps ensure that all aspects relating to the issue are being considered. When analyzing scanning hits, the four-quadrant matrix can be used to help identify trends or discontinuities that might otherwise escape notice. For example, the analyst might identify a trend towards fewer people voting. If the analysis stopped there, one might conclude that people are less interested in politics. Taking an integral perspective, however, one would consider the psychological aspects accompanying the behavior and discover that people are actually very interested and involved in politics. But they are expressing that interest by focusing on single issues personally important to them, through mechanisms such as volunteer work with community groups or non-governmental organizations. An integral perspective helps ensure that scanning hits and the resulting forecasts consider a broad array of possibilities.

When exploring visions, plans, and actions, an integral perspective again broadens the range of possibilities. It is useful to run the potential options and actions through the integral matrix and consider whether they adequately address the four perspectives. Take, for example, a study exploring an increase in travel to China. The behavioral aspects could explore the measurable behavior involved—the actual increase in miles traveled to China. The intentional aspect could look into the individual motivations for going to China. The cultural aspect could look into why other cultures are increasingly interested in China. The physical aspect might look at how the Chinese infrastructure will, or won't, be able to cope with the increased travel.

Benefits

An integral perspective enriches the depth of the activity and helps an organization avoid getting blindsided. It involves more time and effort to think through multiple perspectives, so it may be tempting to skip or gloss over it. Many analyses, however, are undone by a seemingly unrelated trend or stakeholder that escapes an analysis team operating from a single or limited perspective.

Example

An analyst at a Fortune 500 company used an integral perspective to inform foresight activities involving the exploration of new business opportunities. His environmental scanning identified dozens of relevant trends from each of the four perspectives, which were synthesized into a list of potential discontinuities. These were then analyzed from an integral perspective. The resulting analysis firmly convinced the analyst that eight of the discontinuities were solid and would be credible with the business units. The analyst understood their nuances well enough to answer questions along the lines of, "Why should we pay attention to this?" The eight discontinuities were prioritized for use by several of the company's new-business teams, and later used successfully in several business-opportunity workshops.

Further reading

Hines, A. (2003, Winter). Applying Integral Futures to Environmental Scanning. *Futures Research Quarterly, 19* (4).

Slaughter, R. (1999). A New Framework for Environmental Scanning. *foresight: the journal of futures studies, strategic thinking, and policy, 1* (5), 387 - 397. (Available at Www.foresightinternational.com.au.)

Voros, J. (2001). Reframing Environmental Scanning: An Integral Approach. *foresight: the journal of futures studies, strategic thinking, and policy, 3* (6).

Wilber, K. (2000). *A Theory of Everything: An Integral Vision for Business, Politics, Science, and Spirituality*. Boston: Shambala.

2.1.4 Conduct a Stakeholder Analysis

Stakeholder analysis identifies individuals or groups that may influence or be influenced by the foresight activity, and explores the implications of their involvement. Stakeholder analysis may be undertaken individually or with a team. It is best performed after the issue is clearly defined, and should be updated as the understanding of the issue and the system in which it is embedded evolves. It is preferable to convene a diverse group with different perspectives on the issue to ensure all relevant stakeholders are identified.

Stakeholder analysis entails various approaches and formats, but all of these follow the basic steps described below.

Key steps

The first step is to identify the stakeholders: the people, groups, and institutions that currently or potentially influence the issue, either positively or negatively. Second, identify the specific interests these stakeholders have in the issue being analyzed. Will they be positively or adversely affected? Will it require them to take action or make changes? Kees van der Heijden (2002) suggests the following useful interview questions to help elicit the needed information:

- Who is key to decision-making at this time?
- What really matters to these parties—what keeps them awake at night?
- Who are the customers with a high interest in the organization?
- Who are the predatory stakeholders seeking to do the organization harm?

Third, assess the relative importance of each set of stakeholders to resolving the issue. How important are they to success or failure? Identify the interests or goals of each group, or at least the most important ones. Rearrange the list according to those with the most influence, be it positive or negative.

Finally, consider options for gaining stakeholder support and reducing opposition. Think about ways to engage the stakeholders in the activity, perhaps by interviewing them or inviting them to participate in a workshop.

Benefits

A stakeholder analysis enables the team to anticipate positive and negative influences from relevant individuals or groups. A primary benefit is to avoid being blindsided by unforeseen objections. Being proactive in anticipating stakeholder influence enables the team to prepare and develop strategies to get the most effective support possible for the analysis and reduce obstacles to successful implementation.

A common danger in strategic foresight work is to assume that stakeholders will behave in a "reasonable" fashion. The analysis team may have a view of "reasonable" that differs from those of certain stakeholders. The stakeholder analysis will uncover these potential obstacles early in the process, before paths are firmly set, and enable the team to devise appropriate strategies for addressing them. Analysts often go astray by locking into a preferred path or solution too early, then getting defensive when it proves inadequate, rather than seeking out and incorporating alternative viewpoints.

Example

Decision-science expert Paul Nutt (2002) explores how failure to pay sufficient heed to stakeholder concerns led to a debacle for Shell during the disposal of the Brent Spar floating platform. The Brent Spar was a floating oil storage facility

137 meters high and weighing 14,500 tons. Shell needed to discard it, and decided to dispose of it at sea. Government officials approved and Shell made a public announcement.

To the company's surprise, the announcement triggered a firestorm. Greenpeace began a high-profile campaign claiming Shell was environmentally irresponsible, even though it had gone through all proper channels and judged disposal at sea to be the most environmentally benign option. Eventually, Shell had to find another option. Nutt found that the Shell team's desire to keep costs reasonable led them "away from questions about potential opposition and towards the technical problems of disposal." Thus they missed the opposition of a key stakeholder.

Further reading

Van der Heijden, K. (2002). *The Sixth Sense: Accelerating Organizational Learning with Scenarios*. New York: Wiley.

Senge, P. 1994. *The Fifth Discipline: The Art and Practice of the Learning Organization*. New York: Doubleday.

Nutt, P. (2002). *Why Decisions Fail: Avoiding the Blunders and Traps That Lead to Debacles*. San Francisco: Berrett-Koehler.

2.2 Study History

2.2.1 Start by Looking Backwards

All the data an analyst has to work with lies in either the past or the present. Bertrand de Jouvenel (1967) was the first to say, "There are no future facts," meaning there is no data from the future. Similarly, former World Future Society President Ed Cornish (2001) observed, "It is important to recognize very clearly that our ideas about the future cannot come from the future itself because the future, by definition, is not a physical reality. The future exists only in the ideas we have about it." Before launching into the future, therefore, recognize that the facts are uniformly from the past and the present.

Key steps

Given that facts are always present- or past-based, it makes sense that strategic foresight entails good use of historical data. A reasonable early-stage assumption is that the patterns of the past will continue into the future, at least within the timeframe of the analysis. As the activity proceeds, this assumption will be challenged and often revised, but it can be a useful starting point.

Historical data comes in two forms—*qualitative data* and *quantitative data*. The most important kind of qualitative data is an event: a discrete occurrence of something. Big events are crucial for understanding the past—and therefore the future—because they divide the past into eras. An era is a relatively coherent period of time separated by major events. For example, the Cold War was an era. It opened with the Yalta conference and the explosion of the first nuclear weapon by the United States. It ended with the collapse of the Soviet Union. The New Deal in the United States, and the Enlightenment, which began in Europe, are other examples of eras.

Eras help the analyst understand the past. While they are thought of as historical, the present is also an era. It is a coherent period of time that began with one or more significant events, and it will give way to a new era defined by future milestone events. It has not yet ended so it is not clear how much longer it will go on, what will end it, or what future historians will call it. Nevertheless, recognizing that the present is an era puts one's thinking into the flow of history and provides excellent grounds for speculation about how the current era compares to past eras, how it might end, and what it might give way to. For more on eras see *Guideline 3.1.5 Look for Turning Points*.

Quantitative data involves using numbers to express some underlying variable or concept—such as GNP for the size of a nation's economy; the global temperature for the heat in the atmosphere; or a nation's birthrate for the fecundity of its population. Comparing numbers over time exposes a trend, also called a *time series*—a fundamental starting point for quantitative forecasting. The forecaster discerns the pattern of change in a quantity over time, assumes that the pattern will continue until the time horizon, and extrapolates that quantity to that horizon. The assumption of continuity is a pretty good assumption in the short run, although it becomes increasingly suspect for longer-term horizons. Thus, trend extrapolation is useful for short-term horizons, less useful for longer ones.

Benefits

Historical and current data may appear as a discrete instance (an event or quantity) or as a series of events (eras) or quantities (time series). On the qualitative side, events can be used to delineate past eras, further understand the current era, and forecast alternative future eras. Past conditions that are similar to current conditions can also be used as historical analogies, forecasting that the same conditions might occur in the future.

On the quantitative side, numerical data can be arranged as a time series, in which a pattern of change is extrapolated into the future.

In both cases, use of historical data is mandatory for reasonable and valid forecasts.

Example

Some knowledge of the past, and data from the past and present, are required for even the most extreme alternative scenarios. To illustrate this point, futurist Joel Barker (1992) refers to paradigm shifts as "changes in the fundamental rules." He gives the example of how the era of Swiss dominance in watchmaking came to a close: in 1968, the Swiss watch industry commanded 65% of global sales and 80% of profits. By 1980, these numbers had dropped to less than 10% and 20% respectively. What happened? The mechanical watch gave way to the electronic watch. This illustrates how understanding the numbers can help assess the context or current state from which the strategic foresight activity is starting.

Further reading

Barker, J.A. (1992). *Paradigms: The Business of Discovering the Future*. New York: HarperBusiness.

Cornish, E. (2001, July - August). How We Can Anticipate Future Events. *The Futurist*.

De Jouvenel, B. (1967). *The Art of Conjecture*. Translated by Nikita Lary. New York: Basic Books.

2.2.2 Don't Reinvent the Wheel

The analyst doesn't need to start from scratch when undertaking a strategic foresight activity. During the last fifty years or so, a range of methodological approaches and a considerable number of scenarios and other substantive assessments of the future have been produced. A strategic foresight activity should start with a collection of the existing substantive material. Right at the beginning, take advantage of any good studies or scenarios already published that are relevant to the issue at hand.

Avoiding reinventing the wheel means doing the homework: search for links and material, read, talk to experts in the field and ask them to help identify the best resources and most competent people to be interviewed. A lot of time and money can be saved when this is done as thoroughly as possible in the beginning.

Key steps

Clarifying the goals of the activity, resources available, and deadlines will help focus the search for existing relevant methodological and substantive futures material. It helps if expertise in futures research is available inside the company, but it can be brought in from outside. Myriad public sources of futures material and links exist. International futures organizations and projects, such as the Association of Professional Futurists (APF), the Millennium Project, the World Future Society (WFS), and the World Futures Studies Federation (WFSF), are well-regarded neutral sources. Many of the futures consulting companies offer public material on their Web pages. There are also many good literary sources. (see Bell 1997, Glenn 2004.)

Benefits

Not reinventing the wheel means saving time and money. For example, if time and resources are scarce it may make sense to take some general, already-published scenarios as a starting point. Using methodological competence and substantive knowledge from outside the organization does not mean borrowing someone else's thinking; rather, since every situation is unique, they are simply a starting point that frees up the analyst's energy and creativity for re-thinking the issues at hand.

Example

A large multinational was exploring the possibilities for new business opportunities regarding water. The team had scant subject-matter expertise in water, and was initially excited about the prospect of using scenario planning to help them come up to speed. In doing their homework, however, they quickly discovered that there were already excellent scenarios about the future of water publicly available. Rather than create new scenarios, they decided to use a set of existing scenarios as a jumping-off point from which to explore options specific to the company. This homework saved time and money, and helped the team reached the next milestone in their project successfully.

Further reading

Bell, W. (1997). *Foundations of Futures Studies*. (Vol. 1). New Brunswick: Transaction Publishers.

Glenn, J.C. and Gordon, T. (2004). *2004 State of the Future*. Washington, DC: American Council for the United Nations University and The Millennium Project.

Mannermaa, M. (2002). Politics + Science = Futures Studies? In J. Dator, ed. *Advancing Futures* (161 - 175). Westport, Connecticut: Praeger.

2.2.3 Be Wary of Past Success That Leads to Thinking in a Rut

Past success can be difficult for strategic foresight. The effort put into that success and the benefits gained from it provide a compelling rationale to use the success model over and over again. While "If it ain't broke, don't fix it!" is sound advice, when it becomes dogma, it is an obstacle to effective strategic foresight. The analyst needs to remind the organization that all performance follows an "S-curve": first, slow progress; then rapid improvement, and finally diminishing returns. When improvements slow down, it's time to seek new methods, better processes, and greater challenges.

Going beyond past successes requires a shift in mindset. The goal should never be just one success, but rather a never-ending staircase of goals, each one leading to a higher level of performance. When the slope of one goal levels off, it's time to set a new, higher one.

Key steps

Avoiding rut-thinking depends on influencing two aspects of organizational culture: "How do we handle risk?" and more importantly, "How do we handle failure?" One reason organizations find themselves thinking in a rut is that it's safe there. In pop psychology terms, the organization can find itself in a "well-furnished rut."

The analyst must convince an organization that if people get punished—or, even worse, fired—when their business experiments don't succeed, then the organization is ensuring that successes will become end-points rather than launchpads into the future. Organizations are often incapable of recognizing that failure may be evidence of an effort to achieve greater success. In most organizations ruts are like foxholes: they protect from incoming missiles. The goal for the analyst is to enable people to risk existing success in order to achieve future and greater success.

The analyst can draw upon plenty of evidence to make this case. One need only read the business news to find multiple articles about the need for constant improvement. Not a single industry is invulnerable to change. Three industries currently under fire include:

- The music industry's entire distribution infrastructure is under assault from the Internet.
- The IT industry in North America/Europe is under assault from outsourcing.
- The newspaper industry is losing readership to ubiquitous access to information.

Many of the driving forces at work in business suggest that every success is temporary—but perhaps none is stronger than competition. Those with success under their belts tend towards contentment; those without it are hungry, eager, and striving for an edge. Like the old bit of sage advice: If a fox is chasing a rabbit, bet on the rabbit—the fox is running for his dinner, the rabbit is running for his life. The problem, of course, is that this common−sense advice is too obvious. It's read, nodded at in agreement, and then either discounted or forgotten.

Benefits

Some successes are so hard-won that, once they are attained, people feel a natural desire to stop, rest, and enjoy them. While there's nothing inherently wrong with basking in the glory of a well-fought battle, the danger is that the organization becomes too comfortable with success. The little voice that mutters, "Why should we change? This is working so well!" can become very convincing in the face of attempts to reach a higher goal. The current process has delivered success, it's been achieved, it's here... while the proposed attempt to become even better involves unknowns and risk. However, staying in the same place is an even riskier proposition in today's rapidly changing environment.

Example

Canadian vintners are renowned for their production of Ice Wine. Ice Wine is made from a late harvest of grapes that are still hanging on the vine during the first freeze. The frostbitten grapes yield a sweet, delicious, limited-quantity dessert wine that can sell for around $100 for a small bottle. Canadian Ice Wine is recognized as the best in the world, and Canadians "own" the global market. Or they did. Vintners in Australia and New Zealand decided that relying on weather to randomly freeze the grapes was, in a word, inefficient. They tried using refrigeration as a more reliable freezing method and confirmed that, once the grapes were frozen, the natural sublimation process that ensued increased the sugar content and provided the basis for new versions of Ice Wine. While Canadian vintners cried foul—and even contracted with Brock University to prove that genuine Ice Wine is chemically different than the refrigerated variety—their protests amount to not only staying in their rut, but insisting that their rut is the only legal one. Their lack of foresight shows how thinking in a rut can be dangerous when the competition thinks outside of the rut.

Further reading

Christensen, C. (1997). *The Innovator's Dilemma*. New York: HarperBusiness.

Hamel, G. (2002). *Leading the Revolution: How to Thrive in Turbulent Times by Making Innovation a Way of Life*. New York: Penguin Books.

2.3 Scan the Environment

2.3.1 Scan the Environment for Awareness of How the Context Is Changing

A key skill for analysts is scanning the external environment for information useful to the organization. The analyst typically has an important role as the external eyes and ears of an organization, providing an awareness of how the context is changing.

There are two principal forms of environmental scanning, which can be referred to as "scanning" and "the scan." *Scanning* is the ongoing, year-round process of looking for trends and events in the external environment that may have implications for the organization. It is independent of any other activity. It may lead to discovery of issues that the analyst can proactively bring to the attention of the organization, or it may provide information that will later prove useful to a particular foresight activity.

The scan refers to the same process of looking for trends and events in the external environment, but is focused on a particular activity. This process is emphasized early on, when the team is gathering data around the focal issue, but will continue to a lesser extent throughout the activity.

Key steps

There are many different methods for environmental scanning. The four steps below cover the essential elements, which may be combined, re-ordered, or called something else. The key point is to cover these four activities—in whatever way works best for the analyst.

- Finding: exploring for scanning hits
- Analyzing: developing insights about what is found
- Framing: developing a framework for organizing insights
- Applying: using the insights in strategic foresight activities

Finding is about uncovering scanning hits. The sophistication of Internet search tools has made finding raw data fairly easy, and has shifted the emphasis in scanning to getting to different and deeper insights. This requires looking outside one's normal comfort zone. A key value-added the analyst brings to the organization is being able to find and connect things that staff normally don't see. Three key suggestions to improving finding include:

- Go beyond the norm and access a wide range of sources

- Be aware of cognitive filters and don't let them get in the way
- Use scanning to build a mental model for making sense of what is going on out there

Analyzing involves making sense of what is found. Typically, individual scanning hits are synthesized into trends. The trends can serve as the fundamental unit of analysis. New tools are emerging in this realm: Joseph Voros of the Australian Foresight Institute has developed Cross-level Analysis, which applies the insights of Integral philosopher Ken Wilber (see *Guideline 2.1.3 Take an Integral View of the Issue*). Sohail Inayatullah of Queensland University has developed Causal Layered Analysis, based on the work of Richard Slaughter, which probes beneath the surface of the data for insights (see *Guideline 3.1.2 Use a Layered Approach to Get Below the Surface and See the Different Types and Levels of Change*).

Framing involves creating a framework for organizing the trends. A simple model created by Hines (2003) is called the Trend Universe. It is represented by a graphic, with the organization as a planet in the center of the universe, ringed by two sets of trends. The closer ring—market trends—represents the immediate or transactional environment which includes customers, competitors, regulators, and such. The farther ring—contextual trends—contains broad trends in the world at large (the STEEP environment).

Applying involves acting on the insights generated from scanning in a strategic foresight activity. It provides the vital backdrop upon which forecasting is built.

Two key problems in scanning are information overload and the need to glean something meaningful and interesting from the deluge of information. Following the four steps above will help deal with both issues.

Benefits

Environmental scanning helps build a mental model of the environment. The analyst, after performing environmental scans for a number of years, is likely to build up a fairly robust mental model of the external environment. Subsequent scanning then serves to enhance and occasionally challenge that model. Experienced scanners, however, notice that some of the fun drains out of the process because they are not finding much that is truly new. At the same time, they are better scanners because they can tell the difference between a truly novel scanning hit from one that might just be new to the scanner. Analysts can improve their craft by exploring their own internal development—being aware of their personal biases and how these influence what they see as important in the external world, and opening their minds to a wider range of sources, perspectives, and interpretations.

Example

A team inside a multinational company innovated its own approach to environmental scanning, by combining its scanning hits into trends and then combining the trends into discontinuities. One of the resulting discontinuities was "Dematerialization: From Pounds to Sense." The idea was that more and more of the value of products will come from their information content (the sense) rather than their physical content (the pounds).

While developing this discontinuity, the analyst incorporated a key learning from scenarist Pierre Wack (1984) and his colleagues about uncertainties in scenario work. *Uncertainties* are issues that are both important and uncertain, while *predetermineds* are those that are important and fairly certain. Wack and colleagues identified uncertainties early on, and then, through very deep and thorough research, sought to "convert" the most important of them into predetermineds. Thus, when Wack pitched the concept of the rise of OPEC to the executive team, it was no longer an uncertainty in his mind, but a predetermined element. And this was only possible because he and his team did the in-depth research to really understand what was going on.

When the analyst applied this insight back to the discontinuity, he realized that he was in effect converting the uncertainty of dematerialization into a predetermined for his organization.

Further reading

Hamel, G. and Prahalad, C.K. (1996). *Competing for the Future*. Cambridge, MA: Harvard Business School Press.

Hines, A. (2003, Winter). Applying Integral Futures to Environmental Scanning. *Futures Research Quarterly*.

Slaughter, R. (1999). A New Framework for Environmental Scanning. *foresight: the journal of futures studies, strategic thinking, and policy, 1* (5), 387 - 397. (Available at www.foresightinternational.com.au.)

Voros, J. (2001). Reframing Environmental Scanning: An Integral Approach. *foresight: the journal of futures studies, strategic thinking, and policy, 3* (6), 533 - 552.

Wack, P. (1984). Scenarios: The Gentle Art of Reperceiving. Reprinted by Global Business Network from President and Fellows of Harvard College, Working Paper 9-785-042.

2.3.2 Integrate the External and Internal

Strategic foresight explores and makes sense of the organization's external world through environmental scanning. At the same time, a foresight activity needs to be aware of developments within the organization. The analyst thus needs to integrate external and internal scanning for a successful activity.

Gathering external intelligence, as *Guideline 2.3.1 Scan the Environment for Awareness of How the Context Is Changing* suggests, is both a continuous (scanning) and a dedicated activity (the scan). The analysis team should always be looking for interesting weak signals that may be indicators of trends, and developing a framework to organize and maintain this information.

Gathering internal intelligence has the same dual role. The team should be keeping up with internal developments, but it will also undertake more focused activities, working with specific functions and people relevant to each activity. The internal work will often involve some kind of visioning activity, in which the analysis team seeks to uncover the aspirations and goals of the organization (see *4.0 Visioning* for specifics).

Key steps

Scanning and Visioning may proceed simultaneously, or one may precede the other. Start with the organization's vision, if one is available. Look for visionary material during scanning if one is not. The scan may be a key input to the visioning. Similarly, the visioning may inform what the scan should look for. Whatever the chronology, the important task is to integrate the two.

The vision needs to be plausible, given the external trends and developments uncovered in the scan, and the scanning material needs to be relevant to the vision. However, integrating the vision with the scan results may not be as straightforward as it seems. Typically, an experienced foresight analyst or team may become skilled in spotting relevant developments in the external environment, whereas the organization will often be more skilled in internal systems and politics. This mismatch can lead to communication difficulties. The organization may not see the relevance of the analysis team's findings about the external world, while the analysis team is vulnerable to misreading an internal situation or producing information that is tangential or irrelevant.

Benefits

Marrying the internal and external is a key value-add the analyst brings to the organization. In too many companies, the groups responsible for internal and external information do not talk to each other. They often sit in different places and maintain different functions with different responsibilities. As a result, they can miss opportunities and become vulnerable to undetected or poorly communicated threats. Meanwhile, the systemic and holistic orientation of strategic foresight makes it well-suited for this integration task.

Example

The segregation between internal and external monitoring was evident in a multinational whose business-development function included a small strategic-foresight activity, designed to scan the external environment for trends and uncover potential business opportunities. Separately, another team developed strategy for the business units, relying heavily on internally generated data and paying little attention to the external environment beyond trends and developments within each unit's own industry.

The two teams rarely interacted, as they reported to different leaders, but they gradually became aware of one another's work. Someone suggested the two groups should collaborate. The internal strategy team initiated the collaboration by offering to pilot a workshop, involving techniques from a foresight activity this team used in its strategy process. When the pilot turned out successfully, the collaboration between the two teams became institutionalized, and it greatly benefited both sides. The new-business function had greater awareness of the long-term strategic outlook of the business units, while the business units tapped into the greater external awareness of the analysis team. This cross-fertilization led to insights and opportunities that were previously untapped.

Further reading

Hines, A. (2005, June). Using Foresight to Generate Insight: A Sampler of Futures Tools. Competia Online Magazine.

Marien, M. (1991). Scanning: An Imperfect Activity in an Era of Fragmentation and Uncertainty. *Futures Research Quarterly 7*, 82 - 90.

2.3.3 Explore Unfamiliar and "Uninteresting" Areas

Read a golf magazine despite having no interest in golf, or the *Journal of the American Medical Association* despite having no background in medicine. The ads alone will introduce you to new ideas and potential applications that may benefit a strategic foresight activity. Stepping outside the box is not as time-consuming as organizations tend to believe: it consumes only a tiny percentage of resources—one unusual magazine here, a unique conference there—and can yield benefits far beyond the cost, by creating a flow of new information.

The most difficult aspect of this guideline is convincing the organization that exploring unfamiliar or uninteresting areas is a productive use of time. It is difficult enough to stay current with the existing deluge of industry-related material. It can be a challenge to justify devoting scarce resources to something that seems unlikely to have an immediate or even a foreseeable impact.

Key steps

The best approach is to start slowly. Suggest that participants in a foresight activity pick out a magazine at random—simply pick the one three rows over and two shelves down. Have them read it from cover to cover and see what happens. Did it spark any ideas? Did anything interesting emerge of relevance to the activity? If the answer is no, at worst a few dollars and an hour or so were wasted. But it is a safe wager is that a dedicated professional cannot help but find a useful idea in any magazine. An unfamiliar field is filled with ideas not previously encountered. This tactic is a gentle way to generate new ideas.

Next, have participants pick an industry they know nothing about. Have them identify the undisputed leader in that industry, then determine how they achieved prominence. What could the organization learn from that success? Equally important, have them identify an industry leader in another field who has just crashed and burned in some dramatic manner. What can the clothing industry learn from Exxon? What could the construction industry learn from the imminent demise of the way the music industry has traditionally delivered its product?

Benefits

To expand horizons—and opportunities—a constant influx of new information is necessary. The adage "Think outside the box" is perhaps the most useful bit of advice regarding the creative process. The irony is that just as there is far too much to read within one's field, there is an infinite quantity of additional information outside the field. But once the analyst convinces the organization to get outside the box, the resulting discovery of new information and insights will make the familiar box seem old-fashioned and out-of-date.

Example

Great ideas frequently come from unexpected sources. Rolf Smith (1997), former director of the US Air Force's Office of Strategic Innovation, formed the Virtual Thinking Expedition Co. (www.thinking-expedition.com) as a unique way to teach innovation to organizational clients. The company leads four- and eight-day "thinking expeditions" with diverse teams—including customers, suppliers, and outsiders—who learn innovation during a mountain-climbing expedition. Smith asserts, "Thinking different gets to different results." The unfamiliar settings, activities, and challenges of mountain climbing get clients totally out of their familiar boxes and, according to Smith, have been "amazingly successful in both team impact and bottom-line results." According to the firm, a Fortune 100 company expedition oriented around a human-resources challenge targeted $50 million in savings over five years; conservative estimates now put its benefits at $130 million.

Further reading

De Bono, E. (1993). *Serious Creativity*. New York: HarperBusiness.

Kodama, F. (1992, July). Technology Fusion and the New R&D. *Harvard Business Review*.

Smith, R. (2002). *The 7 Levels of Change: Different Thinking for Different Results*. 2nd ed. Irving, TX: Tapestry Press.

Smith, R. (1997, January 1). The Virtual Thinking Expedition Company: A Difffernt Idea…. Exploring the Unknown on Adventures with the Mind. Viewed July 2005, www.thinking-expedition.com/news.html.

2.3.4 Don't Try to Win with Research—Not All the Data Exists

Foresight involves exploring the future, which is challenging from a research perspective. There is plenty of data one would like to have, but a lot of it just does not exist. The analyst must learn to depend on whatever clues are available and be ready to grab information whenever and wherever it can be found.

It is important to recognize when beating the bushes for a certain piece of data becomes a waste of valuable time. On the other hand, if instinct says a certain piece of information ought to exist, it may be worth the effort to try to find it. A balance needs to be struck between these two objectives—finding valuable nuggets, yet using one's time cost-effectively—but this guideline emphasizes the former. One is more likely to waste time looking for the hidden gem, and such excursions should be taken with caution. Many times, the data simply does not exist.

Key steps

When exploring the future of a topic in a foresight activity, keep the reading and research open to serendipitous discoveries. Limit the time spent trying to find certain data to support trends that may be early in their formation. With research staff, set a time limit. Ask them to report early in the process how the hunt is going. That way they can be called off the hunt and redirected to other tasks if necessary.

Meanwhile, be ready to capture what else is found in the process. Accidental discoveries in research offer the chance to find different, but potentially valuable, insights on the changing world. Let alternative information help build the case for the conclusions. It is important when researching trends and issues not to fall too easily for enticing data that seems to be just the right thing. For example, an entire industry produces market forecasts for specific sectors, market segments, and even products. Not all of it is credible. It may not be valid enough to even bother with.

Benefits

Recognizing the limits to data's value means understanding that strategic foresight is a different kind of work. Trend and foresight research is different from working with issues based squarely in the present, with the supporting data readily available. The future hasn't happened yet, so the data record for it doesn't exist. Clues can be found, but not comprehensive evidence for what's emerging. Once you adopt this perspective, more time and energy will be available for a richer exploration of trends and issues that are truly important. Also, by not getting bogged down in small sections of the research, one keeps sight of the broader strategic view as well.

Example

A Fortune 100 company assigned a team of executives to develop a ten-year vision. The executives worked extensively on identifying forces and trends shaping their markets. This led them to a series of issues and trends they wanted to know more about. They organized themselves into small teams and assigned topics for further research. Several of the teams got stuck. They had initially decided what data would best demonstrate the validity of the trends they were studying. They couldn't find the data, and they couldn't find good forecasts that project those trends into the future either. Their work ground to a halt. Most likely, their Holy Grail information didn't exist.

After dozens of hours of effort they were advised to stop the hunt and rethink their research strategy. They got past the problem and found compelling information to analyze and share with their colleagues.

Further reading

Hines, A. (2000, October). Where Do Your Trends Come From? *foresight: the journal of futures studies, strategic thinking, and policy, 2* (5).

Markley, O.W. and Wygant, A.C. (1988). *Information and the Future: A Handbook of Sources and Strategies.* New York: Greenwood Press.

2.4 Involve Colleagues and Outsiders

2.4.1 Consult "Remarkable People"

The term "remarkable people" was coined by philosopher G.I. Gurdjieff (1960) to describe "someone who stands out from those around him by the resourcefulness of his mind." An ongoing part of strategic foresight is to build and maintain a network of remarkable people who can be consulted during an activity across a wide range of topics.

The timing behind using remarkable people depends upon the needs of the activity. It is best to target their entry into the process at the point where the greatest challenge or bottleneck exists, or where the infusion of alternative ideas is at a premium. For instance, remarkable people are particularly well-suited to questioning assumptions during the Framing of an issue, brainstorming creative ideas and alternatives during Forecasting, and identifying and expanding the range of options during Visioning. They are typically good at generating unexpected, fresh thinking when it is needed.

Key steps

Building a network of remarkable people is an ongoing task. The characteristics one looks for are experts who have different perspectives, are skilled at challenging prevailing views, and are able to bring alternative interpretations to situations. Kees van der Heijden (2002) describes them as "intensely curious but sharp observers, who understand the way the world works and have their finger on the pulse of change."

Remarkable people are not narrow experts. They are more often intellectual jacks-of-all-trades who are skilled at bringing insight to practically any activity. Their broad knowledge can be supplemented with subject-matter expertise from specialists. Where possible, it is helpful to bring more than one remarkable person into the activity. Not only will this help the activity, it will also provide an incentive for them to participate—the chance to meet other remarkable people is a great motivator.

Benefits

A key principle underpinning the use of remarkable people, according to Kees van der Heijden (2002), is that "the search for innovative thinking needs to take place outside the organization." Bringing in their higher-level perspective can shift the activity in new directions. Remarkable people can challenge the team's assumptions and preconceived notions, enabling consideration of a wider range of ideas. A challenge, however, is they can also take the activity off-course into areas of intellectual pursuit that are irrelevant to the activity.

Example

Royal Dutch/Shell introduced the "remarkable people" concept into the corporate world in the 1970s by systematically seeking out provocative thinkers to help challenge and inform the company's planning. Pierre Wack, who pioneered scenario development at Shell along with Ted Newland and others, introduced the concept from Gurdjieff and integrated it into the scenario planning process. Wack and colleague Napier Collyns were instrumental in building a network of remarkable people, a strategy to which they attribute a great deal of the success of scenario planning at Shell.

Shell's initial success in anticipating the Arab oil embargo was followed by other scenario-planning achievements, such as anticipating the commoditization of oil and the fall of the Soviet Union. Remarkable people were and still are a fundamental part of scenario planning at Shell. Several Shell scenario planners adopted the remarkable-person concept as fundamental to the operations of the consulting company they later founded, Global Business Network (GBN), which boasts a roster of more than 100 remarkable persons GBN can call upon to enrich its meetings and consulting projects.

Further reading

Collyns, N. (2002, September). Scenarios in Business. *GBN Book Club Newsletter*.

Gurdjieff, G.I. (1960). *Meetings with Remarkable Men*. London: Penguin.

Kelly, E. and Leyden, P. (2002). *What's Next: Exploring the New Terrain for Business*, New York: Perseus/Wiley.

Schwartz, P. (1997). *The Art of the Long View*, New York: Wiley.

Van der Heijden, K. et al. (2002). *The Sixth Sense: Accelerating Organizational Learning with Scenarios*. New York: Wiley.

Wack, P. (1984). Scenarios: The Gentle Art of Reperceiving. Reprinted by Global Business Network from President and Fellows of Harvard College, Working Paper 9-785-042.

2.4.2 Consult Unusual Sources, People, and Places—Including Outliers, Complainers, and Troublemakers

One important function of strategic foresight is the opening of the future. The inclusion of different perspectives is one way to assure this opening. Analysts should look for competent people inside and outside who bring a different way of thinking to the table.

Key steps

The selection of these participants should be done with care. Not every unusual or non-obvious individual qualifies. In the first place, they should be selected based on their authority in a particular domain. They should not bring "just another perspective," but a well-studied and well-articulated different view. The other participants should feel challenged by the ideas they bring in. This sense of challenge can result either from a deeper view of closely related subjects or from a subject that functions by analogy.

The world of business and decision-making favors the rational and bottom-line approach to gathering information. Prusak (1998) suggests that the higher up in the organization a presentation goes, the blander it becomes. Consulting unusual sources is a way to refresh the information flow by tapping into edgy or offbeat sources that challenge prevailing norms. In fact, many of today's norms were yesterday's novel and unusual ideas. The kinds of sources and approaches to look for and identify include:

- Sources at the edge of the organization—Find those in the organization who may be cynical or complaining, but have tried something different, and talk to them to see what they are thinking, reading, and doing.
- Sources outside the organization—Interview young people. Meet with teachers, designers, artists, economists, movers and shakers of the broader society. For example, observing and interviewing tribal elders has been used as a means of raising public interest in traditional storytelling.
- Sources inside and outside the industry—Interview leaders, regulators, politicians, activists, etc., and understand their motivations. Ask them who is doing the thinking at the leading edge.

The approaches for this activity will vary according to the analyst's ability and willingness to invest time in it. One can go onsite and observe, interview, and then collate the learned insights into a meaningful output. It is helpful to have a partner to make sure all the insights are captured. It is not always easy to consult the outliers—they are typically in that position because they are not easy to deal with. Analysts may need to employ tact and diplomacy if they are to gain anything useful from these encounters.

Benefits

Much as yesterday's fringe becomes tomorrow's mainstream, an organization's edge may someday become its center. Some industries, such telecommunications, transport, and retail, have gone through a dusk-and-dawn shift in the past ten years and are seeing their edges become mainstream while the tried-and-true formulas of the past crumble. Companies including Nokia, Sony, and Casio are redefining themselves and coming up with whole new ways of viewing the role of the industry in our everyday lives. They have incorporated their "edge" into their strategic and tactical behaviors.

Example

The World Water Vision exercise (Cosgrove, 1998) is an example of a global strategic foresight program (1998 - 2000) that used outsiders' perspectives to show the importance of using a wide scope to understand the world's water challenges. To initiate several sub-exercises, expert panels were devised blending water and non-water experts. The panels discussed potential institutional shifts and developments in ICT, biotechnology, and energy—four topics very rarely considered among water professionals.

The panels were organized early in the process on a temporary basis of one or two days each. Their output, four small reports highlighting some major ideas, was fed into the overall exercise in order to serve two objectives. On the one hand, the reports made clear the relevance of the four non-water topics for water professionals. On the other, they showed the relevance of a long-term perspective, by elaborating future possibilities and potential long-term developments. As such, they helped to overcome initial skepticism about the value of using remarkable persons and strategic foresight to expand and extend the debate.

Further reading

Collins, J. and Porras, J. (1997). *Built to Last: Successful Habits of Visionary Companies*. New York: Harper Business.

Cosgrove, W.J. and Rijsberman, F.R. (2000) *World Water Vision: Making Water Everybody's Business*. London: Earthscan/James & James.

Kleiner, A. (1996). *The Age of Heretics*. New York: Currency Doubleday.

Marsh, N., McAllum, M. and Purcell, D. (2002). *Strategic Foresight: The Power of Standing in the Future*. Melbourne: Crown Content.

Prusak, L., ed. (1997). *Knowledge in Organizations*. St. Louis, MO: Butterworth-Heinemann.

Steinbock, D. (2001). *The Nokia Revolution: Success Factors of an Extraordinary Company*. New York: AMACOM.

2.4.3 Design Workshops So Learning Can Be Integrated in a Group Setting

Workshops are a useful tool for adult learning. They provide a forum to generate and evaluate ideas and integrate learning. They enable the organization to actively work with the ideas generated by strategic foresight—which leads to more lasting integration of new thinking than can be gained from a passive presentation by an analyst.

There are several points in a strategic foresight activity where a workshop makes sense, in addition to Scanning. During Framing, for example, a workshop can serve the dual purpose of clarifying the focal issue as well as aiding team-building. Whether this is necessary or desirable depends on the situation. A problem clearly framed, and a work team that knows each other well, suggests no need for a workshop—which could actually harm the activity if it is perceived by team members as a waste of time. In the opposite case, where the focal issue is murky and participants don't know one another well, a workshop clearly makes sense.

Another typical place for a workshop is in Forecasting. Whereas scanning workshops are more about problem-finding (what are the key trends and drivers?), forecasting workshops are more about problem-solving (what are the alternative futures to be planned for?). Problem-finding workshops are a form of fact-finding. Problem-solving workshops take the key trends, forces, and issues relevant to the activity and convert them into forecasts of alternative futures around which the team will later vision, plan, and act.

Key steps

Once it is determined that a workshop is needed, several steps apply in any workshop approach. First, creativity expert Gene Anderson (www.geneanderson.biz) suggests four questions that should be answered affirmatively before undertaking any workshop:

- Is it worth doing? (Is a workshop the best approach?)
- Is it do-able? (Can a workshop be staged that will deliver the needed results?)
- Do we have the right people? (Is the organization appropriately represented?)
- Are you willing to do it? (Is the analyst willing to deal with the issues that might arise?)

Four generic steps provide a useful framework for structuring any workshop. While there are myriad approaches to workshop design, they all tend to incorporate the following four steps, captured by creativity guru Gerald Haman (www.solutionpeople.com).

1. *Investigate needs*—Identify the problems, needs, concerns, etc., around the focal issue, and what data, trends, and information are relevant to them. This step is most relevant during *Framing* and *Scanning*.

2. *Create ideas*—Generate ideas for meeting the needs and problems identified, and flesh out the most promising ones.

3. *Evaluate solutions*—Prioritize the best ideas according to predetermined criteria. Evaluating and the step above, creating, are most pertinent during *Forecasting* and *Visioning*.

4. *Activate plans*—Develop the strategy and plans for implementing the prioritized ideas. This step is most useful during *Planning* and *Acting*.

While each workshop step has its most appropriate stage during an activity, there is significant overlap—the steps are more continuous than they are discrete.

Benefits

The benefits of workshops are twofold. First, they help the team learn by drawing on the brains and skills of other participants. Second, by including decision-makers, they encourage the organization's buy-in to the larger activity and its outcomes. It is more difficult to reject results when you have been involved in producing them.

Of course, decision-makers' participation does not ensure acceptance of the results. In fact, their participation can skew the direction of an activity. A forceful participant may intentionally or unintentionally influence the workshop in a preconceived direction that is at odds with the direction the analysis team would naturally take. Strong, opinionated participants must be coached beforehand, whenever possible, about their influence over other participants and to wield that power carefully, if at all.

Example

An example of the value of the workshop comes from the industrial design firm IDEO. IDEO's "Deep Dive" (1999) methodology was featured on the ABC program *Nightline*, where staff members were tasked with redesigning the shopping cart in one week. The show chronicled the intense, immersive workshop process the group used to generate creative ideas and reach a solution. The intensity of the process is a key factor that increases buy-in and, in this case, led to a quite remarkable shopping-cart redesign and to a boom in business for IDEO.

Further reading

Dator, J. (1993, Winter). From Future Workshops to Envisioning Alternative Futures. *Futures Research Quarterly*. Viewed August 2005, www.futures.hawaii.edu/dator/futures/Workshops.html.

Koppel, T. (1999, July 13). The Deep Dive. *ABC News Nightline*. New York: ABC News.

Doyle, M. and Strauss, D. (1993). *How to Make Meetings Work: The New Interaction Method*. East Rutherford, NJ: Berkley Publishing Group.

Schrage, M. (2000). *Serious Play: How the World's Best Companies Simulate to Innovate*. Cambridge, MA: Harvard Business School Press.

3 ▶ Forecasting

3.0 Forecasting

"The surprise-free future isn't." —Herman Kahn

Forecasting involves creating alternative futures. Most organizations, if not challenged, tend to believe the future is going to be pretty much like the past. If the analyst probes at an organization's view of the future, he or she will find an array of unexamined assumptions, which tend to converge around incremental changes—a.k.a. the "official future" or "baseline forecast"—that pretty much preserves the current paradigm or way of doing things. A key task for the analyst, therefore, is to challenge this view and prod the organization to take seriously the possibility that things may not continue as they have—in practice, they rarely do!

In essence, forecasting involves generating the widest range of creative possibilities, then consolidating and prioritizing the most useful for the organization to actively consider or prepare for as it moves forward.

A principal means of challenging the official future is to develop alternative futures. A key tenet of strategic foresight is that the future is inherently unknowable and efforts to get it exactly right are futile. What the analyst *can* offer is to expand the range and depth of possibilities for the organization to consider, thereby reducing the likelihood and magnitude of surprise. This in turn enables the organization to successfully navigate through what does emerge. The analyst may be asked to produce the "correct" future, that is, to predict what will happen. Organizations prefer the clarity of dealing with a single possibility rather than the messiness of alternatives. In response, the analyst must get across the idea that single-point forecasting is doomed and the organization will be better served by understanding and preparing for a range of possibilities.

Forecasting alternative futures does not mean developing detailed plans for every contingency, however. Rather it means monitoring the external environment for leading indicators—signs or guideposts that suggest events are heading towards one or more of the alternatives.

The guidelines in this section suggest how the organization can produce a useful set of alternative futures. A useful forecast challenges existing assumptions about the future, gets the organization to consider "what if," and thereby motivates it to plan and act differently. An alternative future that turns out to be off-base can still be useful if it has prompted the organization to take the future seriously, to consider and prepare for possibilities in a way that yields helpful learning and experience.

The preparatory work done in Framing begins to pay dividends here, incidentally. If Framing has helped the team function well, produced a work environment that is conducive to creativity, and so forth, the work done in Forecasting will be that much better.

The first set of forecasting guidelines, *3.1 Identify Drivers and Uncertainties*, gets to the gist of the raw material needed to create alternative futures. Here the analyst helps the organization understand what is really driving change into the future and to separate those drivers into relative degrees of certainty. Some drivers are fairly well understood. The aging baby boomers, for example, are going to continue to age, and they must be reckoned with in any alternative future that hinges on demographics. Other forces are far less certain. Will nanotechnology provide breakthroughs in materials science? It's difficult to know, but a materials-focused organization would do well to consider how this force could play out even though it may never reach fruition.

The second set, *3.2 Choose Forecasting Tool(s)*, suggests the value of using a formal approach to construct alternative futures. Strategic foresight may be viewed as a black box by those more accustomed to facts and figures, since it relies heavily on interpretation and subjective judgment. So it is important to show that proven tools and methods exist, and to use them in a way that is transparent to the organization. In some cases, of course, the organization will not really be concerned with the "how," so the analyst simply needs to be aware of how much or how little to involve the organization in the methodology.

The third set, *3.3 Diverge—Generate Ideas*, provides guidance on employing the concepts and tools of creative problem-solving and futures thinking to generate a wide range of ideas that may be included in the alternative futures. The goal here is quantity, rather than quality—which is addressed in the next set.

The fourth set, *3.4 Converge—Prioritize Ideas*, provides concepts and tools for narrowing down the long list of generated ideas into a manageable set for inclusion in the alternative futures. It is very useful here to have a predetermined set of criteria by which to rank the ideas. Two simple but perennially useful criteria are *importance and likelihood*.

The fifth set, *3.5 Form Alternatives*, involves the actual crafting of alternative futures. There is no ideal number of alternative futures—one is too few, more than six is probably too many. Different organizations will have different capabilities and preferences. The guidelines here delineate the types of alternatives that can and should be produced and how to ensure they are high-quality. More important than the number of alternatives is that each one be distinct, so that collectively they challenge as many assumptions as possible.

These guidelines are the core of a strategic foresight activity. The analyst must be skillful in persuading the organization to stretch as far as possible beyond its typical boundaries, and then equally skillful in making the connection back to the organization's bottom line. It can be a delicate balancing act, but one that these guidelines are designed to help with.

3.1 Identify Drivers and Uncertainties

3.1.1 Uncover the Underlying Drivers

Drivers are major factors shaping change. Here, they are defined broadly as trends and other changes that shape future conditions. Analysts need to recognize that effective foresight must be grounded in an understanding of the social, technological, economic, environmental, and political (STEEP) factors that either drive or block change, i.e., the strategic context or landscape. In any case, it is useful to take a broader perspective—a longer look back and an anticipatory look forward.

Drivers have both a forecasting utility—in that they provide information on potential futures—and a disruptive dimension in that they call into question assumptions about the present. Some are "no-brainers," or well-understood big changes that affect strategic aims, while others are barely visible yet useful for challenging the organization's present thinking.

It is occasionally difficult to spot or name drivers. They are often affected by interrelationships across issues. And their impacts may not be felt for years or decades.

Key steps

While your scanning activities may reveal many apparent drivers, it is important to determine which are strategically relevant. A suite of interlocking techniques is available to determine relevant drivers, including:

- reviewing credible literature and seeking expert opinion
- ensuring team diversity and a respect for both analytical and intuitive thinking
- looking at fringe ideas, identifying anomalies
- brainstorming issues and how they might be affected over time by larger forces
- employing timelines or scenario planning

If environmental scanning systems are in place, they can draw attention to approaching opportunities and risks whose significance has not yet commonly registered. Scanning groups can be on the lookout for long-term developments, such as general consumption patterns or public attitudes, which will influence the organization's current or future strategy.

Benefits

Identifying and investigating the underlying drivers of visible developments—and questioning whether these drivers will slow down, reverse, move in new directions, or interact with each other—shifts the strategic focus away from predicting what will happen to anticipating discontinuities and alternative future contexts. This fosters a deeper understanding of the dynamics of change and the range of possible future developments.

Examining drivers in depth also helps to discern what can be influenced and when, thus enabling identification of the strategic drivers most important to the organization. Exploratory conversations about strategic drivers can sometimes reveal a different future significance for a specific driver than initially expected.

Other benefits include developing a broader understanding across the strategic foresight process by recognizing those factors that could affect, constrain, block, or influence strategic outcomes. It helps make explicit the assumptions behind strategies. It also helps make clear the organization's "political will" for adjusting to change.

Example

Beginning in 2003, the Australian Communications Authority (ACA) explored the future of communications regulation. It undertook a project to build understanding about the future communications environment. The project team developed a sense of the drivers by environmental scanning, reviewing the literature, interviewing experts and people from other fields, bringing together a diverse group of stakeholders in a series of workshops that identified issues/drivers, developing scenarios, and road-testing ideas internationally in Asia, America, and Europe.

Four strategic drivers of change for the communications sector were identified: digitization, pervasive computing, seamless connectivity, and globalization. These drivers suggested a move to a network-centric approach of interconnected, decentralized, spectrum-efficient, and distributed network intelligence. This thinking about the future regulatory system contributed to a government decision to merge the ACA with the Australian Broadcasting Authority (ABA), and legislation is pending on a new Australian Communications and Media Authority.

Further reading

Australian Communications Authority. (2004, October). *Vision 2020: Preliminary Report*. http://internet.aca.gov.au/ACAINTER:STANDARD::pp=PC_1535,pc=PC_1538.

Buzan, B. and Segal, G. (1998). *Anticipating the Future*. Sydney: Simon & Schuster.

Lindgren, M. and Bandhold, H. (2003). *Scenario Planning*. Hampshire, UK: Palgrave MacMillan.

May, G.H. (1996). *The Future Is Ours*. Westport, CT: Praeger.

Schwartz, P. (2003). *Inevitable Surprises: Thinking Ahead in a Time of Turbulence*. New York: Gotham Books.

Van der Heijden, K. (2002). *The Sixth Sense: Accelerating Organizational Learning with Scenarios*. New York: Wiley.

3.1.2 Use a Layered Approach to Get Below the Surface and See Different Types and Levels of Change

Change occurs on many levels. Many organizations, short on time and beset with operational issues, spend little time examining and understanding the deeper levels of change—those levels below the latest consumer fad or most recent regulatory issue.

The typical approach to identifying trends and emerging issues is to take a horizontal approach, organizing trends into sectors or areas such as STEEP (social, technological, economic, environmental, and political). In contrast, layered approaches take a vertical perspective, identifying the levels of changes. Several futurists have posited layered frameworks, with a prominent example being Sohail Inayatullah's Causal Layered Analysis (CLA). CLA identifies four layers: (1) surface/litany, (2) social causes/systems, (3) discourse/worldview, and (4) metaphor/myth.

Key steps

The layered framework enables comparison of vertical "slices" of reality and change. Layered approaches divide the world into two or more layers, each of which addresses a different type of change or different depth of issue. The basic assumption is that change happens at different levels and at different rates. The deeper the level, the more basic the change—but also the longer it takes. The deepest layers involve values, world views, and belief systems. The highest layers tend to correspond to superficial and fast-changing trends, such as Nielsen media ratings or computer prices.

It is useful to adopt a particular framework and then use it to identify the deep range of change that will impact the organization. The analyst can begin with an existing set of official trends and emerging issues, or use the layered approach to brainstorm them from scratch. When sorting the trends and issues into different layers, it can then be determined which level(s) the organization has been most attentive to. This will identify potential gaps in the organization's thinking and attention. It is often the case that an organization applying a layered approach to its own thinking finds it is spending most of its attention on here-today, gone-tomorrow issues, while missing the more fundamental but less visible issues that are slowly but surely changing the rules of the game.

Benefits

Layered approaches are important because organizations often become narrowly focused on immediate problems. An organizational culture that relies on CNN-like, up-to-the-minute reporting will be distracted by fast-moving, relatively trivial issues. Layered approaches add to the value of foresight activities by expanding the scope of thinking and supporting a broader and deeper exploration and understanding of the environment in which the organization lives and operates.

Specifically, layered approaches can ensure that organizations clearly identify the types of issues and trends they have been focusing on. Layered approaches assist organizations in classifying their issues according to the rate and impact of the change they create. They may reveal to a group that it has been focused on the wrong things, help it identify deeper changes that will impact the organization, and prompt the organization to develop the foresight to address those deeper changes early enough to influence the outcomes—rather than just reacting to them after the fact.

Example

A tourism company traditionally focused on serving the maximum number of visitors in the most profitable manner possible. When the company included a layered trends activity in one of its strategic planning sessions, however, it was forced to identify trends and issues below the traditional visitor statistics. The company worked hard to define more foundational trends at work in the external environment, and through this process came to discuss a range of issues not previously considered, such as urban development, demographic changes in the local population, climate change, and changing local social values and identity. Ultimately, it identified a fundamental shift in the public's perception of long-term and, in some cases, damaging effects of the traditional visitor industry, and considered the need to recast its role and services.

Further reading

Inayatullah, S. (n.d.). The Growth of Aviation and Some Major Constraints. Viewed July 2005, http://library.uws.edu.au/adt-NUWS/uploads/approved/adt-NUWS20050218.120843/public/04Chapter3.pdf.

Inayatullah, S. (2005). Causal Layered Analysis: Post-Structuralism as Method. *The Knowledge Base of Futures Studies* (R. Slaughter, ed.). (Vol. 2). (Professional Edition CD-ROM). Indooroopilly, Australia: Foresight International. (Available at www.foresightinternational.com.au.)

Inayatullah, S., ed. (2004). *The Causal Layered Analysis* (CLA) Reader: *Theory and Case Studies of an Integrative and Transformative Methodology*. Taipei: Tamkang University Press.

Slaughter, R. (1989, October). Probing Beneath the Surface. *Futures*, 21(5), 447 - 65. (Available at www.foresightinternational.com.au.)

3.1.3 Assess Fundamental Shifts That Could Impact Business-As-Usual

Fundamental shifts are those external forces that have the potential of shaking the core assumptions of an organization. These forces are referred to as megatrends, discontinuities, tsunamis, or drivers of change depending on the practitioner. Regardless of what they are called, they have the potential to surprise an organization—unless the analyst can help it anticipate and prepare.

A fundamental shift differs from other trends in that it tends to be pervasive to an industry, an existing business model, and an organizational culture. It has the potential to alter the way the world works. Its impacts are rarely white or black, all-positive or all-negative.

Key steps

To identify fundamental shifts, start with the basics. Basic changes surrounding the organization come from a number of sectors, such as the social, technological, environmental, economic, or political (STEEP) arenas. Start by identifying the significant changes underway in these key areas.

Next, create your criteria for a fundamental shift and prioritize the trends according to them. The criteria might be, for example:

- potential for disrupting the existing industry
- potential for diverting part of the revenue stream to competitors
- potential for altering the organizational ecosystem, or how the players interact

Then, study the collision points among trends, as well as potential paradoxes which could trigger explosive shifts in the business model or purpose. Too often, trends are treated as if they exist in isolation, when in fact they exist in an eco-system of other trends fighting to survive.

Finally, once the fundamental-shift candidates (for example, miniaturization, digitization, globalization, sustainability, convergence, work/life balance, aging) have been identified, assess their meaning for the business-as-usual models and approaches.

Once an analyst has identified a potential fundamental shift, its impacts need to be explored. The initial analysis typically leads to identifying some opportunities and threats to the organization's business model and purpose. Later analysis leads to a deeper understanding of impacts across many areas of the business.

Ideally this assessment should be part of the strategic foresight process, linked to ongoing strategic decision-making (see *Guideline 6.3.1: Create an Intelligence System Aligned by Strategic Foresight and Linked to the Planning Process*). It should be professionally facilitated by those with expertise in facilitation and foresight. Analysts may be able to do it themselves, or team up with internal or external experts. The key is to provide an approach and tools that fit the context of assessment and the organizational culture. It requires understanding how thinking proactively about the future can best be done according to the organization's readiness and foresight process status.

A potential caveat: be wary of the organization wanting to use only criteria that fit its business-as-usual model. If this occurs the assessment will reinforce the organization's existing assumptions about its business, miss potential opportunities, and be vulnerable to potential threats.

Benefits

The time allotted to assessing fundamental shifts will be repaid multifold once the organization starts accounting for these shifts in its business decisions. This work is at the core of the strategic agenda, so analysts must involve and communicate with senior management. Listening to a thirty-minute presentation is not the same as an internalized understanding gained by directly engaging with the material.

Example

An excellent example of assessing fundamental shifts was Nokia's proactive shift from paper and pulp, rubber boots, PCs, and TVs to a focus on telecommunications and mobile communications. (Steinbock 2001.) Nokia was established in 1865 as a wood-pulp mill and later expanded into rubber products. After World War II, Nokia acquired Finnish Cable Works, a producer of telephone and telegraph cables, which led gradually to a deep immersion in telecommunications. Today, none of its paper, pulp, or rubber origins are visible in the company.

Through its nimble response to changing markets, Nokia showed that assessing fundamental shifts is important both to choosing new strategic directions and to understanding the best timing for them. Some shifts might be placed into the "maybe in ten years bucket," while others should be dealt with immediately.

Further reading

Collins, J.C. and Porras, J.I. (1997). *Built to Last: Successful Habits of Visionary Companies*. New York: HarperBusiness.

Marsh, N., McAllum, M., and Purcell, D. (2002). *Strategic Foresight: The Power of Standing in the Future*. Melbourne: Crown Content.

Nokia: History. Wikipedia. Viewed August 2005, http://en.wikipedia.org/wiki/Nokia.

Schwartz, P. (1991). *The Art of the Long View*. New York: Currency Doubleday.

Steinbock, D. (2001). *The Nokia Revolution: Success Factors of an Extraordinary Company*. New York: AMACOM.

3.1.4 Look for Colliding Change Trajectories

In *Systems I* (1980), Draper Kauffman wrote, "You can't do just one thing." This means that anything that one intends to do has consequences, and they are often far beyond the initial intentions. By the same token, "Nothing changes by itself." In a world of accelerating change, many, if not most, things are changing at the same time. Yet when thinking of the future, particularly when extrapolating trends, organizations tend to look only at the future of that trend and perhaps its immediate implications, while holding the rest of the world more or less constant. They often do not consider how the trend itself will change because of changes in other conditions and trends.

The longer the forecasted time horizon, the more changes the analyst has to take into account. Organizations can act in a relatively focused way in the short run. Disciplines and domains do have an internal logic and pattern of change that explains most change for a while. But after that short while, the domain itself is changed by changes underway in other domains. That is why strategic-foresight analysts use frameworks like STEEP—to be sure they are taking account of all the changes that could affect their focal domain.

Key steps

Futurist Ted Gordon has developed a technique called *Trend Impact Analysis* (TIA) to account for sudden events that perturb a long-term trend. He assumes that the perturbing event creates a short-term deviation from, but eventually a return to, the long-term trend pattern. The process then is to estimate the duration and magnitude of the deviation. To do this, he recommends the analyst answer the following questions:

- When does the event occur?
- When does the trend begin to deviate?
- When is the deviation at its peak?
- How large is the deviation at the peak?
- When does the deviation return to the trend line?

Unfortunately, none of these estimates has much quantitative support, unless similar events have intervened before. If there have been only a few prior impacts, then the conditions must be quite similar if they are to be useful as historical analogies. The larger the number of impacts, however, the more one can apply statistical measures to calculate the average deviation, and the variation in deviations, to those impacts. Nevertheless, TIA reinforces that most trends are not smooth curves stretching indefinitely into the future. The analyst must ask, "What might happen along the way to skew the trend we have extrapolated?"

A second, more quantitative tool is *cross-impact analysis*. Created in 1966 by Olaf Helmer (1983) and Ted Gordon, the cross-impact tool is a square matrix in which each row and column is a set of events or trends, or both. The cells represent the impacts of the row event or trend on the column event or trend. In the event version, the cell would be the conditional probability of the column event occurring if the row event had already occurred. In the trend version, the cell would be a regression coefficient that translates units of change in the row trend to units of change in the column trend. Using a random start, and random events throughout, thousands of runs of the same matrix would produce a probability distribution of events or trends in a Monte Carlo fashion.

Benefits

Trends change over time. Trend impact analysis and the cross-impact matrix are two tools the analyst can use to identify and track these changes. Thinking systematically about deviations from the norm, and the impacts of trends upon one another, will allow the analyst to help organizations avoid being blindsided by colliding change trajectories. Anticipating these collisions can help the organization to prepare strategies for coping with the change, instilling confidence in the organization that it is ready for the future.

Example

An example of a cross-impact approach involves the research and technology commercialization enterprise at Battelle in Columbus, Ohio, spearheaded by technology analyst Steven Millett. Battelle developed a cross-impact technique called Interactive Future Simulations to build scenarios. One project involved a large multinational company exploring new business opportunities in the "Healthy Home Market in 2010." The project combined trend analysis done by Battelle with that of the client organization, and brought the two together using Interactive Future Simulations to study the cross-impacts—the impacts that the two trend sets had on one another. The resulting scenarios were a key piece of supporting data that enabled the business team to convince the home organization to take the business opportunity to the next stage.

Further reading

Gordon. T.J. (2003). Trend Impact Analysis. In J. Glenn and T.J. Gordon, eds. *Futures Research Methodology, Version 2.0*. Washington, DC: American Council for the United Nations.

Helmer, O. (1983). *Looking Forward*. Beverly Hills, CA: Sage.

IFS. (n.d.). Viewed August 2005, www.battelle.org/dr-futuring/IFS/default.stm.

Kauffman, D. (1980). *Systems I: An Introduction to Systems Thinking*. Minneapolis, MN: Futures Systems.

3.1.5 Look for Turning Points

The flow of time and the degree of change can be divided into *eras*. An era is a coherent period characterized by a set of structures, beliefs, values, trends, and issues. The point between eras is a turning point, tipping point, or discontinuity, usually marked by one or more events that close the previous era and open the new one. The new era is not completely different from the old; fundamental things carry over. But enough changes to make a recognizable transition.

Analysts can characterize the past and present in terms of eras, and look for trends that move across eras. Characterizing the past as a set of eras reinforces the awareness that change happens at different rates at different times. The rate of change speeds up considerably during the transition from one era to the next. The present era can end just as abruptly as past eras have.

Key steps

The first step is to characterize the past as a set of eras. Different eras occur in different domains, at different levels, and at different times, so the characterization is never perfect. Take the history of the United States. Historians might divide that history into nine eras:

Discontinuous event	Time period	Era
Columbus lands in Western Hemisphere	1492–1604	1. Discovery and exploration
Establishment of Jamestown	1604–1775	2. Colonialism
American Revolution, Articles of Confederation	1777–1785	3. Confederation of states
American Constitution	1785–1860	4. Early democracy
Civil War	1865–1914	5. Industrialism
World War I	1919–1929	6. Inter-war period
Stock market collapse	1929–1941	7. Great Depression
World War II	1945–1989	8. Cold War
Collapse of Soviet Union	1991–present	9. US dominance

The basic idea is that the past consists of relatively long periods of time punctuated by discontinuous events that demarcate one time period from the next. The level of detail is a matter of choice depending on the objective. This rendition includes nine eras. One could skip or combine any one or more, such as the Articles of Confederation, and have fewer eras.

If the analyst was exploring technological eras rather than sociopolitical ones, then items like the railroad, automobiles, airplanes, electricity, telephones, and computers would figure as the discontinuous events. Again, what is the purpose of the activity? Placing oneself into the flow of history is the first step to understanding the past and the future.

The next step is characterizing the present era compared to the last era. What is different about today compared to yesterday, some of which people only barely realize? While it is hard to answer that question definitively, even some inkling about the differences between the past and present era can be a competitive advantage if not everyone has grasped that yet. One cannot wait for future historians to describe the characteristics of the age one is living in because then it is too late to do anything about it.

Finally, the present is an era and will also come to an end, perhaps abruptly in some event or other, and a whole new era will begin. While it cannot be predicted how the current era will end or what the new era will be, it is worthwhile to consider some plausible alternatives in order to avoid surprise and perhaps even to develop some rough contingency plans against the more important scenarios. Speculating about the future is useful when it leads to awareness, insight, and perhaps more adequate preparation for major changes that are just around the corner.

Benefits

The analyst should recognize that most forecasting deals with trends and incremental change. Incremental change is the most common form of change, lasting at least through one era and usually across many of them. However, one must deal with turning points to avoid being surprised by change and to prepare adequately for it. When the Corporate Strategy Board surveyed its members, it found that "identifying discontinuous change" was one of the five most important skills identified, yet was not a skill most respondents felt they were very good at. Discontinuities are unpredictable and, therefore, will be surprising to some extent. But being aware that discontinuities are always possible, even likely, and trying to discern what difference the discontinuity and the new era will make are significantly more useful than simply extrapolating the trends of the current era indefinitely—and inaccurately—into the future.

Example

IBM invented the personal computer and introduced it in 1981. The PC was, of course, a major discontinuity. But IBM did not fully comprehend what it had done. Not only had it transformed the computer industry, it had accelerated the process of innovation.

In 1982, Compaq introduced the first portable PC, eighteen months before IBM's first portable. At the time, Intel was releasing new processors almost annually. The IBM-PC relied on the Intel 8088 processor; its next PC, the popular PC-AT, used the 80286 processor. In 1985 Intel released the 80386 processor, but IBM did not use it because it did not want to limit the market for the profitable AT models. This was the discontinuity that gave Compaq the opening to introduce its own Deskpro model, based on the 80386, in September 1986, six months before IBM came out with its PS/2. So IBM's dominance of a major computer market had ended.

Further reading

Bishop, P. (2004). Era System. (Unpublished manuscript).

Corporate Strategy Board. (2000). *State of the Union: 2000 Member Survey*. Washington, DC: Corporate Strategy Board.

3.1.6 Improve Decision-Making by Reducing Uncertainty

Decisions can be improved and uncertainty reduced by widening the ability to read the strategic environment—seeking new information, creating new mental models, and focusing on residual uncertainty. Residual uncertainty is the uncertainty left over after collecting, collating, and analyzing relevant, available information from internal and external sources. Look for uncertainties that have both a forecasting utility—providing information on potential alternative futures—and a disruptive dimension, calling into question the organization's assumptions about the present.

When facing frequent surprises or major changes affecting capital spending, resource allocation, direction-setting, or the organization's long-term viability, sorting the known from the unknown allows the organization to build and work from a common evidence base. It also alerts it to diverse interpretations of information which may need to be reconciled.

Key steps

The simplest approach to identifying strategic uncertainty is to engage key decision-makers in a strategic conversation about what is uncertain. The conversation may use a simple or complex tool. Tools such as *Mitroff's impact-uncertainty grid, emerging-issues analysis, or scenario planning* are means to ignite these discussions. There is no one-size-fits-all answer. Tools are devices to start the conversation and should not be adhered to slavishly.

Identify and record what is fundamentally uncertain or even unknowable within the time horizon. Taking these uncertainties, identify the different directions in which they might lead. Select for further analysis those that will most help the organization think about the future, in ways that will shape and influence present decisions. In addition, identify those things that are fairly certain. Strategies designed around these known elements can anchor the more dynamic elements of strategy that are built around the uncertainties.

When designing a conversational process about uncertainties, take into account organizational culture, organizational philosophy—"the way we do things around here"—and especially the time commitments of key participants. Some organizations favor "fixers" over thought pioneers, so be wary of the tendency to stack the deck with one type or the other. As a rule of thumb the participants will be focused on their immediate priorities, such as marketing, operations, or finance, and will need to be persuaded to devote time to think about uncertainty. Accordingly, the conversation should cover emerging changes, framed in a way that creates an impression of urgency. The organization is more likely to be persuaded when new evidence arrives in support of the emerging changes identified.

Benefits

Thinking through uncertainty enables a level of strategic thinking, strategic conversation, and strategic planning that is more sophisticated than activities that are limited to business-as-usual. As Paul Schoemaker suggests, "Firms can shift the boundaries of what they control and don't, through superior anticipation, flexible strategies, and dynamic monitoring." Other benefits of discussing uncertainty include:

- providing a benchmark for what can and cannot be known when developing strategies
- providing guidance on which assumptions are most appropriate in any given situation
- challenging perceptions of the world and sensitizing the organization to the soft signals that may eventually influence perceptions or become major trends in their own right
- helping find things that are "just not done" in the industry, and providing an impetus to go ahead and do them

Example

In 2002, an analysis team was asked to assess the viability of purchasing a high-cost ocean vessel for use in Australia's Southern Ocean. The senior executive team of the organization was considering financial and cost profiles for three different vessels and wanted to explore a range of uncertainties, including the potential for:

- increased government surveillance, regulation, and enforcement of commercial fisheries
- increased global competition amongst commercial fisheries fleets
- the impacts of climate change on ocean conditions and fish populations
- more stringent marine environmental-protection standards

Although the initial financial and cost profiles favored a costlier vessel, the strategic conversation suggested that a more basic vessel would do the job, particularly given the uncertainty about the nature and the size of the fisheries fleets over the longer term.

Further reading

Courtney, H. (2001). *20/20 Foresight: Crafting Strategy in an Uncertain World*. Boston: Harvard Business School Press.

Delaney, K. (2003, August). Decision Corridors as a Futures Technique. *Journal of Futures Studies 8* (1), 53 - 60.

Kahneman, D., Slovic, P., and Tversky, A. (1982). *Judgment under Uncertainty: Heuristics and Biases*. Cambridge, UK: Cambridge University Press.

Mitroff, I. and Linstone, H.A. (1993). *The Unbounded Mind: Breaking the Chains of Traditional Business Thinking*. New York: Oxford University Press.

Schoemaker, P.J.H. (2002). *Profiting from Uncertainty*. New York: Free Press.

Van der Heijden, K. (2002). *The Sixth Sense: Accelerating Organizational Learning with Scenarios*. New York: Wiley.

3.2 Choose Forecasting Tool(s)

3.2.1 Use the Right Approach and Tool(s)

There are many different approaches or tools an analyst can choose from for performing strategic foresight. An *approach* can be defined as the design of the overall process, while *tools* are aimed at specific tasks within the approach. There will be times when the approach and the tool are one and the same, but quite often an approach will require multiple tools. It is important to choose an approach and tools well-suited to the activity at hand. Here, choosing the right tool or approach is discussed in terms of the forecasting phase, although there may be other phases where one needs to choose an approach or tools.

There is no single "right" approach or tool for each situation. Most analysts develop a feel for these choices over time. Choosing the right approach and tools is greatly aided by accurately framing the issue, so the first step is to revisit and check the accuracy of the framing. At a high level, know whether the task is to answer a specific question or to generate a range of potential options for decision-makers to choose from.

Key steps

Hugh Courtney (2001) offers a framework for helping to select tools, based on the nature of the uncertainty involved in the activity.

Level	Possible Tools
Level 1: A clear, single view of the future	Market research Porter's 5 Forces Value chain analysis Trend extrapolation
Level 2: A limited set of possible future outcomes, one of which will occur	Decision analysis Real options
Level 3: A range of possible future outcomes	Forecasting Scenarios
Level 4: A limitless range of possible future outcomes	Game theory Systems dynamics

Other factors to consider in choosing an approach or tool are the time availability, size, skill, and style of the analysis team and the members' comfort with the approach or tool. Whether outside consulting help is available should also be factored in. As a rule, it is a good idea to bring in an outside expert versed in a particular tool or approach, as this typically enhances the credibility of the activity.

Benefits

Choosing the right approach and tool to fit the problem at hand can sometimes make or break an activity. Using the wrong tool will not only distort results, but can lead to demoralization of the team and sap energy from the activity. A common pitfall is becoming enamored with personal-favorite approaches and tools and using them for every situation, even when they are inappropriate. It is good practice to keep current with emerging tools and approaches through reading, conferences, networking, and the like.

Example

An analyst relates how the importance of choosing the right tool was brought home to him in his work as a consulting futurist. In one instance, the approach to a foresight project involving the future of science and technology used the approach of alternative scenarios. The organization felt uncomfortable with the wide range of scenarios being generated and asked instead for the team to put together its single-best guess or baseline forecast. As a result the project got back on track and became a huge success for the organization and the consultants alike.

In another case, the analysis team generated reams of data about emerging information technologies. Again, the client felt uncomfortable with the enormous report and challenged the team to come up with single-page scenarios describing potential alternatives. The analysis team hired a professional cartoonist to generate graphics depicting the scenarios on a single page each. In this case, the activity was useful in generating the background for the scenarios, but the move to graphics enabled the organization to plug the scenarios into its planning system in a way that was highly convenient and useful.

Further reading

Courtney, H. (2001). *20/20 Foresight: Crafting Strategy in an Uncertain World*. Cambridge, MA: Harvard Business School.

Hines, A. (1999, April). The Simple Facts of Business Life. *foresight: the journal of futures studies, strategic thinking, and policy, 1* (2).

3.2.2 Use at Least One Formal Method

Strategic foresight work should be transparent to clients. That is, they should be able to understand how the conclusions were reached. Using a formal method is the most effective means to demonstrate transparency.

A formal method is fundamental to generating a forecast. It follows a proven process to generate results and thus lends credibility to the results. The method or methods used in an activity should be explained in a way that is understandable to the organization, in order to gain their buy-in to the activity.

Formal methods may also be used at other points of a strategic foresight activity. In Framing, for example, the method of stakeholder analysis (see *Guideline 2.1.4: Conduct a Stakeholder Analysis*) can be used to assess the needs of stakeholders.

There are also various methods for team-building that can be useful in Framing. Environmental scanning is a method typically employed to gather external intelligence that will feed the forecast. There are also methods for exploring implications during the Planning phase, such as the Futures Wheel developed by Jerome Glenn (2003) and the Implications Wheel developed by Joel Barker (www.implicationswheel.com); see *Guideline 4.1.2 Get to the Second- and Third-order Implications*.

Key steps

Choosing a method is an art, not a science. No single method is right for every situation, or even for a particular situation. Choosing one depends on the judgment of the analyst to assess the best approach for the circumstances. Analysts may have preferred methods, which of course should be taken into account, but not necessarily be decisive.

Work with the client to select the best method, whenever possible. While this may slow the process down, it will increase the organization's buy-in if it has a say in the method. It may also require educating the organization about the various options. Again, the time is worth investing.

Sometimes an analyst may seek to try a new method. It is best to be upfront with the organization when attempting to engage in something new. Many clients are excited by the potential of doing something innovative. It will help your case if you can point to examples where the approach has been used successfully by other consultants or organizations.

Formal methods should never be a straitjacket. Analysts must rely on their judgment to adapt and take the appropriate steps. As long as the reasoning is made explicit, the organization is likely to understand and appreciate the necessity. In fact, innovating during an activity is often how existing methods are improved and new ones are developed.

Benefits

Strategic foresight is vulnerable to the charge that it is based on guesswork and lacking in credibility as it projects into the future. Its results cannot be validated until the future actually occurs. Thus, it is important to be able to demonstrate credibility by relying on proven methods.

Using formal methods also serves as a discipline for the analysis team. It tightens up the process and helps ensure steps are not overlooked or missed. It can be used to support the results when making the case to a client. It demonstrates how the conclusions were reached, in a way the client can understand.

A caveat is to beware of over-reliance on method, risking false confidence in the results. Using a method is not a guarantee of a successful activity, but rather improves the likelihood of success.

Example

An example of how the use of methodology helped build the credibility of a forecast comes from the early experience of the Association of Professional Futurists. The clients in this case were the association's own members. The activity involved setting the long-term direction of the newly formed association. A workshop was organized that used the scenario-planning method to explore possible futures for the futures field and the association. The method produced several potential futures for the organization that became the basis for subsequent branding and strategic planning. A branding activity drew heavily upon the results generated by the method, which was often invoked as providing support for the decisions made.

Two years after this initial scenario planning, a second workshop was organized around specific strategies and plans to carry the association forward. Here again, the scenario work was invoked at the basis for moving forward. The membership was clearly able to see how the plans and activities being devised were based upon results that were generated by a method they understood and were comfortable with.

Further reading

Glenn, J. and Gordon, T.J., eds. (2003). *Futures Research Methodology, Version 2.0*. Washington, DC: AC/UNU Millennium Project.

Hines, A. (2003). The Futures of Futures: A Scenario Salon. *foresight: the journal of futures studies, strategic thinking, and policy, 5* (4), 28 - 35.

3.2.3 Adapt Existing Methods and Models to the Situation

Most analysts are accustomed to working with standard, static, and rigid methods to produce and analyze information, because these methods are battle-tested and have been useful in the past. But the context for strategic foresight—the social reality—is flexible, open, complex, and changing; thus the methods used to analyze it should be flexible too.

There are no standard recipes to produce and analyze strategic information. Although some general references must be considered, every case is unique. So, most of time, the success in an activity depends on the way analysts are able to adapt the existing methods and models to the specific situation.

Key steps

To choose the best forecasting methods, begin with some simple diagnostic questions, such as:

- What do we expect of the process?
- What do the team and/ or our clients expect of the process?
- Does the team want to explore alternative action plans?
- Does the team want to justify a concrete action plan?

Strategic foresight is inspired by generic challenges that can be addressed as specific targets. So the second step should be to clearly identify the targets of the forecasting activity. This may seem naïve, but as discussed in Framing above, sometimes an activity can start without the participants understanding exactly what is expected of it. Sometimes the organization itself has serious problems defining what it expects of the future and what it wants and needs in the present. Thus, clearly identifying the activity's targets is an important precursor.

The next step should be a diagnostic of the available resources, both internal and external, to approach the foresight activity. This means defining available time, money, people, and knowledge.

Benefits

Rethinking the methods to produce and analyze information should be a preliminary routine in any process of strategic foresight. A systematic effort to adapt existing models to the specific situation confers several benefits. First, it manages expectations by recognizing that there is no perfect method for analyzing and understanding social reality. Current methods and tools for social research are attempts to model social reality under systematic assumptions—but not perfect recipes.

Second, it acknowledges that "objectivity" is an extremely difficult achievement in social research. Behind every method lies a worldview, whether tacit or explicit. Even the traditional frontier between quantitative and qualitative methods highlights the diversity of approaches to any given subject of study.

Finally, existing methods for the analysis of social reality should be understood as open, not closed and definitive. Methods evolve in response to new insights and learnings, often gaining added sophistication and efficacy. Thus, innovative approaches should be welcomed.

Most of the methods used in foresight today are a product of this understanding of innovation in social research. They have been developed and adapted to the context and/ or the subject under study. For example, earlier tools like the group interview or the survey poll were reinterpreted to create a new standard such as the Delphi technique.

Example

Discontinuities in the social realm, such as the spread of AIDS in the 1980s, the 9/11 attacks, or the emergence of China as a major producer/consumer, highlight the need to continually rethink traditional analysis methods. Social research is not bounded and unchanging, as research in the natural sciences often is; even complex econometric models that predict the course of the world's economy can be quickly invalidated by an isolated action like the 9/11 terror attacks. Innovation and openness are needed because the methods traditionally used to predict future events are ineffective in the unstable context of social reality. Traditional methods must be complemented with new ones, as well as undergoing rethinking and revision themselves.

Further reading

Bas, E. (1999). The Sociology of the 21st Century, or How to Be Ready for Facing the Future. *International Review of Sociology, 9* (3), 287 - 293.

Bell, W. (1997). *Foundations of Futures Studies*. (Vol. 1). New Brunswick: Transaction Publishers.

Slaughter, R. (1995). *The Foresight Principle: Cultural Recovery in the 21st Century*. Westport, CT: Praeger Press and London: Adamantine Press Ltd. 52.

3.2.4 Combine Different Techniques to Envision a Broader Range of Possible Futures

Organizations are often tempted to use a single tool for forecasting, usually one they are already familiar with. This attitude restricts their capacity for foresight, though, as it will allow them to explore only certain aspects of a problem. By combining different foresight tools, they can avoid the risk of incomplete analysis.

Different tools should be explored and applied in order to assure a multidimensional approach, both before and during the analysis of the problem. At the end of the analysis, it also makes sense to do a post-check to see if the outcomes of different methods are being fully taken into consideration—no single source should be overrepresented.

Key steps

Each problem and situation needs to be analyzed in order to understand what kind of future-oriented information is needed for the activity. The needs should be matched with tools that are best suited for gathering and analyzing that particular kind of data.

It is also important to match complementary methods, meaning that the weaknesses of one method should be balanced by the strengths of another. One way is to apply the selected methods separately, investigating the problem first with one method, then with another. The outcomes can then be harmonized and structured to support the activity. A good example would be to define the attitudes of certain customer groups by comparing the data from a statistical database with opinions gained through a Delphi process.

Another possibility is to apply the methods consecutively, with the outcomes of one method acting as inputs to the next. Interviewing experts about a certain phenomenon could give valuable insights about which trends need further investigation, for instance.

Finally, it is important to check the output of the work to see if the outcomes of each method have been fully considered. Again, many experts tend to value certain methods over others and thus risk overestimating their importance.

Benefits

Combining different foresight tools has several benefits. More complex dimensions of the problem or situation can be uncovered, giving the analyst a deeper understanding of the key factors for decision-making.

Every method has strengths and weaknesses. Using multiple methods helps to leverage the strengths and offset the weaknesses of each, and enables a synergistic solution that fits the uniqueness of the situation. In addition, using multiple tools provides flexibility, since certain sources of information may be restricted or unavailable and the analysis team may be compelled to turn to other methods to gain the information.

Finally, creativity and sensibility can be enhanced by applying different methods—as they can provide valuable insights to the problem and provoke new ideas.

Example

A study for a large chemical company explored the future of the industry, looking particularly for "gamechanger" events: potential discontinuities that could shift the basis of competition in an industry. The analysis team, working with an external consulting company, used scenario planning to create a range of alternative futures. However, they felt the study lacked the supporting detail necessary to truly deliver an impact for their data-hungry client. They decided to introduce a cross-impact analysis, which measured the impacts of the scenario variables upon one another. The resulting table greatly enriched the details upon which the scenarios could draw, and led to new insights that were especially helpful in suggesting pathways from the present to the future and identifying leading indicators the organization could track. This combination—scenarios to sketch out the big picture and the cross-impact matrix to help fill in the details— created a rich resource that proved useful in several applications at the company in subsequent years.

Further reading

Belliveau, P., Griffin, A., and Somermeyer, S. (2002). *The PDMA Toolbook for New Product Development*. New York: John Wiley & Sons.

Hines, A. (2005, June). Using Foresight to Generate Insight: A Sampler of Futures Tools. Competia Online Magazine.

3.3 Diverge—Generate Ideas

3.3.1 Provoke New Lines of Thinking with Creative Approaches and Tools

"The time will come when our descendants will be amazed that we were not able to see the obvious," according to Seneca. Many solutions for today's problems are already available, but not yet discovered. Use tools for creative thinking to reveal more opportunities for successful organizational development, alternatives to take action or solve a problem, and ways to improve a product, service, process, or system.

Key steps

Analysts can draw from the following useful archetypes for strategic innovation.

The *strategic relatives* archetype suggests learning from other industries. Most of the strategic issues and problems in an organization have been handled before—but in other fields and industries. Identify these "strategic relatives," i.e., businesses that have similar missions, strategies, and structures. A hospital might discover new opportunities for processes in car production. Banks learn from retailers about their strategic options. Who are the "strategic relatives" and what opportunities do they bear for the organization?

The *biostrategy* archetype suggests learning from nature. Nature is the most successful organization in history. For some five billion years it has experienced no real bankruptcy and performed very efficiently. Fractal-shaped production plants, network strategies in knowledge management, participatory leadership as well as the political principle of subsidiarity—all have been invented by nature. How would nature organize the organization?

The *science fiction* archetype suggests learning from fiction. A science fiction writer's job is to think of alternative futures and alternative realities. Non-invasive injections, communicators, voice control, and pervasive computing on the technical side, US-Russian cooperation, feminization, and race integration on the sociopolitical side were in books and on television screens long before they diffused to everyday life. What does science fiction say about alternative views in your organization?

The *value analysis* archetype suggests concentrating on the desired outcome. Customers don't pay for products and services, but for their outcomes. Provide holes, not drilling machines; increasing crop yields, not pesticides; homes, not mortgages. In short, be a specialist not in either products or solutions, but in outcomes.

Benefits

Using thinking models like those above benefits organizations in several ways. Foremost, the organization will have a broader field of vision by seeing more alternatives. As the saying goes: where there are two alternatives, choose the third. The Chinese use this paradox to point out that there are always more alternatives than assumed.

Moreover, thinking models save organizations time by furnishing mental shortcuts. They facilitate idea generation more effectively than pure, unstructured brainstorming.

Thinking models also help an organization anticipate the future well enough to seize a pioneering position. Creative-thinking models describe common paths of strategic innovation: someone, somewhere, at some time in the future will arrive at the same idea. Be first. They also help organizations to differentiate strategically from their competitors, by looking differently at their industry and developing original ideas.

Example

In the early 1980s Roland Kamm, CEO of Kärcher, today the world's leading supplier of cleaning technology, attended a corporate strategy seminar. One of the presenters, biologist Hans Hass, spoke about biostrategic approaches to corporate strategy. He described the finches on the Galapagos Islands which, in the 1830s, inspired Charles Darwin to develop his hypotheses about the origins of species. The Galapagos finches are special in that they differentiated through the shapes of their beaks—i.e., they specialized around different forms of food, so that finches of every sub-species could have a competitive advantage in their own niche.

Kamm left the four-day seminar after the first day. Inspired by the finches story, he stopped or sold all of Kärcher's businesses except high-pressure washers. This product was something like the primeval finch. Then, like the Galapagos finches, Kamm started to differentiate the high-pressure washers into a comprehensive set of cleaning technologies for every cleaning need (i.e., every form of "food"). He created a new mission statement: "Kärcher—Cleaning Is Our Matter," and went on to make his company the world leader in cleaning technologies. A single analogy to biostrategy laid the foundation for world-class success. (Hass, 1988)

Further reading

de Bono, E. (1992). *Opportunities: A Handbook of Business Opportunity Search*. London: Penguin.

Burke, W. (1996). *Wide Angle Vision*. New York: Wiley.

Hass, H. (1988). *Der Hai im Management*. Berlin, Germany: Ullstein.

Micic, P. (2003). *Der ZukunftsManager*. Munich, Germany: Haufe.

Micic, P. and Marx, A. (2004). *Die Bank von Morgen denken und gestalten*. Eltville, Germany: ADG.

3.3.2 Go Beyond Brainstorming

Brainstorming has become so widely used as a creative-thinking technique that it is practically synonymous with idea generation. But it is just one technique, and a fairly limited one at that. Brainstorming is about downloading or emptying out the ideas one already has about a topic. It is popular because it is so simple: participants literally just speak or write what comes to mind around the topic. But it is a poor means for generating new thinking, unless it is combined with other techniques.

Key steps

A good time to use brainstorming is at the beginning of an idea generation session. This gets all the preexisting ideas out on the table. While almost everybody is familiar with brainstorming, there are some best practices to keep in mind. It is important to establish clear rules, such as "There are no dumb ideas" and "Don't criticize or evaluate ideas during the brainstorm." Also, keep brainstorms short. A brainstorm should release energy quickly, and stop as soon as the flow of contributions starts drying up. The key is to enable participants to contribute freely without fear of being judged by their fellows.

The group can then prioritize those ideas that are useful and discard the rest. A particularly bold approach suggested by Gene Anderson, co-developer of Bottom Line Innovation, is to discard all ideas generated during brainstorming, on the grounds that they are things people have already thought of and therefore are not new or creative. This may trigger a near-rebellion, but in the end, most groups are surprised to find they were indeed able to generate fresher ideas when they let go of their preexisting ones.

After a brainstorm, other creativity tools aimed at forcing people to think differently can be used to help the group come to new insights. Creativity guru Edward de Bono, for instance, has developed a wide array of tools around the concept of lateral thinking. He notes that the brain prefers to work linearly, and that a way to generate new thinking is to force it to go sideways, or laterally. Besides de Bono's, hundreds of techniques exist for "tricking" the brain off its normal path and getting it to think differently. Arthur van Gundy (1995) and Michael Michalko (1991) have particularly useful catalogues of these kinds of tools.

Benefits

Brainstorms have substantive and process benefits. They yield some ideas and they establish a norm of group participation. Going beyond brainstorming will yield even richer benefits, as it gets to tools that will help generate ideas that are truly breakthrough and innovative.

Example

Examples of unsuccessful brainstorming are legion. A common complaint is that nothing really new emerges from these sessions. As suggested above, if one relies primarily on brainstorming, this is likely to be an accurate complaint since if people draw only upon their existing ideas, they will keep getting the same results. This is particularly common in organizations with a long history and stable workforce. Often, eyes will roll and groans emerge when another brainstorm is suggested. The good news is that myriad alternative tools for idea generation are available, challenging participants to think differently (which may generate another round of complaints) and stand a better chance of generating ideas that are truly creative and innovative.

Further reading

de Bono, E. (1996). *Serious Creativity: Using the Power of Lateral Thinking to Create New Ideas*. Hammersmith, UK: Harper Collins Business.

Glenn, J. (1994). Participatory Methods. In J. Glenn and T. Gordon, eds. *Futures Research Methodology—Version 2.0.* Washington, DC: AC/UNU Millennium Project.

Hall, D. (1995). *Jump Start Your Brain.* New York: Warner Books.

Michalko, M. (1991). *Thinkertoys: A Handbook of Business Creativity.* Berkeley, CA: Ten Speed Press.

Van Gundy, A.B. (1995). *Brain Boosters for Business Advantage: Ticklers, Grab Bags, Blue Skies, and Other Bionic Ideas.* San Diego, CA: Pfeiffer & Co.

3.3.3 Adapt the Tried-and-True Approaches of Creative People to New Contexts

Creativity is the ability to consistently produce new ideas. Innovation is the adoption of these new and useful ideas by people in organizations. Creative thinking is a skill that can be learned, contrary to the popular myth that one is either born with creativity or not. Clearly, there are differences in natural creative ability. Sports provide an analogy: not everyone is born with professional ability, but even someone without much natural ability can improve by using the right equipment and practicing the proper techniques.

The great psychologist Carl Jung suggested: "[We humans have] the distinctive power to create something new in the real sense of the word, just as nature, in the course of long periods of time, succeeds in creating new forms." Each person has unique capacities for creativity in the ways they solve problems, manage people, participate on a team, resolve conflict, turn seminal ideas into marketable products and services, or motivate others to reach their potentials. Analysts need to know how to enlist the creativity within an organization and foster a culture of innovation. This requires understanding the varieties of creativity, and of ways to ignite curiosity and passion.

Key steps

Jung developed a theory about eight equally valuable, equally creative ways of knowing. To make his model more accessible, Katharine Briggs and Isabel Myers developed the Myers Briggs Type Indicator (MBTI), a validated, tested, and easily accessible personality inventory. Building on their work, Levesque (2001) focused on using the MBTI to develop creative potential. She posits eight creative types and the creative contributions they typically make. For example, the *Adventurer* (ESTP, ESFP—extravert, sensor, thinker or feeler, and perceiver) is a daredevil type who seeks fun and unique experiences, is a clever innovator, and uses skillful adaptations to solve novel challenges. Another type, the *Navigator* (ISTJ, ISFJ—introvert, sensor, thinker or feeler, and judgmental) plans the voyage, keeps logs and charts, and enables discoveries and practical adaptations of what others have initiated.

Developing creative thinking and a culture for innovation requires a certain mindset. This mindset acknowledges that while genius and outstanding ability do exist, each member of the team has the potential to generate creative solutions within an environment that respects and values their unique talents. A substantial body of literature on creativity, by authors such as Edward de Bono, Michael Gelb, and Tony Buzan, can help foster such a mindset and culture. There are also considerable resources targeted at helping groups in specific contexts to tap their creative potential; for example, Warren Bennis and Peter Senge have published extensively on creativity and innovation in leadership and management.

Benefits

Creativity, and its corollary innovation, helps achieve extraordinary results not only for the organization but for creative people themselves. Developing individuals' creative capacity opens the door to greater flexibility, self-expression, and personal reward. People tend to receive more recognition and to see themselves as valuable contributors to the team. For the organization, it builds resilience and competitive edge—and the ability to recognize when only minor modifications, or none at all, are the best approach.

A culture of innovation also supports new levels of synergy and dynamism for the organization. By creating this culture of innovation, the organization will build its capacity to excel in the undefined, unstructured change environment of today's business world.

Example

In 1965, Yale University undergraduate Frederick W. Smith wrote a term paper about the fact that most airfreight shippers relied on passenger routes, a strategy he viewed as inefficient and expensive. Smith also wrote of how slow and unresponsive the US Postal Service was to business needs. He received a grade of "C" on the paper, but it led him to imagine a shipping system designed specifically for airfreight that could accommodate time-sensitive shipments such as medicines, computer parts, and electronics. With a vision of guaranteed next-day delivery, he revolutionized a static industry by pioneering a new process of sorting and delivering letters and freight. Thus was born FDX, later Fedex—and a stellar example of adapting tried-and-true approaches to new contexts.

Further reading

Bennis, W. (2003). *On Becoming a Leader*. Philadelphia, PA: Perseus Books.

Burton, L.E. (2004). Creativity, Innovation, and Visionary Thinking: Becoming All You Can Become. In H. Didsbury, ed. *Thinking Creatively in Turbulent Times*. Bethesda, MD: World Future Society.

De Bono, E. (1985). *Six Thinking Hats*. New York: Little, Brown and Co.

FedEx Corporate History. Viewed August 2005, www.fedex.com/us/about/today/history/?link=4.

Gelb, M.J. (1998). *How to Think Like Leonardo da Vinci: Seven Steps to Genius Every Day*. New York: Dell Publishing.

Levesque, L.C. (2001). *Breakthrough Creativity: Achieving Top Performance Using the Eight Creative Talents*. Mountain View, CA: Davies-Black.

Ross, B. and Segal, C. (2002). *Breakthrough Thinking for Nonprofit Organizations: Creative Strategies for Extraordinary Results*. San Francisco: Jossey-Bass.

Senge, P., Kleiner, A., Roberts, C., Ross, R., and Smith, B. (1994). *The Fifth Discipline Fieldbook*. New York: Currency Doubleday.

3.3.4 Assume that What Is Known for Certain...Is False

Foresight typically involves dismantling preconceived notions. Creativity techniques can be useful for this. Creativity is sometimes less about dreaming up something original than it is about daring to question what is already known. This is not always necessary—it's more often a tactic of last resort, when everything else has failed. Organizations are more amenable to attacking the sacred cows of thought when they have no other choice.

Key steps

The first step in eliminating outworn preconceptions is to identify the aspect of the problem that seems most intractable or causes the greatest concern. For example, retailers have a problem with customers returning goods the day after Christmas. Cash flow in stores is typically negative that day, as money is refunded for returned goods. One thing is known for certain: "customers returning goods" is an undesirable event.

The second step is to create a reversal—to assume that "customers returning goods" is now a good thing. Then find a way to pretend that this reversal is a reality. One solution is to reward people who return goods. Instead of refunding the purchase price, customers could be given the option of a gift certificate (non-redeemable for cash) for 110% of the value of the purchase.

The result of this particular reversal tactic would be to retain revenues that were already received, at the acceptable cost of taking a discount on their value. An even more positive byproduct is that when customers use the gift certificates to make a purchase, they will inevitably purchase something of greater value than the gift certificate.

The primary objection to the reversal tactic is that people believe it is impossible to reverse a certainty. The other failing is that there is no guarantee this technique will succeed every time. The good news is that when it does work, the results are often astounding.

Benefits

The challenge in any problem-solving activity is to think outside the proverbial box. But the real problem is that one seldom knows one is in a box. Nevertheless, the boundaries of the box constrain action and foster inaccurate perceptions of what is and is not possible. Keep in mind that the box and the boundaries are usually self-constructed. In addition, they are often so ingrained that they become invisible. Creative problem-solving approaches are a way out.

This guideline can be applied widely because it is always possible to list what is "known for certain." That list then defines the "box." The reversal tactic is guaranteed to generate fresh thinking. A significant prerequisite, however, is the courage to handle the contrarian conclusions as well as what may be perfectly legitimate objections to the wild assertions generated by the technique. It requires an equally strong faith in the process.

Example

The technology used to build a stone arch bridge testifies to the value of the reversal tactic. Consider the problems encountered in building a bridge out of stone blocks across a river. Chiefly, gravity would constantly pull the structure down. Assume for certain that "gravity is the problem," and then reverse it to "gravity is the solution." Then the task is to make this statement come true, even if one has no idea how to make it happen.

Getting gravity to push sideways instead of down is relatively easy: just make it impossible to move straight down. An arch takes care of that need. The next problem is to make sure the stones can't "bulge" out to the side. That is done by blocking the sides with rubble. That structure would stand up because of gravity. Of course, first one would have to put up a temporary wooden scaffold on which to build the gravity-exploiting structure. Once the stone structure is completed, the wooden scaffold is removed and the stones cannot fall down.

Further reading

Coates, J.F. (1999). Getting at Assumptions Is Troublesome. *Technological Forecasting & Social Change, 62,* 97 - 99.

Smith, R. (2002). *The 7 Levels of Change: Different Thinking for Different Results.* 2nd Ed. Irving, TX: Tapestry Press.

3.3.5 Explore Ideas that Cause Discomfort

When conducting a strategic foresight activity—whether for exploring new business opportunities, designing a strategy, developing a marketing or hiring plan, or simply brainstorming—seek out ideas that make the organization feel uneasy. These include ideas that would counteract the current strategy, put the organization out of business, make a new product obsolete, be perceived as too "weird," or be contrary to the organization's culture or notions about how the world works.

Seeking out uncomfortable ideas is not an activity that should be pursued for every organizational decision. There are times, however, when it is a necessity: in developing hiring and training strategies, making strategic decisions, designing products, and any activity requiring the generation of new ideas.

Key steps

Many techniques and idioms exist for seeking out and exploring ideas that cause discomfort. At a basic level, the analyst can suggest that the organization hire people who make them uncomfortable, and include them in foresight activities. For example, an executive vice president at Motorola deliberately looks for people who will annoy him and tell him he is wrong. Similarly, the founder and chairman of the design firm IDEO says that when employees in his company feel uncomfortable around new hires, he knows that he has done something right.

One doesn't always have to go outside the organization to find things that make one uncomfortable. People in the organization who have never been good at science, for example, could be challenged to visit the research and development department, or those phobic about math could go talk to someone from accounting, and so on. The cross-pollination this engenders, and the exposure to considering problems from different angles, could be very valuable.

Sutton (2002) explores various practical methods for benefiting from discomfiting ideas. One is to assign someone at any business meeting to be the official devil's advocate. This person is tasked with "...pointing out flaws in the assumptions, beliefs, facts, and decisions..." of the group. To avoid "groupthink," an organization must have people who are willing to challenge their colleagues' assumptions, even if those colleagues are in senior positions.

Taking this a step further is the practice of dialectical inquiry. Here the devil's advocate not only challenges the group's assumptions; he or she also develops contrary assumptions and puts them to the group, which may lead to new recommendations. Another idea from Sutton is to generate ideas that may seem impractical, ridiculous, or dumb when compared to the industry standard. In effect, the analyst dares the organization to defy conventional wisdom and risk being wrong, in order to widen the range of ideas considered.

Benefits

The benefits of exploring uncomfortable ideas are akin to the explanation one gives a child for why she should eat her vegetables: "because it's good for you." Seeking out contrarian ideas and people may seem counterintuitive, and does not always leave a great taste in one's mouth, yet is necessary for organizational health. Other benefits include avoiding groupthink, promoting a diversity of beliefs and ideas, uncovering new opportunities, and preventing the organization from becoming intellectually homogeneous.

If this principle isn't followed, an organization runs the risk of entering a downward spiral. The creative capital of the organization is tapped out in shorter and shorter amounts of time, since the same types of people are generating the same types of ideas. That's why it is important to have someone drag their feet, point out potential downsides and problems, and highlight weak points and critical flaws. If everyone thinks an idea is great, it probably means it is not unique or innovative enough.

Example

The story of John Boyd, as chronicled by Coram (2002), is an excellent case study in innovation and controversial personalities. Boyd was a gifted fighter pilot who was also, among other things, loud, brash, brilliant, and unconcerned with making people feel comfortable. At one point in his career he was asked to work on an experimental Air Force program for a next-generation airplane. The standard mindset of the Air Force was that each successive plane should be bigger and fly faster, farther, and higher. This led to multipurpose planes that were too heavy, too complex, and too expensive. Boyd took the opposite approach and, at great professional risk, advocated a cheap, simple, high-performance fighter. He made some progress that initially led to the F-15, but ultimately his work led to the F-16, one of the greatest fighter aircraft of all time.

Further reading

Coram, R. (2002). *Boyd: The Fighter Pilot That Changed the Art of War*. New York: Little, Brown and Company.

Farber, B. (2001, February). Get Uncomfortable. *Entrepreneur*. Viewed December 2004, www.entrepreneur.com/Magazines/ Copy_of_MA_SegArticle/0,4453,285542,00.html.

Kelley, T. (2001). *The Art of Innovation: Lessons in Creativity from IDEO, America's Leading Design Firm*. New York: Currency Doubleday.

Sutton, R.I. (2002). *Weird Ideas That Work: 11 Practices for Promoting, Managing, and Sustaining Innovation*. New York: Free Press.

3.3.6 Combine Rigor with Creativity

Many people assume that rigor and creativity don't mix. But when properly balanced, the mix can be very powerful. In fact, one without the other leads to problems. Creativity without rigor can wander off topic and fail to inform the activity. Rigor without creativity often generates the obvious and fails to deliver insight. The combination of the two maximizes potential. Rigor helps keep creativity focused, and creativity keeps rigor from becoming stale or failing to generate insights.

Key steps

This guideline is especially important during idea generation. The analyst needs to think through a process that will free the participants to think creatively, yet be rigorous in keeping the participants focused on the issue at hand and yielding practical, actionable results.

For instance, rigor may be brought to bear as a series of steps designed to achieve the desired outcome. After this process is outlined, the analyst should then select creativity tools that fit the desired outcomes and the dynamics of the team involved. The process should flow in a way that the selected tools generate ideas that in turn help produce insights at the core of the activity. Of course, it may be necessary to make adjustments to the process—rigor does not mean inflexibility or inability to adapt. One typical trap to avoid is an overly rigorous process that stifles creativity. At the opposite end of the spectrum, too much creativity without sufficient rigor can generate interesting and creative ideas, but fail to serve the purposes and outcomes required by the activity.

Benefits

Typically, the purpose of a strategic foresight activity is to derive insights that escape routine consideration. As creativity guru Mihaly Csikszentmihalyi (1990) observes, "It seems that the most basic requirement is to provide a clear set of challenges." Being sufficiently rigorous in undertaking creativity maximizes the chances of generating insights that will be useful.

Example

Craig Wynett, former head of Corporate New Ventures (CNV) at Procter & Gamble, has long been preaching the gospel of bringing discipline to creativity and innovation. Ideas bubbling up from P&G's far-flung workforce of 110,000 people were routed to a CNV innovation panel via My Idea, a corporate collaboration network. CNV teams then brought rigor to these ideas by putting them under the microscope—using the Web to analyze markets, demographics, and cost information to make sure a new-product idea was feasible. Once the team decided to go ahead, a project was launched within days.

The program delivered results. At the time of writing, it had put fifty-eight products onto the market. One of CNV's first items was a new household-cleaning tool called the Swiffer, which got out the door in just ten months—less than half the usual time—and has since become a staple of P&G's household-products portfolio.

Further reading

Csikszentmihalyi, M. (1990). *Flow: The Psychology of Optimal Experience*. New York: HarperCollins.

Stepanek, M. (1999, December 13). Using the Net for Brainstorming. BusinessWeek Online.

Wynett, C. (2002, August). Inspiring Innovation. *Harvard Business Review, 80*, 39 - 49.

3.3.7 Incorporate Analytical and Emotional Elements for Compelling Strategic Conversations

Conversations are central to strategic foresight. They are how people in organizations gain information about the future, make sense of that information, and deliberate how to go forward. To get creative outputs from conversations, it is important to combine the rational data of analysis with opportunities for people to exercise their imagination, desires, hunches, and beliefs. Creative conversations are relevant to many aspects of the strategic process—wherever new ideas are sought and it is important to develop a shared commitment among people to move forward.

Key steps

Gratton and Ghoshal (2002:221) argue, "The vice grip of relentless pragmatism needs to be softened by the invigorating spirit of romanticism. Big, broad questions must be legitimized again, as a driver of the constant endeavor not only to execute for today but also to renew for tomorrow." Their research indicates a number of ways to jumpstart creative conversations.

One way is to encourage a climate of questioning and doubt. Many organizations either implicitly or explicitly give messages that doubt is a sign of weakness, indecision, or insubordination. However, a willingness to question, to give voice to feelings of unease, to wonder how things could be different, provides the environment for creative conversations to occur. This can be achieved through approaches such as scenario planning; through the role modeling of the analyst; and by the organization trusting its staff to participate in the conversations that are important to them.

Another way to balance analysis with emotion is to set out topics that are energizing, broad, and personally meaningful. Such topics get engagement from people because they are exciting and regarded as worthwhile. The research discipline of *appreciative inquiry* has long understood that "organizations move in the direction of what they study." (Ludema, Cooperrider, and Barrett, 2001:192). An example of a meaningful topic is: "How do we create the best possible health system that unites the achievements of the past with the aspirations of the future?" Compare this with the more limited and negative topic: "How do we fix the problems with the health system"? See *4.3.4 You Get What You Think*.

A third way is to provide the time and space for creative conversations. Dedicated time must be set aside if such conversations are not to be squeezed out by daily busy-ness. Whether this time is scheduled weekly or monthly depends on the purpose of the conversation. The important thing is to make the time, and for the leadership to endorse the importance of this. Also, sustained time must be allowed for people to develop a level of trust with each other that in turn takes the group to a deeper level, where the sharing of more emotional information is possible. Of similar importance is carefully choosing the place where such conversations might occur. The venue needs to stimulate all the senses and provide an environment for thinking and feeling.

A fourth way is to mix up the participants and the rules. A diverse mix of people leads to more varied and interesting conversations. People could be from different levels and parts of the organization as well as from external agencies. Similarly, including some novel rules about how the conversation is to be conducted can provide the conditions for fresh outcomes.

Benefits

There are two key reasons why combining the analytical and the emotional is so important to effective creative conversations. First, Hardin Tibbs (2000) makes the point that people have a great desire to "know" the future. Most foresight activity focuses on gaining information in the belief that the more one has, the clearer it will become how to act. However, the future is far more "alive" than that: it is "a psychological space into which we project our hopes and fears, our dreams and expectations" (Tibbs, 2000:1). Therefore, when action is taken for the future, it is inevitably a combination of thoughts, feelings, and desires. This reflects the conviction that management is an art as much as a science, and that analysis is an important part of the process but cannot by itself yield truly innovative strategies (Roos, 2004).

Second, when dealing with new or complex issues, as strategic foresight typically does, answers often emerge in the process of questioning and discussion. That is, they are "invented in the act of answering" (Waldenfels, cited in Statler and Jacobs, 2003:11). These are called "productive" answers, in contrast with "reproductive" answers which are drawn from previous situations and precedents. Therefore, creative conversations, and their combination of the analytical and emotional, can allow these new and unformed answers to emerge. This can lead to early understanding of new phenomena and innovations that others have yet to see.

Example

Gratton and Ghoshal (2002:217) cite the example of BP's decision to create a new brand identity, which led to many conversations that combined the analytical and the emotional. In the late 1990s BP purchased two other companies, Amoco and Arco, and as a result had a workforce with a diverse heritage. The new brand was seen as a way of bringing these diverse groups together around a common future aspiration.

For one year, over 15,000 employees from all over BP engaged in deep conversations about the fundamental values of the new firm, and how they could be expressed in concrete actions or what came to be called "proof points." With the help of external research partners, the brand team collected an enormous amount of data ranging from industry trends to government policies, NGO aspirations, and employee surveys. Beyond data, the conversations were also about the hopes and aspirations of the many different kinds of people who worked at BP. Their views—expressing a passion that surprised management—shaped the attributes that would underlie the new brand: progressive, green, innovative, and performance-driven. By the time the new brand—Beyond Petroleum—was launched on July 24, 2001, those values and the overall theme of becoming a force for good had created a level of internal energy, enthusiasm, and commitment unprecedented in BP's history. "We are now a very successful company, making after-tax profits of over $1 billion per month," said Rodney Chase, then deputy CEO. "I am absolutely convinced that we could not have achieved this state without that energy and commitment."

Further reading

Gratton, L. and Ghoshal, S. (2002). Improving the Quality of Conversations. *Organizational Dynamics, 31* (3), 209 - 223.

Hussey, D. (2001). Creative Strategic Thinking and the Analytical Process: Critical Factors for Strategic Success. *Strategic Change, 10* (4), 201 - 213.

Ludema, J.D., Cooperrider, D.L., and Barrett, F.J. (2001). Appreciative Inquiry: The Power of the Unconditional Positive Question. In *Handbook of Action Research: Participative Inquiry and Practice*. (P. Reason and H. Bradbury, eds.). London: Sage Publications.

Roos, J. (2004). Sparking Strategic Imagination. *MIT Sloan Management Review, 46* (1), 96.

Statler, M. and Jacobs, C. (2003). *Active Responsiveness through Adaptive Play: Casting New Light on Strategy Genesis*. Retrieved from www.imagilab.org.

Tibbs, H. (2000). Making the Future Visible: Psychology, Scenarios, and Strategy. Global Business Network. Viewed March 2005, www.hardintibbs.com/pdfs/GBN_Tibbs3_00.pdf.

3.3.8 Experience the Future First-Hand—Make Use of Different Sensory Experiences

Strategic foresight is often very abstract. Although this is not in itself a negative, getting to actionable results often requires concrete, tangible thinking. One way to balance the abstract and concrete is to provide a variety of sensory experiences, combining sight, smell, taste, touch, and hearing.

Moving from abstract thinking to more experience-based approaches may not be easy. In many organizations, sensory inputs are ignored or even suppressed. An analyst should be prepared to spend quite some time communicating the relevance of such a shift. It can be helpful to apply certain simple techniques to help the organization open up to sensory approaches.

Key steps

Any sensory-based approach should contain at least two main steps:

- collection of sensory experiences through activities and excursions "in the field"
- integration of these particular, individual experiences into more general conclusions and observations

Whereas the first task requires a degree of perseverance, the second demands a specific effort to bring these experiences back to the foresight activity. Mutual exchange of experiences through a group activity is a necessary step. While the experiences may or may not replace the initial abstract notions, they will add meaning to them.

Benefits

Although many issues can be dealt with in theoretical terms, others require experience-based approaches. This is especially the case when an organization gets trapped in a web of abstract terms it has coined to understand potential future changes. Although people are in general very familiar with abstract thinking, particular notions may lose their meaning along the way. Many strategic terms require a more experience-based approach to regain meaning—such as "power relations," "environmental pollution," and even "profit." Sensory experiences can be very helpful in making abstract notions more concrete. How does profit smell? What noise do power relations make? What is the color of environmental pollution? The answers to these and similar questions will lead to a different set of elements that lends meaning to hard-to-grasp notions.

Other abstract concepts that might benefit from experience-based approaches include "economic growth" (usually framed in the very abstract GNP) or "population density" (what does it really mean to live very closely together, or to have your nearest neighbor more than ten miles from your home, etc.).

Example

A facilitator had to work out solutions for the work pressures within a hospital. After several unsuccessful attempts to discuss the issue, he decided to take the management group to the hospital and ask them to describe how work pressure smells and feels. Suddenly, work pressure was no longer an abstract entity; it was a collection of sensations. For example, the participants discovered that work pressure is sticky (sticky door handles, tables, etc.) and, hence, one of its manifestations was a lack of hygiene (Wouters, 1999).

Further reading

Shupp, L. (2004). Ethnofuturism. Viewed August 2005, www.cheskin.com/p/ar.asp?mlid=7&arid=13&art=1.

Wouters, P. (1999). *Denkgereedschap: Een Filosofische Onderhoudsbeurt*. Rotterdam: Lemniscaat (in Dutch). *(Thinking Tools. A Philosophical Overhaul.)*

3.3.9 When Blocked, Put It Aside and Sleep

When problem-solving, it is common to find oneself exploring the same unsuccessful paths towards a solution. It is easy to forget that a given solution was tried before and didn't work. The only way out of the maze is to break away from the process...and sleep does this very effectively.

Putting the issue aside cannot work until one has become saturated in the problem-solving effort. It requires a certain level of obsession and frustration with the problem. One indicator the situation has reached this point is that a sense of déjà vu is the norm rather than the exception. If people are paying attention to their own behavior, it is relatively easy to be aware that their thoughts are going in circles. Or they may become aware of the box, à la "Think outside the box." Walking away then becomes like putting energy into a flywheel: the wheel spins faster and faster as energy goes into it, then, when the instigator walks away, continues spinning on its own without deliberate effort. It works undercover while the instigator's consciousness is elsewhere.

Key steps

Using this tactic is extremely simple. Many people end up using it by accident as they put their problems aside when they leave the office. It can be triggered deliberately, however. Try working on the problem for two or three hours, then consciously go off and do something different, turning the problem over to the subconscious to work out.

The "something different" should be an activity that doesn't require the same type of thinking as the original problem. Turning attention to an equally demanding task isn't going to free the mind to work on the first problem. The new task should be different. If the original challenge was an analytical problem, then the secondary task should involve watching a movie or video, reading a book, going for a walk, or having a conversation.

If sleep is used as the alternative task, then working on the problem for about half an hour before sleeping is often enough to ensure that one focuses on the problem while sleeping. Keeping pen and paper at hand to capture the solution is recommended. Of course, this strategy comes with no guarantee of success. But the cost of experimentation is low, so that even if the success rate is one in a hundred, the return on investment is positive.

Benefits

Myriad problem-solving techniques are available, with the vast majority requiring deep study in some form of analytical thinking. This technique is different; it requires nothing more than a faith that the subconscious will continue to work on a problem while conscious attention is turned to something else. Sadly, its very simplicity is enough for many people to discount this as a useful problem-solving technique. One additional weakness associated with the technique is that it works best on technical/analytical types of problems, and is less successful for people-management problems.

Example

Perhaps the most famous example of this technique is the discovery of benzene's chemical structure. Friedrich August Kekulé von Stradonitz was a chemist wrestling with the structures of carbon-based substances. In his own words, this is how Kekulé discovered the structure of benzene (Roberts, 1989):

> *I was sitting writing on my textbook, but the work did not progress; my thoughts were elsewhere. I turned my chair to the fire and dozed. Again the atoms were gamboling before my eyes. This time the smaller groups kept modestly in the background. My mental eye, rendered more acute by the repeated visions of the kind, could now distinguish larger structures of manifold conformation; long rows sometimes more closely fitted together*

all twining and twisting in snake-like motion. But look! What was that? One of the snakes had seized hold of its own tail, and the form whirled mockingly before my eyes. As if by a flash of lightning I awoke; and this time also I spent the rest of the night in working out the consequences of the hypothesis.

Further reading

Ray, M. and Myers, R. (1986). *Creativity in Business*. New York: Doubleday.

Roberts, R.M. (1989). *Serendipity: Accidental Discoveries in Science*. New York: Wiley.

3.3.10 Avoid Early Convergence of Ideas

An early convergence of ideas occurs when a group generating ideas rapidly agrees on a limited set of issues or solutions. This obstructs the broadness of scope critical to a strategic foresight activity. Although a broad scope in itself is not a guarantee of good strategic foresight, a limited scope is likely to suppress potentially relevant issues or solutions.

Convergence of ideas is not a bad thing, but it is a bad sign when it occurs early in an activity. This usually means significant issues have been underplayed, or underlying controversial themes have been suppressed. Analysts should therefore be keen on keeping processes open for as long as practical, even by adding new subjects or people, before moving to convergence.

Key steps

Bringing different people into the activity will naturally widen the process before it narrows down, unless the group is very homogeneous or hierarchical. Early in an activity, the analyst can steer away from convergence by facilitating activities that widen the group's scope. These can be various creative problem-solving tools and futures techniques such as environmental scanning or futures wheels. It may also be important to bring in some non-obvious participants (see *Guideline 2.4.2: Consult Unusual Sources, People, and Places—Including Outliers, Complainers, and Troublemakers*).

With smaller groups, one can assign specific tasks to people to avoid convergence. Simply scheduling sufficient time between different points in the process will make it possible to evolve more slowly towards convergence. In the case of large groups, convergence of ideas is often more problematic due to the numbers.

In general, analysts will not find it too hard to get some wide-ranging ideas, and it may be temping to lead the group quickly to convergence. However, it is important to continue with broadening exercises as long as possible to work out additional ideas and to move beyond the results of the initial list. Unless the activity has a strict and pressing deadline, it is important to take sufficient time for reflection in order to fully develop novel ideas. As a rule of thumb, a new idea is not typically understood on the spot, but requires reflection and more in-depth consideration.

Benefits

A major lesson of Bertrand de Jouvenel's classic *The Art of Conjecture* is that the value of strategic foresight activities comes from opening the future—i.e., widening the scope of possible futures. Although this may nowadays seem trivial, it remains a powerful message for any activity. While participants may understand conceptually that many different futures are possible, truly believing this is inherently difficult—and organizations still tend to prefer their "official future."

One advantage of strategic foresight is that it almost automatically forces one to think in broader terms. Nevertheless, it is important that all who commit themselves to the activity are aware of this particular characteristic and to see it as an important benefit. Avoiding early convergence is, so to speak, "part of the strategic deal." By analogy, an activity should be like an accordion: first it widens to take in sufficient air, then it compresses to produce sound and, if the holder knows how to play it, music. The more air it takes in, the more music it can make.

Example

Paul Nutt (2002) illustrates what he calls the strategic blunder of "premature commitment" in the case of a medium-sized firm that was doing well, but faced an important customer's complaint about products being out-of-stock, leading to late shipments. The vice president responded by advocating that the company adopt an up-to-date production system recommended by the customer. He sold the CEO on the idea and a new person was hired to implement the new system. Even after the system was up and running, however, the out-of-stock problem continued. Further study revealed that the problem had nothing do with the production system. Because the company converged on the first solution proffered, it failed to adequately investigate the problem and to choose an appropriate solution.

Further reading

de Jouvenel, B. (1967). *The Art of Conjecture*. New York: Basic Books.

Glenn, J. (1994). Participatory Methods. In J. Glenn and T. Gordon, eds. *Futures Research Methodology—Version 2.0*. Washington, DC: AC/UNU Millennium Project.

Nutt, P. C. (2002). *Why Decisions Fail: Avoiding the Blunders and Traps That Lead to Debacles*. San Francisco: Berrett-Koehler.

3.4 Converge—Prioritize Ideas

3.4.1 Identify and Prioritize Areas of Common Ground

Common ground is a set of issues or concerns that most stakeholders consider both important and within the scope of interest or influence of the organization. If a strategic foresight activity is being applied in a context of multiple, potentially controversial interests, then identifying common ground becomes crucial. A multi-actor, controversial setting in which underlying controversy might hamper communication among participants can lead to obstruction without some common ground to fall back on. That said, finding common ground does not automatically resolve open conflict or non-cooperative behavior.

Key steps

The search for common ground relies to a large extent on skilled facilitation by the analyst. It demands that participants can express their concerns and learn those of others. A group exercise can reveal these concerns. The analyst's task then is to identify which issues are shared among the participants. Finally, agreement should be sought on which issues have to be addressed.

Common ground should not be used to suppress different points of view. On the contrary, diversity is needed to develop contrasting views of how issues could develop and to what extent they can be influenced. As soon as the group has stabilized around a common set of issues, it can work on them in greater depth. In a later phase, when participants have learned to work together and to appreciate different points of view, the common ground might be enlarged by going back to the initial exercise and taking up some of the other issues which the group didn't agree on.

Benefits

Common ground is a valuable asset when working with diverse actors. It serves two important purposes. First, it can strengthen the process internally: without a common basis among the participants, the activity is likely to fail. Second, it is also an important output of the process. Since the activity aims at influencing decision-making behavior and exploiting the potential for change, common ground will make it possible to develop strategic plans and to stimulate joint action.

The objective of common ground is therefore to provide some kind of harmonization within a group of actors. Obviously, not all activities require this kind of harmonization. Sometimes the group of participants is already rather homogeneous, or the objective may be to explore the strategic consequences of a controversy. But many activities require at least a set of shared basic premises in order to achieve any strategic result.

Example

During many years of experience, the "father" of the common ground concept, Marvin Weisbord (2000), has accumulated diverse experiences. His approach has been published as a very detailed and practical manual, which lays out a step-by-step approach to help practitioners find common ground. The approach is a complete design to harmonize a group of actors so they can work together actively on particular issues of concern. As Weisbord himself emphasizes, the outcome of his approach is not an action plan, but a "change [of] the conditions under which people interact. That much we can control and it leads to surprising outcomes." And, he adds, "We don't expect dramatic individual change, only a change in the action potential among individuals, based on discovering new alignments." The analyst can either follow Weisbord's approach faithfully or adapt his ideas using other designs.

Weisbord (2004) recalls how his team once believed that only projects and programs lasting two to three years could alter a large system's policies, procedures, and norms. Using their process that gets to common ground much more quickly, they have been able to dramatically shorten this timeframe. In a meeting with the global furniture retailer IKEA, the team applied the principle of "whole system in the room": fifty-two stakeholders examined the existing system, developed a new design, created a strategic plan, and formed task forces led by key executives to implement it in just eighteen hours. The analysts first suggested that one way to change a system in real-time is for those with critical stakes in the process to share what they know, under conditions that enable action without asking permission from anyone who is not present. Next, they asked the mixed groups to identify their common ground: what they all agreed were the "minimum critical specifications." These were posted and discussed until every stakeholder was satisfied. The agreed-upon specs were surprisingly concrete, many reflecting the most far-reaching of the future scenarios. In an intense hour or so, the design was validated and seven key areas for action agreed to by all.

Further reading

Weisbord, M. and Janoff, S. (2000). *Future Search: An Action Guide to Finding Common Ground in Organizations and Communities*. (2nd Edition, Updated and Expanded). San Francisco: Berrett-Koehler.

Weisbord, M. and Janoff, S. (2004). Faster, Shorter, Cheaper May Be Simple; It's Never Easy. *The Journal of Applied Behavioral Science 20* (10).

3.4.2 Balance "Realism" with a Critical Approach

Strategic foresight entails thinking ahead to improve the current situation. The final aim is to obtain future success by developing a strategy today. This pragmatic approach to management does not imply an absence of values; on the contrary, pragmatic realism can go hand-in-hand with moral values that are part of a critical approach.

Pragmatism and realism are the normal attitudes in an activity—to consider only what is visible and fits with existing data and standard approaches. But foresight analysts need to look ahead in a *critical* way—trying to look beyond the obvious, to probe deeper, and to innovate when necessary. A critical approach means looking ahead without prejudice and going beyond the rational and probable. Thinking about the future with an open attitude suggests acknowledging and setting aside personal assumptions and mental models.

Key steps

Seeing reality not as a dogma—a given truth that cannot be deciphered—but as a mental construction—a relative image, complex and questionable—leads directly to a relativistic perception of reality. Any statement or idea about the present situation, or about what the future "will be" or "should be," is merely a construction whose accuracy depends on many different things, such as the variables considered or the method used. If these parameters are changed, perceptions about the present and the future can change dramatically.

Thus, this point of view suggests that reality is not obvious. Any assumption—general or concrete—about society, the economy, technology, etc., should not be considered final, because there are myriad ways of understanding reality. Reality is complex, multidimensional, and perhaps even multiple. So, being realistic is not so straightforward, and suggests a need for a complementary critical approach that does not accept a given view of reality at face value.

It is probably better to err on the side of being too critical than too realistic. Realism is typically guided by conformity and conservative attitudes. Being critical introduces relativity and complexity throughout the activity—challenging the conventional view of reality, enabling the complex thinking needed for complex issues, and opening up the possibility of groundbreaking innovation. That said, being overly critical can be counterproductive and lead to impractical plans. The best advice is "to keep your head in the clouds and your feet on the ground."

Benefits

Balancing realism with a critical perspective enables the best of both worlds—challenging conventional wisdom yet keeping one's feet on the ground. It is easy for an organization to treat the "official future," its conventional wisdom about the future, as a given. A critical approach helps avoid this trap. Yet an approach that is solely critical can generate inertia. Tearing down assumptions and conventional wisdom is only half the job; the other half is building options to address the reality the critical perspective has uncovered.

Example

Spain's recent political history offers a good example of the two extremes of realism and criticality. Whereas the former conservative government tended towards a realistic attitude, the new socialist government leans towards the critical. Critical perspectives, which involve rethinking the current situation, tended to be viewed as destabilizing.

Defenders of the conservative government point out how the realistic approach succeeded in maintaining stability. In the international arena, the conservative regime tended to favor realistic approaches that did not threaten the status quo. Conversely, defenders of the current government emphasize change and the domestic agenda, and tend to deemphasize global realpolitik. This guideline suggests that balancing the two—or at least accounting for the other—is the optimum strategy.

Further research

Barbieri, E. (1984). Futures Research and Global Change. *Futures, 15*, 468 - 470.

Bas, E. (1999). The Sociology of the 21st Century, or How to Be Ready for Facing the Future. *International Review of Sociology, 9* (3), 287 - 293.

Bell, W. (1996). The Sociology of the Future and the Future of Sociology. *Sociological Perspectives, 39*, 40 - 57.

Berger, P. and Luckman, T. (1966). *The Social Construction of Reality*. New York: Doubleday.

Kleiner, A. (1999, Spring). Doing Scenarios. *Whole Earth Review*.

Slaughter, R. (2001, October). Knowledge Creation, Futures Methodologies, and the Integral Agenda. *foresight: the journal of futures studies, strategic thinking, and policy, 3* (5), 407 - 418. (Available at www.foresightinternational.com.au)

3.4.3 Approach Trends with Skepticism

Question the most trusted trends regularly and approach new ones with skepticism. Most organizations are subject to *trend-faith*—a tacit belief that current trends represent regular patterns of change: linear, exponential, logistic, cyclical, or combinations thereof. Trend-thinking is a basic human way of understanding change. But extrapolating current trends is rarely an accurate way to foretell the future, and foresight analysts should adopt a critical perspective towards trends. Analysts should ask not merely whether an important trend is going to break down, but when.

Key steps

Early in an activity, when identifying basic beliefs of the organization, the analyst should address the questions: "What are the main trends the organization believes in; when did it start to believe in them; why; and are those reasons still relevant?"

A group exercise is a good way to confront these questions. The group can start by making a list of trends that have been among the basic beliefs of management, including those trends the group thinks have been "well-behaved" during the previous ten or more years. If the group is able to identify some of these, they should be asked whether they believe these trends are going to behave well in the future. And for how long? And based on what assumptions? If, after answering these questions, the group still believes in the continuation of these trends, the trends may qualify as ones that should be continually monitored.

In addition to updating the group's beliefs concerning existing trends, time should be taken to analyze potential new trends. Important new trends may be revealed that the organization is not sufficiently taking into account. What is needed is a way to pay systematic attention to the premises of the existing trends and also to weak signals, some of which may turn into trends or even megatrends in the future.

Benefits

Most organizations tend to believe that today's trends and patterns will hold true in the future, too. Econometric models popular in many organizations use variables, parameters, and equations to express this message in a more complicated way than straightforward trend extrapolation, but the result is the same: continuing today's visible patterns of change into the future. In fact, some patterns do hold constant, and this unchangeability must be included in analyses too. If something has not changed in the past, and it is believed that it will not change in the future, then that may be held constant.

At the same time, organizations exist in a world of increasing complexity and risk: globalization, regionalization, fragmentation, tensions between different cultures and religions and between the rich North and the poor South, increasing pace of change, etc. Today's is a world of turbulence and trend breaks. Perhaps more than ever before, analysts need to pay considerable and conscious attention to new trends.

Example

In 1929 the US Department of Labor suggested, "1930 will be a splendid employment year." On the eve of the Great Depression, trend-faith led the US government into a gross forecasting error. Similar examples are plentiful. Even nowadays, with supercomputers and extensive data and competence available in futures work, economic recessions and structural changes, like the collapse of the Socialist bloc in 1989, are very difficult to forecast. Meanwhile, critical analysis of trends has produced good results in reorienting the dominant thinking and activities of organizations.

Further reading

Bell, W. (1997). *Foundations of Futures Studies*. (Vol. 1). New Brunswick: Transaction Publishers.

Mannermaa, M. (2004). Traps in Futures Thinking—and How to Overcome Them. In H. Didsbury Jr., ed. *Thinking Creatively in Turbulent Times*. Bethesda, MD: World Future Society, 41 - 53.

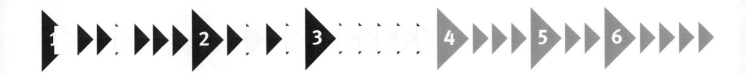

3.5 Form Alternatives

3.5.1 Recognize that the Baseline Forecast Is Almost Always Wrong

Conclusions are supported by data. In the case of strategic foresight, conclusions are often forecasts or descriptions of future conditions or events. While forecasts that are well-supported with good empirical data often turn out to be true, they don't always. The reason is that data, no matter how much there is or how good it is, never automatically leads to one and only one conclusion. Alternative conclusions are always possible. Put another way, all data, no matter how obvious, needs to be interpreted correctly. Or in a third way, drawing conclusions from data is not a deductive process of rigorous logic.

Interpreting data always requires making one or more assumptions, which can bias the interpretation to support these preconceived conclusions. These assumptions are called warrants—permission to use the data to support the conclusion. Even the most reasonable warrants are sometimes wrong; so data that seems to point to an obvious conclusion can be correct while the conclusion (the forecast) can be wrong. All data may point in the same direction, and yet the future can turn out differently.

Key steps

The best method for uncovering assumptions is to accept the data as is—assume it is true—but to imagine that the forecast is wrong. How could that happen? The answer will always be one or more hidden assumptions. Most assumptions are unconscious: they are taken for granted, made automatically without thinking. But that is where the trouble begins. Thinking about how the forecast could be wrong even when the data is correct is the process of revealing those assumptions.

Revealing assumptions, however, is not the same as rejecting them. In fact, most of the time one will affirm that the assumption is reasonable. But making them explicit allows an examination of their limits and weaknesses. And once in a while, the alternative assumption might look reasonable as well. "Rising stock prices might be a market bubble that could burst before the forecast's time horizon." Then the analyst must state the alternative assumptions, along with their implications, so the client can decide with full knowledge which forecast to accept, what decision to make, and what action to take. Advancing forecasts without making their assumptions explicit is unprofessional, or even unethical if it is done intentionally. Good analysts always discover their assumptions by first imagining how their forecasts could be wrong.

Benefits

Whenever empirical data is being used to support a forecast, the analyst should consider how the data could be correct but the forecast could be wrong. Forecasting requires making one or more assumptions about the support for the forecast. Uncovering those assumptions, testing them for reasonableness, and considering the implications if they are wrong is a necessary step in drawing data-based conclusions in forecasting.

Example

The failure to find weapons of mass destruction in Iraq was one of the most serious failures in forecasting in recent history. The table below summarizes the evidence and the supporting assumptions.

Evidence	Assumptions	Realities
1. Iraqi exiles said WMDs were there.	They had access to that knowledge. They had no reason to lie.	They probably did not have the knowledge. They did have reason to lie: to get America to act.
2. High-ranking Iraqi defectors said they were there.	They had seen the weapons. Or, Saddam told them about the weapons.	They hadn't seen the weapons. Saddam did so to boost morale.
3. Aluminum tubes similar to the type used to enrich uranium were found.	The aluminum tubes were the same size as those used to enrich uranium.	They were not the same size.
4. Saddam was reported to be trying to buy "yellow cake"—un-enriched uranium—from Niger.	Those reports were accurate.	Those reports were not accurate.
5. Saddam would not reveal weapons to the inspectors.	Saddam was being difficult and evasive.	Saddam was not being evasive. He didn't have weapons to reveal. For once he was telling the truth.
6. The inspectors did not find weapons while they were there.	The weapons were well hidden. The inspectors were not looking hard enough.	They were not hidden; they didn't exist. The inspectors probably were looking hard enough.

George Tenet, then-head of the CIA, called the conclusion that Saddam Hussein had weapons of mass destruction "a slam dunk" based on all this evidence. He and his analysts obviously had not applied the test that all the evidence was true (and it was, as stated in the left-hand column) but that the forecast—weapons of mass destruction would be found—was wrong. Thus they failed to detect that each piece of evidence was based on one or more assumptions that later turned out to be wrong.

Further reading

Senate Select Committee on Intelligence (2005). Report of the Select Committee on Intelligence on the US Intelligence Community's Prewar Intelligence Assessments on Iraq. Washington, DC: Government Printing Office.

Toulmin, S. (1972). *Human Understanding*. Princeton NJ: Princeton University Press.

Zarefsky, D. Argumentation: The Study of Effective Reasoning. Course #499, Lecture 9. Chantilly VA: The Teaching Company.

3.5.2 Explore and Craft Alternative Futures

Most forecasters make predictions: single-valued statements about how the future will be. A prediction either happens or it does not. Predictions are meant to be precise; the organizations served by them want them to be precise; stakeholders believe they are precise—yet most predictions are wrong. Everyone knows predicting is inaccurate, but few seek a better way.

The opposite blunder is not to speak about the future at all. "It's too complicated; we don't know enough; predictions are always wrong," etc. Many groups take that tack.

The middle road is to make forecasts instead of predictions. Forecasts are alternative futures that might occur, even though any one of them probably will not occur exactly as stated. Each forecast can be thought of as a scenario, a story about the future that could plausibly occur. The set of all plausible forecasts has a much better chance of capturing the actual future than a single-valued prediction does. By way of analogy, bird hunters use shotguns, not rifles.

Key steps

The more turbulent the external environment, the more likely a precise prediction will be wrong. But even in stable environments, it is easy to imagine how that stability might disappear. Even if the stability persists, an organization benefits from considering destabilization and preparing, at least mentally, for the implications.

Myriad techniques are available for developing forecasts. Some of the simpler ones include:

- Identify what is expected to happen in the future. This is the baseline forecast. Then imagine that this expectation is wrong. How could that be? What might happen instead?
- Identify five to six aspects of the current situation that have been true for a long time. Now, one by one, list their opposites. For instance, if education has always been conducted in schools, then the opposite would be that education is not conducted in schools or is conducted outside of schools. Then come up with a way that the opposite could happen. Note: These are not predictions, and some of them might not even be plausible, but they do stretch the imagination and open up a wider range of possibilities.

- Identify parts of the future that everyone agrees are very uncertain. For example, is China's economy in a bubble—that is, growing too quickly—that is about to burst? Then write two scenarios: one in which the bubble bursts and one in which it does not, with the appropriate supporting evidence and detail for each one.
- Identify two important trends that are shaping the future, such as biotechnology and oil depletion. Then write a scenario where these two are the most important driving forces over the next twenty years, with enough detail to make the story plausible.

Benefits

The purpose of forecasting is not to get the future "right"—to accurately predict what will happen. That is impossible to any realistic degree. The purpose of forecasting is to be prepared for change. One can be well-prepared without knowing exactly what will happen. A homeowner buys insurance because of the slight chance his house will burn down. He doesn't wait for the year that he thinks it will burn down; he buys it every year—and the same is true of a savings account, healthy eating, leaving early to go to the airport, etc.

The analyst thus presents a set of plausible alternative futures (scenarios) to decision-makers so they can be prepared for contingencies they may not have thought of. Even when most of those contingencies do not transpire—and they won't—the organization is prepared for the one that does.

Example

Peter Schwartz (1996) relates a story about Royal Dutch Shell that demonstrates the power of scenarios. The price of oil skyrocketed in the late 1970s. It reached $40 per barrel, and some forecasters were predicting $100 per barrel as OPEC squeezed production. Shell's Strategic Planning Unit, a pioneer in using scenarios for business planning, understood these forecasts but also created a forecast involving the collapse of the oil market. The planners reasoned that if the oil market collapsed, long-term contracts with the oil-producing countries (which had been the primary contractual vehicle to that time) would give way to a spot market where producers sold their oil to traders. Shell reasoned there would be a new market in trading oil, not just producing and refining it. So they developed a contingency plan to set up just such a trading company should the oil price collapse—which it did in 1981. Shell immediately launched its trading company, far ahead of its competitors who were still trying to figure out what was going on, and made money that year even though the value of its reserves had plummeted.

Further reading

Fahey, L. and Randall, R., eds. (1998). *Learning from the Future: Competitive Foresight Scenarios*. New York: Wiley.

Lindgren, M. and Bandhold, H. (2003). *Scenario Planning: The Link between Future and Strategy*. New York: Macmillan.

Ogilvy, J.A. (2002). Creating Better Futures: *Scenario Planning as a Tool for a Better Tomorrow*. Oxford: Oxford University Press.

Ringland, G. (1998). *Scenario Planning: Managing for the Future*. New York: Wiley.

Schwartz, P. (1991). *The Art of the Long View*. New York: Currency Doubleday.

Van der Heijden, K. (1996). *Scenarios: The Art of Strategic Conversation*. New York: Wiley.

3.5.3 Develop Possible, Plausible, Probable, and Preferable Solutions

The purpose of a strategic foresight activity is to help an organization envision and act upon alternative future possibilities. Four types of futures are developed:

- The broadest range are possible futures: anything positive or negative, probable or improbable, that could potentially happen in the future.

- A more bounded set is plausible futures: reasonable outcomes, with a discernable pathway from the present to the future. For example, discovering extraterrestrial life within the next decade is possible, but not plausible.

- Still narrower are probable futures: the most likely outcomes. Most organizations have an "official future," which is their view of how the future is likely to unfold. It is reasonably probable that it will occur, even if not very likely.

- The last type of future is the preferable future: the most desirable outcome for the organization. This one is often developed through a visioning process, discussed in the next chapter.

Key steps

A wide variety of techniques are used to generate futures. Initially, some form of idea generation process is typically used. The guidelines for such a process include the following:

- Set general boundaries for the session.
- Generate as many ideas as possible.
- Defer judgment. Do not criticize during a brainstorming session.
- Build on the ideas of others. Combine and improve ideas.
- Encourage wild thinking.
- Write down every idea verbatim to ensure that no idea or seed of an idea gets lost.

One successful idea-generation process tailored to strategic foresight is the *Future Workshop*, developed by the late Robert Jungk. Jungk developed this as a result of his experience as a victim of Adolf Hitler's regime. He sought a process to help empower the least powerful people. The Future Workshop uses a facilitated idea-generation approach, at a three-day meeting of usually eighteen to twenty people affected by a complex problem.

The first day of the meeting is called the Critique Phase. The facilitator asks, "What's bothering you? What are your complaints?" The facilitator records the proceedings on strategically placed flipcharts. When the complaints dwindle, the facilitator seeks clarification, helps link the comments, and organizes the results in clusters of similar problems.

In the Fantasy Phase, usually held the next day, problems identified in the Critique Phase are rephrased in a positive manner. For example, "no space for kids" becomes "plenty of room for kids." Now the group brainstorms all possibilities, however improbable and infeasible. Again, at the end, the facilitator summarizes the findings.

In the final Implementation Phase, the group looks at its preferred solutions and tempers them with the reality of what is plausible. Members explore what can be done to bring about solutions. They identify the obstacles to be overcome. An action plan is developed, including a schedule, and responsibility for action is assigned.

Benefits

Using the Future Workshop structural overlay, or some variation thereof, empowers people closest to the issue to become problem-solvers. Participants take responsibility for creating their preferred futures from a full range of possible, plausible, and probable futures. They can then determine what actions are necessary to move from the probable future of the victim, to the preferable future of the empowered.

Example

An example of how this guideline is being applied comes from a group of futurists who started the Applied Foresight Network. These futurists are marshalling the research resources of universities around the globe in support of informed dialogue and practical action on issues of critical importance to humanity. The aim is to create a web of strategically located Applied Foresight Centers around the world, connected by online forums for professors, students, teachers, and concerned citizens. This Applied Foresight Network will use idea generation with a modified Future Workshop overlay to address critical issues such as climate change, options for peace in Iraq, and cloning.

Further reading

Bell, W. (1997). *Foundations of Futures Studies: Human Science for a New Era*. New Jersey: Transaction Publishers.

Burton, L. (2004). Creativity, Innovation, and Visionary Thinking: Becoming All You Can Become. In H. Didsbury, ed. *Thinking Creatively in Turbulent Times*. Bethesda: World Future Society.

Levesque, L. (2001). *Breakthrough Creativity: Achieving Top Performance Using the Eight Creative Talents*. Mountain View, CA: Davies-Black Publishing.

Schultz, W. (2003). Sidling into Our Futures. In *Futures Fluency: Explorations in Leadership, Vision, and Creativity*. Viewed June 2005, www.infinitefutures.com/essays.

Joseph, E. Futurist Skills, Tools, and Information. *The Minnesota Futurist*. Viewed June 2005, www.mnfuturists.org.

3.5.4 Emphasize Plausible Surprises

Extrapolation is the most common forecasting method—projecting existing conditions, documented trends, and announced plans into the future. But that process yields only the expected or the most likely future. There are no real surprises in that future. Yet it is certain that the future will contain surprises, sometimes many of them. Surprises cannot be predicted—because they are, by definition, unexpected—but they can be prepared for by imagining surprising developments that might actually occur. Even if these precise surprises do not occur, organizations will better prepared for the ones that do.

The more turbulent the environment, the more surprises it contains—and the more an organization is at risk if it fails to prepare. Thus, considering surprises, even if they seem far-fetched, is a good way to prepare to be successful in a turbulent environment.

Key steps

The process of emphasizing plausible surprises is to first identify what is expected and then imagine what might happen instead. This looks easy, but may not be. Expectations for the future are so common that they are often not at the conscious level of awareness. In fact, they usually aren't known until events play out differently—i.e., the organization is surprised. It looks back and realizes it had expected something different.

One place to look for surprises is in the assumptions behind the baseline forecast. What have all the published sources, participants, or mathematics assumed to be true? That question is usually not much easier than dreaming up surprises directly, because assumptions usually remain hidden until they are proven to be wrong. One question to ask is, "What must remain true for these expectations to come about?" Another is, "How could all these data be true, but the future turn out differently?" (see *Guideline 3.5.1: Recognize that the Baseline Forecast Is Almost Always Wrong*).

A more direct way of surfacing surprising futures is simply to ask people. Most people have a more diverse view of the future than they usually talk about, because our culture discourages people from sharing forecasts that are not likely. When asked, however, people readily reveal interesting and surprising futures. One question to elicit this information might be, "What do you think might happen in the future that most people are not paying enough attention to?"

Finally, all the tools and techniques of creativity can be applied to this task. The purpose of being creative, after all, is to think of something that hasn't existed before. In this case, one is trying to imagine futures that haven't been imagined before and that are not part of the extension of current trends and plans into the future.

Benefits

The practice of strategic foresight requires that success be defined appropriately. Success is not getting the future "right," or predicting accurately what will happen. Rather, success is being prepared for the future that eventually does become the present. Being prepared does not require a precise prediction; it requires preparing for multiple eventualities. Although more difficult than preparing for one future, preparing for multiple futures is preferable when the levels of turbulence and uncertainty point to multiple plausible futures. In fact, preparing for only one future carries the enormous risk of preparing for the wrong future.

A better way of defining success, then, is simply to not be surprised—to have thought of and prepared for whichever future actually occurs. The future is going to develop in unexpected (i.e., surprising) ways. That much is known. The surprises can be considered early, while there is still time to prepare, or ignored until they are actually occurring. The better practice is, of course, to consider the surprises earlier, when there is ample time to prepare.

Example

The attacks on the World Trade Center and the Pentagon in September 2001 are the best contemporary examples of failing to anticipate surprise. Warning signs that were underplayed or ignored include:

- The first attack on the World Trade Center in 1993 and the subsequent attacks on the US embassies in Kenya and Tanzania and on the USS Cole in Yemen
- Foreigners known to have terrorist links who had overstayed their US visas
- Individuals taking flight lessons who didn't want to learn how to land or take off
- Warnings from foreign governments that an attack was imminent

And, even if the exact nature of the attack could not have been predicted, the responses of the Federal Aviation Administration, Air Force, and other authorities could have been swifter if they had considered this scenario beforehand. The possibility of airliners being used as weapons had been previously considered—not least by novelist Tom Clancy in *Executive Orders* (1997)—but none of these potential surprises had been taken seriously enough to affect protocols for air defense during times of emergency.

Further reading

Air University. (1996). *Air Force 2025*. Maxwell AFB: Air University Press.

Clancy, T. (1997). *Executive Orders*. New York: Berkley.

Petersen, J. (1997). *Out of the Blue*. Arlington, VA: Arlington Institute.

Schwartz, P. (2004). *Inevitable Surprises*. New York: Gotham.

3.5.5 Describe How the Future Will Be Different from the Present

Talking about the future is difficult and therefore risky. Most people don't like to talk about the future because they can easily be wrong. They have to take all factors into account; they have to make assumptions; they have to use their imaginations. None of this is easy, and all of it is prone to criticism. So people just avoid it if they can. Moreover, people who do stand up to talk about the future often don't really talk about the future at all; they talk about the present. They may speak about things that are shaping the future, such as trends and issues; but trends and issues are not the future, they are the present.

Key steps

After talking about trends and issues, it is necessary to take the next step and describe a real future, not just the forces shaping it. What will it be like? How will the future be different from today? What implications do those differences have for the focal concern or organization? The answers to these questions are the results of trends and issues occurring today—but they are subtly different. They are not just the forces pushing us into the future; they are the details of what the future could actually be like, look like, feel like when it finally arrives. These questions open up a more vivid, compelling, and ultimately more useful image of the future than discussions of trends and issues ever will.

Ask the question, "And what will the world be like when all this has had time to play out?" The answer to that question is more prone to error and therefore to criticism. But its importance can be made clear with the proper disclaimer, such as, "This is not a prediction; it's a story, a plausible alternative future that really could happen. And if it does, you need to know about it ahead of time."

To help people describe the future themselves, after reviewing all the forces shaping the future ask them to imagine being Rip Van Winkle or discovering a time machine. They look around, see the landscape, the buildings, the people. What are these people doing? How are they different from the people of today? Imagine talking to them. What are they concerned about? What are they proud of? What problems have they solved, what problems have they created since our own time? Have them tell a story of how they got from their past to the future.

Historical analogy is another excellent way of painting a vivid picture of the future. Some say, "The future will be like the past, only different." Mark Twain said it even more eloquently: "History doesn't repeat itself, but it rhymes." Everyone has images of the past stored away in pictures and stories. Starting with those and then twisting them into images of the future can be a powerful way to describe the future—which, whatever it is, we are all bound to experience together.

Benefits

If an activity merely recounts the facts of today—even if they are described as trends (facts changing today) and issues (factual disputes going on today)—others can easily discount their effect on the future. "Haven't those trends and issues been going on for a long time now?" "So what if they go on for another ten or twenty years?" "We're doing all right so far." "We still have time to change if we have to." Given those inclinations, how is an organization supposed to get a picture of a different world, a world of change that requires new thinking and new action?

On the other hand, vividly describing a changed world is a dash of cold water in the face. An organization that sees or hears about a real future, a future that is plausibly yet radically different from today, gets chills just thinking about it. Participants see their world, the familiar one, the one in which the organization has been successful, changing in important ways. They don't like the picture; it's the passing of an era. But see it they must.

The job of the analyst is to alert the organization in the most respectful yet persuasive way possible that change will occur and that it needs to start preparing for it, soon if not right away. The alert does not have to be negative or critical of the present, but it does need to be challenging—urging the organization to get ready to leave the past behind and to confront the future and all its differences.

Example

Fiction, in literature and film, is excellent at portraying real futures. Think of *Brave New World*, *1984*, *Blade Runner*, or *2001: A Space Odyssey*. Fiction conjures up images of plausible, interesting, and even frightening futures. Most analysts don't have the talent, time, or resources for full-scale writing or film-making, but they must tend in that direction nevertheless. (Calder)

Analogies from the present and past are also useful for painting pictures of the future. A common analogy to describe the aging of the US population is to point out that the proportion of people over 65 in 2030 will be larger than the proportion of older people who now live in Florida. A whole country of Floridas—now there is a vivid image of a plausible future!

Further reading

Calder, J. *A Futurist at the Movies*. www.futuristmovies.com.

Record, J. (1998). Perils of Reasoning by Historical Analogy: Munich, Vietnam, and American Use of Force Since 1945. Maxwell AFB: Air University. Viewed May 2005, www.au.af.mil/au/awc/awcgate/cst/occppr04.htm.

Schnaars, S. (1989). *Megamistakes: Forecasting and the Myth of Rapid Technological Change*. New York: The Free Press.

3.5.6 Work Backwards to Distinguish How an Extreme Scenario Could Unfold

Follow an idea towards its ultimate conclusion, however ridiculous that might seem, and then work back to see if there is a way it might actually happen. This technique often highlights how an otherwise apparently minor trend might unfold into something much more significant. This is a good technique for identifying interesting aspects of trends that might otherwise go unnoticed. It can be used almost recreationally as part of scenario development, to explore how one or more trends can come together to create an unexpected outcome.

Key steps

Start with a simple trend and quickly think it through as far as it can go, ignoring detail or analyzing all the usual reasons why it would never happen like that. When the ultimate conclusion is reached—perhaps the 50-year point—start working backwards to see what would realistically need to happen to make this outcome possible. This will not be the same path followed to get there, since now realistic paths need to be worked out.

As the exercise is pursued, branching points will become apparent as well as other interesting potential paths into the future. Maybe the original outcome wasn't feasible, but by looking at it in this way, whole areas of possible futures might emerge that wouldn't otherwise have been thought of. If one manages to get all the way back to the present, identifying a plausible path to the ultimate outcome, that can serve as a useful timeline. Since it describes at least one way this outcome could happen, the outcome can be listed as plausible. The exercise will also identify related trends and other outcomes that could be associated with it. So starting with a single thin path to one point in the futures plane can yield a map of a significant area around the path, and probably lots of interesting side roads along the way.

If this exercise is repeated often enough, it will start to reveal side roads that link current trends together. These cross-links—which are hard to find by other means—will help strengthen the future worldview by adding a lot of detail to the map of the future. These are the second- and third-order effects that make the future view both credible and rich.

Benefits

The main advantages of working backwards are that it is a fun way to explore the future, and it helps map out significant areas of the future. In particular, it avoids the constraints of thinking linearly forward from today, by first rushing rapidly to the future, then working backwards. Often an obstacle that would otherwise hide such futures terrain from exploration can be easily circumvented, and working backwards might uncover a path that is not at all obvious from the other direction.

In short, it is a tool to bypass prejudices. But it also helps unlock imagination, allowing organizations to explore terrain they wouldn't normally visit. Even if an ultimate conclusion turns out to be unfeasible, exploring it will often uncover related areas that are feasible, as well as non-obvious relationships among other trends and outcomes.

Example

A good example of backwards-futuring is e-Baybies. A team of analysts started with the trend of genetic manipulation, then took it to the logical conclusion of people being able to design and fabricate their own kids. Thinking back from this outcome, the team was forced to wonder why someone would do this, and realized that some people cannot have kids. But genetic analysis already allows people to have their genome captured on a CD, so they can mix it with someone else's and create digital renderings of any number of potential babies. Protein simulation would be able to give these babies a digital life, and future genetic-assembly technology might allow them to be physically assembled into real, living human beings. Moreover, these potential babies could be created today, and traded on e-Bay, with people collecting celebrity babies. So the exercise had already generated several new ideas. And then, exploring other side roads, the analysts saw that haptics technology would allow physical interaction with digitally emulated kids, so why not use that with ultrasound to explore real fetuses today? And AI might allow digital kids to live in the real world via android technology, or they might be kept in computer games with real-life kids as their "gods." And of course, this simulation technology would allow real embryos to be screened for likely future behaviors, so one might see much more genetic selection. And this potential might quickly make it almost compulsory for parents to give their kids the best possible genetic start in life. So just this one avenue led to lots of very interesting side roads and helped map out a very broad area around genetic manipulation. It works just as well for other problems.

Further reading

Coates, J.F., Mahaffie, J.B., and Hines, A. (1996). *2025: Scenarios of US and Global Society as Reshaped by Science and Technology*. Greensboro, NC: Oakhill Press.

Schultz, W. (1991, September 19).Words, Dreams, and Action: Sharing the Futures Experience. A Presentation to the World Futures Studies Federation, Barcelona, Spain. Viewed August 2005, www.infinitefutures.com/essays/fs12.shtml.

Wang, C.K. and Guild, P.D. (1995). Backcasting as a Tool in Competitive Analysis, ISBM Report 24-1995. University Park, PA: Institute for the Study of Business Markets, Pennsylvania State University.

3.5.7 Game the Future—Explore How the Rules Might Change

Every social system can be thought of as a game. It has players, teams, rules, and goals. Some games are competitive, with winners and losers. Some are cooperative, with everyone working together to achieve a common goal. But it's still a game. Thinking of each system as a game raises certain critical questions: Who are the players? Who works with whom? What are the teams? What is the purpose of the game and how is score kept? Who are the winners and losers, if any? Understanding these aspects of the system is the beginning of learning to play and be successful at that game.

Key steps

The first step is deciding whether the game is fundamentally competitive or cooperative. In other words, are there going to be losers? Do there have to be losers? Some people prefer competitive games, so they tend to turn every situation into a competition. Some prefer cooperative games; they usually do not like people winning at the expense of others or getting more than others do. In many complex games, competition and cooperation are operating at the same time—some people are playing to win, and some are playing to achieve a common goal (see *Guideline 3.1.2: Use a Layered Approach to Get Below the Surface and See the Different Types and Levels of Change*).

If the game is fundamentally cooperative (such as governance), but some people are playing it competitively (as in politics), the question is whether they can be convinced to cooperate or whether they can be ignored. The situation is a Prisoner's Dilemma in which the cooperative solution nets the greatest good for all players, but a unilateral competitive action nets a greater score for the competitive player (Poundstone, 1992). So unfortunately, competition often trumps cooperation, unless the cooperators have enough power to influence or ignore the competitor.

On the other hand, fundamentally competitive games also have their cooperative aspects, since individuals rarely play alone. More often, people are part of teams that cooperate in order to win the overall competition. But the complexity doesn't stop there. People may compete with their teammates when they are supposed to be cooperating. Who gets the ball in the basketball game? Who gets the raise or the promotion when the team succeeds? Trust is the quality that allows people to cooperate with the confidence that their teammates are cooperating as well—although this trust, too, is sometimes misplaced. In the end, few games are purely competitive or purely cooperative.

Understanding the goals of the organization is the next step. What is the organization working for? What counts as success? Being clear about goals is a necessary step to selecting a consistent set of effective strategies that will achieve those goals. Strategies are actions that, ultimately, lead to the goal. They are the game plan in sports, the battle plan in war, the grand strategy in business or politics.

Finally, what are the rules? What can or cannot be done? A common strategy is to take a hard look at the rules and decide which are really rules and which just customs or habits. If the latter, changing that rule might make it easier to achieve the goal.

In sum, identifying the game aspect of these situations highlights requirements for achieving the goal:

1. What is the goal? When will it be known that it has been achieved?

2. What are the other players' goals?

3. Therefore, who can be trusted and worked with? Who must be competed with?

4. What are the rules of the game? Which rules might be broken or bent to achieve the goals?

5. Given that context, what strategies will most effectively achieve the goals?

Benefits

Gaming provides a way to rehearse for the future. It enables the organization to experience types of situations that might emerge in the future. It brings these possibilities to life, and forces participants to make decisions in simulation that they may have to make someday in reality. The experience will prove useful even if the particular alternative does not occur, since the rehearsal gives the organization practice in anticipating multiple futures.

Example

One of the most successful gaming strategies in recent history was mutual assured destruction (MAD). This game was played by the United States and the Soviet Union from 1947 - 1989, the period popularly known as the Cold War. The goal of each player was world domination. Each possessed massive quantities of nuclear weapons with which they could obliterate their opponent. Why didn't they use these weapons? Because, as we know, each side also gave unwavering assurance that any first strike with nuclear weapons would be answered with a second strike, obliterating the aggressor in turn. Use of nuclear weapons by either side would therefore make large areas of the planet unlivable and obliterate much of the opponent's territory. So neither side used their weapons as long as they believed the assurance from the other side that they would be obliterated in turn if they did.

Further reading

Axelrod, R. (1985). *The Evolution of Cooperation*. New York: Basic Books.

Dixit, A.K. and Skeath, S. (1999). *Games of Strategy*. New York: Norton.

Poundstone, W. (1992). *Prisoner's Dilemma*. New York: Doubleday.

Ross, Don. (2004). Game Theory. *The Stanford Encyclopedia of Philosophy, Winter 2004 Edition*. Edward N. Zalta, ed. Viewed May 2005, http://plato.stanford.edu/archives/win2004/entries/game-theory.

3.5.8 Check the Resulting Alternatives for Quality and Consistency

Alternative futures are traditionally evaluated by two principal criteria: *desirability* and *probability*. This guideline suggests two additional criteria: *consistency* and *quality*, on the grounds that these are also fundamental to credible alternatives. An alternative future needs to be internally consistent; that is, any one of its features cannot be logically inconsistent with another. And quality control applies to foresight as to any other discipline, and may be even more fundamental to foresight given its esoteric nature.

Evaluation of consistency in an alternative future should be done late in the Forecasting phase. Having a reference point for internal consistency is as important for decision-making as are reference points for the degree of probability or desirability. Internal consistency is the attribute that permits one to regard (or not) an alternative as a solid option.

Key steps

The first step in building an alternative is to evaluate how and how much every piece of data or information can be taken into account, both at the qualitative and quantitative levels. Several questions should be asked in order to be confident about the impact of the data on the alternative under consideration.

- Are the variables well-defined?
- Do the variables cover a full range of possibilities?
- Is the method used to get and analyze the information appropriate?
- Are the sources of information reliable?
- Are the information suppliers reliable?

The second step is to evaluate the nature and consistency of the observed relationships among those data and/or features. This helps shape the alternative properly, by taking into account how some variables influence others. Questions might include:

- Do they covariate in time?
- Do they have any causal relationship between them?
- What is the real weight of any one factor in the model?

The third step is to check whether the consistency of the variables and their relationships perseveres over time.

Surprisingly, it is not necessarily a routine practice for foresight professionals to check the quality and consistency of the information used in a forecast. While clients may assume the analyst is doing this, factors such as over-reliance on traditional methods, past references, and static rather than creative attitudes, as well as a lack of time, can easily lead analysts to gloss over this guideline.

Benefits

Being creative while working hard to measure the quality and consistency of the alternatives will lead to better future strategies. A principal challenge in working with alternative futures is that the estimated probability and desirability of any of them will determine how much they influence final decisions. Both estimations are needed to define a scenario, but they are sterile if the alternative is not good enough in terms of methodological rigor.

Checking for quality and consistency also will help sort out and prioritize alternatives. Typically, the quality and internal consistency of an alternative future is qualitative and subjective, involving a joint evaluation of all the features and data that, respectively, articulate and justify the entire alternative.

Finally, an account of internal consistency serves as a guarantee for the decision-makers who will work with the scenarios. Lack of confidence in strategic analyses is most often due to a supposed lack of rigor in the process.

Example

Coates (2000) describes how important internal consistency and plausibility have been to scenario planning since its inception. In the 1950s, Herman Kahn popularized scenarios with the US Department of Defense, using the *escalation ladder* concept for thinking about nuclear war. Kahn's escalation ladder defined a series of steps between "war" and "no war." He emphasized, "To lend reality to those steps one has to have detailed accounts on how they may arise, be responded to, and resolved to create a new terminal or baseline situation." He went on to note that "the great value of a scenario is being able to take complex elements and weave them into a story which is coherent, systematic, comprehensive, and plausible." The US military has since found scenarios an invaluable aid, thanks to Kahn and his development of the scenario war game.

Further reading

Bas, E. (2004), *Megatendencias para el Siglo XXI; un Estudio Delfos*. Mexico: FCE.

Coates, J.F. (2000). Scenario Planning. *Technological Forecasting and Social Change, 65*, 115 - 123.

3.5.9 Support Alternative Futures with Empirical Data

Forecasting techniques are generally sorted into quantitative and qualitative categories. Quantitative techniques are about numbers, qualitative techniques about ideas. But the division need not, indeed should not, be absolute. Using both numbers and ideas in the same forecast makes it stronger. Alternative scenarios can and should include calculated quantities that give the organization a chance to see how key variables would change compared to the present or to the baseline or other scenarios.

Future quantities can be calculated for different scenarios as long as the assumptions used are true for those scenarios. So one might calculate the future GDP of the US under different economic policies (Republican or Democratic, for instance), since the underlying relationships used to calculate GDP would stay in place under either future administration. On the other hand, one would have been hard-pressed to calculate the GDP of the Soviet economy in 1985 and project it to 1995, across the fall of the Soviet Union. The measure and meaning of the ruble changed so radically that a billion dollars in the old Soviet economy bore little relation to a billion dollars in the new Russian economy.

Key steps

Forecasters use mathematical models to project quantities in the future, from simple growth rates to complex econometrics. Each model consists of a form—the structure of the model, which identifies rates across time and usually relationships among variables—and parameters, specific numbers that indicate how strong the rates and relationships are.

Thus, a model's output (the projections) can be manipulated in two ways: by varying the form or by varying the parameters. The simpler case is varying the parameters, a technique called *sensitivity analysis*. In this case the model is run with different plausible values for the parameters, and the output is noted. Each set of parameters and its associated projections becomes a mini-scenario. For instance, one of the key parameters in standard econometric models is the interest rate, which in the US is set by the Federal Reserve. In one scenario, the Fed lowers interest rates to encourage economic growth; alternatively, it may raise rates to control growth. Economic variables can also be embedded in a qualitative scenario, such as the prospect of war between China and Taiwan, by positing different interest rates and projecting the growth rates that might result.

The other method of varying a model is to change the form, which is the same as changing the equations that drive the model. A change in form represents a discontinuity in the system the model depicts. So the Montreal Protocol, a qualitative discontinuity that banned CFCs to preserve planetary ozone, changed the form of the model of CFC production from moderate growth to precipitous decline and eventual elimination of CFCs.

Benefits

Numerical quantities strengthen the credibility and precision of any scenario, even highly qualitative ones. They convey the impression that the analyst is working with real-world quantities and how they might change under different conditions. Organizations can use the numbers as inputs to their own models and identify the resulting implications. Finally, numbers ensure the analyst's imagination—a necessary component of any good forecast—stays within the bounds of plausible extrapolation of the key quantities. Just as variables are driven by structures and ideas, so ideas should be bounded by the plausible quantitative extremes.

Example

Much is made today of the potential for alternative energy sources to replace fossil fuels, particularly oil, as a major component of the world's energy supply. Those who advocate or are optimistic about alternative energy often quote the growth rates of these sources over recent years. A scenario that relied on the following quotation would look rosy for alternative energy:

> *World production of solar cells soared to 742 MW in 2003, a jump of 32% in just one year. With solar cell production growing by an average of 27% annually over the past five years, cumulative world production now stands at 3,145 MW, enough to meet the electricity needs of more than a million homes. (RenewableAccess.com, 2004)*

Extrapolating this same rate of growth, 32%, over the next twenty years gives an apparently whopping 191,000 MW of power produced by solar cells. That is over 250 times the capacity produced in 2003. While 3,145 MW seems like a lot of capacity—more than million homes—in fact it represents only 0.09% of the world's total 3,465,000 MW of electrical capacity (EIA 2004). Even growing at 32% per year (compared to the 2.5% growth in overall electrical capacity), the 811,000 MW solar cell capacity in 2023 would still be only about 14% of the world's electrical capacity.

Thus, extrapolating a few numbers in an energy scenario might yield an overly optimistic assessment of how one alternative energy source is going to solve the problem of electricity production in the medium-term future.

Further reading

Energy Information Administration. (2004). "International Energy Annual 2002." Washington, DC: Department of Energy. Viewed May 2005, www.eia.doe.gov/pub/international/iealf/table64.xls.

4 ▶ Visioning

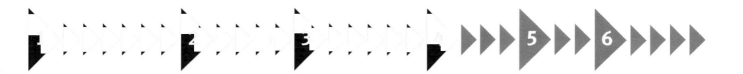

4.0 Visioning

"Whatever you can do or dream you can, begin it. Boldness has genius, power, and magic in it." —Goethe

The ultimate purpose of strategic foresight is to make better, more informed decisions in the present. Forecasting lays out a range of potential futures so decision-makers can consider how to prepare for them more effectively today. The guidelines in *Section 4.0: Visioning* suggest ways to bring the consideration of the future back to the present by addressing the question "So what?" Given the future possibilities outlined by Forecasting, what does the organization want to do?

Failure to ask this question diminishes the activity to just an interesting intellectual exercise. And few organizations have time or patience for that. Like any organizational activity, unless strategic foresight can demonstrate a link to the mission, purpose, effectiveness, performance, and, ultimately, the bottom line, it will quickly lose favor. Because the payoff for strategic foresight comes down the road, the analyst's task is to map the pathway to that payoff.

The first set of guidelines below, *4.1 Identify Implications*, begins the process of connecting the alternative futures identified by Forecasting directly to the organization's present reality. They emphasize the "so what" by asking the organization to consider what it would mean to the organization if each alternative were to occur.

The second set, *4.2 Challenge Assumptions*, advises the analyst to step back and reexamine the work to date before putting together the action options. Have unexamined assumptions or biases crept into the ideas that have been brought forward? It is useful here to reexamine these assumptions and, if necessary, go back and either generate additional ideas or bring forward ideas that were left behind.

The third set, *4.3 Think Visionary*, reminds the analyst that while attention must be paid to the here-and-now and the bottom line, it is also important to "think big." This is the stage where the organization expresses its hopes, dreams, and aspirations about the future, albeit grounded in the "reality" constructed in the preceding stages. The analyst's task here is to encourage the organization to step out of its comfort zone and outside its box to envision and consider a future it would really prefer to have. Erring on the side of over-ambition is preferable at this point, since the next section, *5.0 Planning*, is concerned with bringing that vision into being and can scale it back or fine-tune it as appropriate.

4.1 Identify Implications

4.1.1   Use Alternatives Not as the Answer, But to Help Frame the Important Questions

Forecasting develops potential alternative futures for the issue at hand. These alternatives map out the possibilities. This guideline suggests that these alternatives provide the material from which to frame the questions that will need to be answered to develop strategies and plans. Scenario guru Pierre Wack suggested that a first set of scenarios should be followed by a second set of what he called "decision scenarios." The first set, in effect, provides the key questions to be answered by the second or decision scenarios.

Key steps

The analyst first needs to digest and understand the alternative future possibilities that have been created in Forecasting. The alternatives need to be explored in terms of possibilities, formed as "what if?" questions. The questions should address implications of the alternatives for the key stakeholders identified earlier in the activity. Some basic categories are implications for (1) society, (2) the industry, (3) the organization, and (4) the specific unit or team within the organization.

Ideally, as many decision-makers as possible should be involved in the discussion of these questions since they will be the ones ultimately responsible for taking action. A workshop format is suggested for this task, as the interactions among participants may spur additional insights that would be missed by an email or interview approach.

In a workshop, a place to start is to assume that each alternative in turn has come true. The team can then generate ideas about potential strategies or actions for the organization based on that assumption. Next is to generate a set of specific questions that need to be answered, and to look at how the answers differ according to the different alternative futures. The questions will vary depending on the nature of the organization and the issue at hand. Some representative questions might include:

- What are the likely core competencies needed to respond, and do we have them?
- How would this alternative future affect the balance of power in the industry and our position within it?
- How would this alternative future influence our brand and/or our ability to attract talent?

The responses to the various questions should then be collated and prioritized according to predetermined criteria, which can be weighted according to the specifics of the situation. The initial prioritization can be relatively simple, using a "sticky dot" voting approach in which participants place their votes on the items they feel are most relevant.

Once the initial large list is sorted down into a more manageable number, the next round of prioritization should involve more detailed criteria.

Benefits

Following the approach above effectively translates the alternative futures generated by Forecasting from interesting information to potential action items. This is critical in today's time-stressed and bottom-line oriented organizations. It also helps avoid jumping too quickly into "solution space." Most organizations will be itching to get to solutions after having spent a lot of time generating alternatives. Following this guideline modulates this process and enables the team to clarify the right questions before jumping into strategy formation and action.

Example

A large multinational exploring the future of its information architecture used scenario planning to create four alternative futures. Once the four alternatives were agreed upon, a workshop was organized to explore their implications for the team's strategy. The client agreed that the results from this workshop would tie into the strategy formulation process used by the larger organization. The workshop began with an idea generation session, using "assume this scenario were true" to generate a batch of potential strategic actions. Next the group looked at the implications of each scenario for the key stakeholders identified by the activity, again generating a batch of potential strategic actions. Lastly, the team addressed specific questions relevant to the information architecture and explored how they would be answered by each scenario.

This created a huge pool of ideas, which were then prioritized down to the actions considered most essential. These, in turn, were further modified and reshaped to fit into the larger strategy process. The activity was rated a solid success by the team, with the implications workshop receiving high marks for translating the alternative futures or scenarios into action steps that plugged seamlessly into the company's decision-making process.

Further reading

Inayatullah, S. (n.d.). From Strategy to Transformative Change. Metafuture.org. Viewed August 2005, www.metafuture. org/Articles/teachingfuturestudies.htm.

Ogilvy, J., Gregory, E., and Harris, G. (n.d.). After the Scenarios, Then What? Strategic Conversation, Early Indicators, and the Art of Communicating Scenarios. *Presearch: Provoking Strategic Conversation*. Emeryville, CA: Global Business Network.

Ray, M. and Myers, R. (1986). *Creativity in Business*. New York: Doubleday.

Wack, P. (1984). Scenarios: The Gentle Art of Reperceiving. Reprinted by Global Business Network from President and Fellows of Harvard College, Working Paper 9-785-042.

4.1.2 Get to the Second- and Third-Order Implications

Guideline 3.5.5 Describe How the Future Will Be Different from the Present suggests going beyond just looking at the trends and issues leading to the future, to describing the alternative future itself. But here again, the obvious differences in the imagined future are only the beginning: those differences create differences of their own. The original differences are the first-order implications of change; the implications of those implications are the second-order implications and so on. The real message from foresight often lies in third-order implications, or higher.

Key steps

While implications can simply be thought about one at a time, the traditional method for identifying second- and higher-order implications is the *futures wheel*, developed by Jerome Glenn in 1971 (Glenn 1972). The method is described in detail in the AC/UNU Millennium Project's *Futures Research Methodology* (Glenn and Gordon, 2003).

Constructing a futures wheel begins with identifying one important difference between the present and the future. The difference could be expressed as a new condition (25% of the population will be over 65 years of age by a certain date), a trend leading to that condition (the population is aging), or an event (a major jump in life expectancy in a short period of time). This difference is written in a circle in the middle of a blank sheet or computer screen. Idea generation by one or more people then produces implications of that difference by answering the question, "If that change happens, what else will happen?" Three to eight such implications are listed, each one in a circle around the central difference. (More implications can be listed on a separate sheet, but the limitations of the graphic only allow a certain number around the central difference.) Those are the first-order implications of the central difference.

The same question is then asked about each of the first-order implications, leading to three or four second-order implications for each first-order implication, and so on. The process can go on indefinitely, but it usually stops with the second- or third-order implications because these usually encompass most of the important implications and, beyond them, the relationships get increasingly tenuous. One can also modify the question for the last round of implications to focus on the core issues or organization. Thus: "If that change happens, what are the implications for the focal issue or organization?"

Futures wheels are a subset of a more general thinking tool called *mind mapping*, popularized by Tony Buzan (1996), a creativity and memory specialist. A number of software programs now support mind mapping, such as MindManager (www.mindjet.com/us/products/mindmanager_x5pro/index.php?s=2) and Inspiration (www.inspiration.com/home.cfm). These can easily be used to generate futures wheels.

The noted futurist Joel Barker has also released a training program and software for implications analysis. Barker's technique, called the Implications Wheel (http://jbdl.frontlineproductions.us), is a highly refined and sophisticated version of the futures wheel that promises to measurably improve the ability of a team to carry out this guideline.

Benefits

The key benefit of exploring second- and third-order implications is in going beyond the obvious, first-order implications. Many organizations will stop at these and fail to get to potentially important, downstream implications. But being thorough at the outset reduces the risk of encountering expensive surprises down the road, as WHO did in Borneo. It also increases the chances of identifying a potential solution that would escape routine analysis.

Example

Hunter Lovins, co-founder of the Rocky Mountain Institute, a leading research center for sustainability solutions, tells the story of "parachuting cats" to illustrate the importance of second- and third-order implications. In Borneo in the early 1950s, the World Health Organization (WHO) sprayed DDT to kill mosquitoes carrying malaria. Initially this worked, with both the mosquito population and incidences of malaria declining. Later, however, roofs of people's houses mysteriously began collapsing. The DDT had poisoned wasps, which previously kept a local variety of thatch-eating caterpillars in check. Without the wasps the caterpillars proliferated and ate the thatch in the roofs, and the roofs fell in.

At the same time, DDT entered the food chain. It poisoned insects, which in turn were eaten by lizard-like creatures called geckos, which then were eaten by cats. When the poisoned cats died, rats flourished. Facing outbreaks of sylvatic plague and typhus from the rats, WHO was obliged to parachute live cats into Borneo.

Further reading

Buzan, T. and Buzan, B. (1996). *The Mind Map Book: How to Use Radiant Thinking to Maximize Your Brain's Untapped Potential*. London: Penguin.

Glenn, J.C. (1972, Spring). "Futurizing Teaching vs. Futures Course." *Social Science Record, 9* (3).

Glenn, J. and Gordon, T.J., eds. (2003). *Futures Research Methodology, Version 2.0*. Washington, DC: AC/UNU Millennium Project.

Lovins, H. (1990, Spring). The Parachuting Cats. *InContext*. Viewed February 2005, www.context.org/ICLIB/IC25/Lovins.htm.

Snyder, D.P. (1993). *The Futures Wheel: A Strategic Thinking Exercise*. Bethesda, MD: The Snyder Family Enterprise.

4.1.3 Think of Longer-Term and Unintended Consequences

In strategic foresight one has to check not only the first-, second-, and third-order implications that could manifest in the shorter term, but also those that could take a long while to emerge. When working with plausible futures and thinking through the solutions they suggest for the present, one needs to also check what these proposed solutions could lead to in the long run. This is done by considering their longer-term consequences—including exploring for unintended ones.

Key steps

In foresight activities a complex question is often divided into subsystems in order to better manage the analysis. However, this carries the danger of creating incomplete solutions that address only a part of the issue being explored. It is important to investigate how the different factors influence each other in the longer run, and what kind of unintended consequences may occur that would cause an internal contradiction.

When this is done in the context of scenarios, several tools are available for exploring longer-term consequences, such as the *impossible pairs* table (Finland Futures Academy, 2004).

It is indispensable to have a look at the big picture also. Proposed solutions or scenarios of the different subsystems should be investigated for their influence on the whole system. For instance, a typical unintended consequence of a business solution is longer-term environmental damage. In the case of an organization, a solution that may be ideal for one division or department can endanger the work of another. Thus solutions and alternatives should always be tested on the whole system.

It is not enough to simply uncover the direct consequences, because a complex system contains several feedback loops, which can carry indirect effects. In fact, the feedback mechanisms of a system are an important source of unintended consequences.

Perhaps most important, though, is to establish an effective monitoring system that watches for unexpected consequences over time. Longer-term and unintended consequences, unfortunately, tend to emerge when and where they are not expected. A monitoring process is needed to constantly look for weak signals and enable the organization to react as early as possible.

Benefits

One of foresight's chief strengths is discovering and describing long-term, unintended consequences. While many other decision-making methods may generate good solutions to specific problems, few offer a sophisticated approach for looking at the whole system over time.

Some systems change very slowly, and thus by definition demand investigation of long-term consequences. In fact, these need to be explored in even greater detail since consequences in slow-changing systems can have not only indirect effects, but also could interfere directly with intended changes—for instance, the implementation of our offered solution!

The importance of long-term, unintended consequences should be emphasized when working with alternatives that have a major effect on the future. Usually, these major decisions are complex ones, carrying enormous potential for creating important unintended consequences. Again, as an example, think of the negative environmental consequences that are often neglected and only become visible in the form of environmental catastrophes.

Example

Hungary still struggles with recovering the flora and the fauna of one of its main rivers, the Tisza, which suffered serious poisoning when an accident in one of the chemical factories situated near the river released untreated, toxic effluent into the water. Importantly, the problem was not the accident in itself—no matter how unexpected it may have been— but rather the lack of an emergency scenario, with guidelines for quickly containing environmental damage before it became serious.

The Tisza incident also points to the importance of feedback loops, since accidents like these often undermine the image of the company responsible for them and thereby endanger its position in the market. An ecological catastrophe can therefore easily have unintended consequences for the business side of the company.

Further reading

Coates, J.F. and Coates, V.T. (2003). Next Stages in Technology Assessment: Topics and Tools. *Technological Forecasting and Social Change 70*, 187 - 192.

Hines, A. (1997, July - August). Technology's Revenge: Review of Edward Tenner's Why Things Bite Back: Technology and the Revenge of Unintended Consequences. *The Futurist*, July - August 1997.

How Can We Explore the Future? (2004). Turku: Finland Futures Academy.

Tenner, E. (1997). *Why Things Bite Back: Technology and the Revenge of Unintended Consequences*. London: Random House.

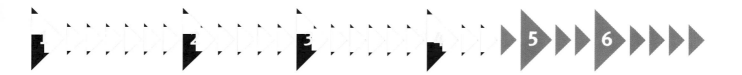

4.2 Challenge Assumptions

4.2.1 Uncover and Clarify Assumptions

It is useful to reconsider assumptions, particularly those of the client organization, as the activity draws closer to the Action phase. As the organization begins to consider what it would like to do with what is has learned to this point, reexamining whether it may have assumptions about itself that have not yet come to light, or whether any new, unexamined assumptions have crept in, will enable a truly robust foresight activity.

Uncovering hidden assumptions is essential to first-rate foresight work. Hidden assumptions often lie at the root of strategic foresight gone awry; that is, plans fail because an unstated assumption turns out to be incorrect. Even more insidiously, an analyst or other member of the foresight team will unconsciously gravitate to evidence that supports a hidden assumption, or ignore evidence that contradicts it.

Thus, throughout a foresight activity the analyst needs to stay alert for hidden assumptions. Methods for uncovering and challenging both overt and hidden assumptions have been described in Framing and Scanning (see especially *1.3.2 Seek to Improve the Mental Model of Decision-makers* and *2.4.1 Consult "Remarkable People"*). It is also intrinsic to good Forecasting, as discussed in *3.1.1 Uncover the Underlying Drivers* and throughout *3.5 Form Alternatives*.

In Visioning—the last phase before strategy begins to be translated into plans and tactics—it is important to step back and formally reexamine the work done to date to root out any remaining hidden assumptions. Identifying and clarifying assumptions at this point may seem redundant, but it will enable the analyst to trace back the pathway along which the analysis has proceeded, uncover any buried biases, and adjust assumptions that have turned out to be false or need readjusting on the basis of new or improved data.

Key steps

A formal approach to uncovering and clarifying assumptions proceeds through several steps:

- First, map the system under consideration. This includes identifying first the key stakeholders, then the forces directly and indirectly influencing the system. See *Guideline 2.1.2 Map the System Under Consideration* for more.
- After the players and forces are identified, prioritize them according to their importance to the issue at hand. Consult *Guideline 2.1.4 Conduct a Stakeholder Analysis*.

- Now identify assumptions about the behavior of the key players and forces. One way to do this is to imagine being granted three questions of someone who knows what the future will be, with each answer costing $100,000. What questions would the organization ask about how its future will look ten years from now? Once the assumptions are identified, look for data and information that supports or weakens them.
- As the activity proceeds and more is learned about the issue involved, revisit this list of assumptions and see if they continue to make sense, revising where necessary.

Uncovering hidden assumptions can be time-consuming, uncomfortable, and sometimes painful. There will often be pressure "to get on with it." Over the course of the activity, however, this upfront investment will pay dividends—since rework based on faulty assumptions is far more time-consuming and difficult than being conscientious at the beginning.

Uncovering assumptions can also be personally challenging to team members. It may force people to reveal thoughts and beliefs they would prefer to keep to themselves, or challenge those who gravitate towards evidence that supports their assumptions and thus distorts the results. It can also force team members to resolve differences in their assumptions—but unless the team is on the same page, the activity will crumble later when the underlying assumptions are put to the test.

Benefits

The benefits of uncovering and clarifying assumptions are manifold. First, it prevents problems down the road when an unidentified assumption trips up the activity. Second, clarifying differences among team members' assumptions provides a common framework upon which the activity can proceed. Third, it enables the team to learn where other members are coming from on the issue, what they are thinking, and what they believe. Resolving the differences builds a solid basis from which the activity can proceed, and also makes it easier to adjust the analysis as new data comes in. Fourth, it keeps the activity honest, enabling the team to objectively view evidence and revise assumptions where it makes sense, and avoid locking into a solution too soon by ignoring contrary evidence. Finally, it provides a basis for testing various solutions to the issue at hand. Different assumptions can be tested to see how they would make the activity come out differently.

Example

Nutt (2002) describes the EuroDisney "debacle," where hidden or unclear assumptions undercut the European theme park's success. Disney assumed its stellar track record of building parks in other regions of the world would translate easily to Europe. Failure seemed unimaginable—and this hidden assumption led the park's developers to ignore hints of trouble which continued to surface and grow. Issues specific to French geography and culture were ignored, or pooh-poohed with a kind of rah-rah, can-do enthusiasm. As the problems snowballed, Disney's earnings and stock price ultimately took a big hit.

Further reading

Nutt, P.C. (2002). *Why Decisions Fail: Avoiding the Blunders and Traps That Lead to Debacles*. San Francisco: Berrett-Koehler.

Coates, J.F. (1999). Getting at Assumptions Is Troublesome. *Technological Forecasting & Social Change, 62*, 97 - 99.

4.2.2 Challenge Conventional Wisdom

Rethink the standard-issue future. People carry around assumptions about the future picked up from the popular press, conversations, the organization's norms, or their own hopes and fears. For example, a common and usually unchallenged assumption in the United States in the 1980s was that Generation-X teens were "slackers": unmotivated, ignorant, etc. Yet experience has borne out that Gen-Xers are quite savvy and shrewd in managing their lives—just with different priorities than the baby boomers. A more extreme example is the hoary belief that before long, flying cars will be common. While a flying car has been technically demonstrated, myriad obstacles prevent it from becoming a practical form of transport in the present. Future ideas like these are typically untested, poorly thought out, or just implausible.

Key steps

A core role for analysts who help organizations focus on change is to examine and challenge the *official future*. In strategic discussions this means discovering and discussing a group's assumptions about the future. Often, people need to be challenged to think more comprehensively about change and get beyond extrapolation of a few prominent trends. There are several steps to challenging the official future.

First, get everyone involved to air their views on the future of the question at hand. Bringing out tacit assumptions immediately invites scrutiny of them. Through the ensuing discussion, colleagues will begin to challenge each other's assumptions as well as their own.

Second, subject these assumptions to further discussion and scrutiny. Bring in more informed views of the future on the topics of interest to the group. That may mean involving a futurist or domain expert.

Third, one of the basic failings of an official future is that it usually makes much of one or two key changes without regard to others. So the next step is to collect a more comprehensive list of issues, trends, and driving forces that are important to the organization's future. This is not hard to initiate—the process of airing assumptions about the future will drive participants to add insights of their own, and to make more reasoned discoveries about likely future outcomes, based on their collective thinking.

Finally, after widening the thinking by looking at additional issues, trends, and forces, the analyst plays a particularly important role by helping the group see how these forces and trends interrelate and shape each other. *Cross-impact analysis* is a great tool for this; see *Guideline 3.1.4 Look for Colliding Change Trajectories* for more on this technique. Many explanations of cross-impact analysis overcomplicate it; essentially, it places trends in a matrix that arrays each trend against every other, then asks how they influence each other. It is an exploratory tool for finding important, perhaps hidden, changes in the future. It can even be performed in a simple group discussion, by taking important trends or issues in turn and discussing how they interrelate.

Benefits

Analysts have a key role in ensuring that strategic discussions don't shortcut thinking, or allow it to be limited to a narrow or even sensationalist view of the future. Aligning with conventional wisdom is easier and more comfortable because it reflects what most people already believe. More challenging, but infinitely more valuable, is to buck conventional wisdom and suggest that things could turn out quite differently from the official future. However (as in the quote by Herman Kahn introducing *Section 3.0 Forecasting*), "The surprise-free future isn't"—in other words, a future that flows seamlessly from today's visible trends is very unlikely.

Example

Across the consumer-products sector, marketers and strategists act in constant awareness of Wal-Mart—often the single most powerful force in their markets. Wal-Mart presses its vendors for price reductions, and makes specific demands that shape their product development, packaging, and distribution. This often reduces vendors' margins and makes them less profitable—and is becoming a permanent bogeyman for growing numbers of consumer-product companies.

The easiest future scenario for executives of these companies to envision is a Wal-Mart dominated world. From a strategic foresight perspective, the problem is that this apparent certainty—Wal-Mart calling the shots for the foreseeable future—prevents them from imagining new kinds of business with new channels. Wal-Mart becomes the inexorable force in their standard-issue future, blinding them to new opportunities.

Savvy consumer-products firms have thought their way past this by setting fear of Wal-Mart aside long enough to explore the wider world of change. They may maintain a focused strategy for their Wal-Mart dealings, but they also look for higher-margin opportunities serving other channels and tapping new business opportunities. They find ways to not be cowed into narrow strategic thinking.

Further reading

Gordon, T. (2004). Cross-Impact Analysis. In Glenn, J.C. and Gordon, T. (2004). *2004 State of the Future*. Washington, DC: American Council for the United Nations University and The Millennium Project.

Hamel, G. (2002). *Leading the Revolution: How to Thrive in Turbulent Times by Making Innovation a Way of Life*. New York: Penguin Books.

4.2.3 Assume Nothing; Question Everything

The analyst must adopt an attitude of complete open-mindedness when evaluating information. Beware of making assumptions before giving the information a fair hearing. Go a step further and see if there is a way to make sense of information before rejecting it.

Key steps

In preparing to evaluate a forecast, analysts should start by clearing their minds. How this is achieved is up to the individual. A meditative exercise may be helpful. Michael Ray (1986), a professor emeritus at Stanford Business School, has a wonderful set of relaxation exercises developed for his graduate students in his book *Creativity in Business*.

Once relaxed, analysts should consider whether they have unconsciously made any assumptions about the information used to develop the forecast. No matter how objective analysts strive to be, bias inevitably creeps in. This is not a problem as long as the analyst is aware of the bias and evaluates its usefulness along with evaluating the information.

Finally, the forecast to be evaluated should be considered from as many different perspectives as possible. A particularly useful approach for this is causal-layered analysis, developed by Sohail Inayatullah (1998) based on the foundational work of Richard Slaughter. Inayatullah offers a questioning technique drawing on the tools of postmodern critique, for evaluating a set of information from multiple perspectives. Five tools he suggests are:

- *Deconstruction*—Who is privileged by this information? Who gains from it at the economic, social, and other levels? Who is silenced? What are the politics of its truth?

- *Genealogy*—Which discourses have been victorious in constituting the present? How have they traveled through history? What have been the points at which the issue has become important or contentious?

- *Distance*—Which scenarios make the present remarkable? Make it unfamiliar? Strange? Denaturalize it?

- *Alternative pasts and futures*—Which interpretation of the past is valorized? What histories make the present problematic? Which vision of the future is used to maintain the present? Which would undo the unity of the present?

- *Reordering knowledge*—How does the ordering of knowledge differ across civilization, gender, and episteme? What or who is "othered?" How does it denaturalize current orderings, making them peculiar instead of universal?

While Inayatullah's questions are cast at a high level, the discipline of thinking them through can help identify hidden assumptions. It challenges the analyst and the organization to be aware of deeply embedded assumptions about how they view the world, and recognizes that there are other ways to do so. One might assume, for example, that the existing world economic order based on the so-called Washington Consensus of free trade, democracy, and open markets is the best and only way that the global economic order will be organized in the future. Going through the questions above will challenge that thinking and reveal there are alternative views, and that these may gain more prominence as the future unfolds.

Benefits

The value-add of a foresight activity is very much about delivering insights that escape traditional analysis. Being open to information others may reject out of hand is central to this. The open-minded approach described above—of trying to make sense of information before rejecting it—is perhaps most important when evaluating a forecast and preparing to envision the organization's preferred future. A forecast may seem implausible at first, but given time and considered from different angles and perspectives it may begin to look more possible. While this approach is particularly useful during evaluation, it is a principle that can serve the analyst well throughout an activity.

Example

A multinational business unit in the midst of a strategy-formulation process devoted two days to coming up with alternative strategies to its current one. The team intended to then evaluate these alternatives to see if they would be likely to produce better results. The facilitator created an environment conducive to open-mindedness through the use of music, toys, and the Disney instruction to "willingly suspend disbelief."

One of the exercises involved challenging orthodoxies or assumptions about the way the unit itself currently operated. This tool, known as *challenging orthodoxies*, was adapted from the consulting firm Strategos (www.strategos.com), founded by Gary Hamel. In the course of the exercise, one the assumptions challenged was that "we would never walk away from our largest customer." When this was first mentioned, laughter in the room signaled agreement with the orthodoxy. Then the team was instructed, in the spirit of open-mindedness and multiple perspectives, to think harder about the challenge before rejecting it. One participant somewhat hesitantly suggested a scenario in which the company could indeed walk away from its biggest customer. Once the ice was broken, others began to suggest additional ways. By the end of the two days, the team ended up selecting a strategy based on walking away from its best customer. A year later, the business unit had replaced the business from the lost customer and even added more.

Further reading

Ray, M. and Myers, R. (1986). *Creativity in Business*. New York: Doubleday.

Inayatullah, S. (1998). Causal Layered Analysis: Poststructuralism as Method. *Futures, 30* (6), 815 - 829.

4.2.4 Identify and Tear Down Taboos Ghosting the Organization

Taboos refer to the issues an organization is afraid to speak of, touch upon, or even think about. There is collective denial that these issues even exist, even though most organizations have them. They can severely impede a strategic foresight activity by prohibiting open discussion of deep structural changes an organization may need for its survival. Upper management often sets the tone for taboos. They can take many shapes and forms, from "no advertising" to refusing to discuss strategy because "it's all about implementation" or "we are not a services company." It's a taboo when members of the organization are afraid to challenge these concepts publicly, for fear of being branded "not a team player" or hurting their career.

Ideally, open discussion of taboos should take place as early in the foresight activity as possible. This aim, however, is paradoxical: how to discuss topics whose existence is denied?

Key steps

Be wary of relying solely on top executives for information about what is going on in the organization. Executives typically see themselves as having answers, rather than knowing the right questions to ask. Organizational reward structures will tend to reinforce this. Recognize that many people in lower levels of the organization have a closer feel for "what is really going on" and can help the analyst avoid being hypnotized into overlooking a taboo. The opportunity for the analyst is to pay attention to what isn't being said publicly, but is being discussed around the water cooler or off-the-record.

Tackling a company's taboos is, by definition, extremely difficult. Few activities even attempt it. One way to come at it indirectly is to expose the organization to odd situations and strange questions posed by outsiders. This may mean visiting seminars, meetings, and websites of people and organizations outside the normal scope of business—even those of enemies. A business leader could do something completely out of the ordinary—take part in a seminar of a feminist activist group, go to a Britney Spears concert, or read some alternative literature such as that of Charles Bukowski. In scenario-building and strategy groups, bring in the most diverse expertise possible. Good ideas may result, even—or especially—about familiar issues, and different perspectives may help the organization confront issues related to its taboos.

If the taboos seem to emanate from what might be called paradigm blindness, one can recall Marshall McLuhan's insight: "We don't know who discovered water, but we are pretty sure it wasn't a fish." Every organization can benefit from periodically getting distance from its normal circumstances and paradigm in order to see better.

It is also useful to assess the implications of the taboos for areas such as:

- Culture and values, e.g., around the organization's willingness to learn, its respect for the individual, achievement, customer satisfaction, and other factors
- Flow of ideas and feedback loops
- Employee satisfaction

Benefits

Taboos can severely limit the ability to think about and discuss future opportunities and threats, trends, scenarios, visions, or weak signals. Still more fundamentally, they can prohibit open discussion concerning the organization's inner issues like structures and policies. Even if the foresight activity uncovers important competitive threats or needs for change, taboos may prevent discussion of the changes required—let alone of their implementation. In less serious cases the company may lose some of its competitive advantage; in more serious ones, taboos can bring a company down.

Example

One company that failed to tackle its taboos was Enron. Kleiner (2003) recounts a letter to the Houston Chronicle that reported an "arrogant, self-satisfied culture" focused on "How can I get a piece?" Another letter described the flip-side—the excitement employees felt: "You walked in the door and got energized. You worked with the best, the most brilliant." Employees received perks like mobile phones, PDAs, laptops, first-class airfare, free food, big-screen TVs in the company lounge, and so on. In this climate, former employees reported, it was impossible to raise taboo questions such as "Is this sustainable?" or even the more basic "Is this legal?" Ultimately, this failure to address taboo questions led to Enron's well-publicized downfall.

Further reading

Kleiner, A. (2003). *Who Really Matters: The Core Group Theory of Power, Privilege, and Success*. New York: Currency Doubleday.

Mannermaa, M. and Glenn, J. (2005, July 30). Wanted! New Paradigms for Futures and Futures Studies. Presentation to World Future Society General Assembly, July 29 - 31, 2005, Chicago, Illinois.

Mitroff, I. (1977). Corporate Taboos as the Key to Unlocking Culture. In H.A. Linstone and C.W.H. Simmonds, eds., *Futures Research: New Directions*. Reading, MA: Addison-Wesley, 1977.

4.2.5 Validate Assumptions by Cross-Checking Them

Once assumptions, taboos, and biases have been uncovered and examined, a set of explicit future assumptions—acknowledged beliefs about the future, which have been clarified and found worthy of supporting the strategic forecasts—will remain. The quality of these future assumptions can make or break the forecasting activity. The best way to ensure their robustness is to cross-check them against the views of other sources—preferably, a group of internal and external experts.

Key steps

The following steps will improve the quality of future assumptions. First, as explained in *Guideline 4.2.1 Uncover and Clarify Assumptions*, identify the organization's critical assumptions about the future.

Second, gather and interview an interdisciplinary group of at least ten experts and non-experts. Let everyone in the group give their own answers to questions about how the organization's future will look. Sum up the answers and formulate a set of forecasts that comprises all the different beliefs.

Third, let every expert attribute an expectational probability to every answer and forecast. Use a scale of one to nine with one indicating low, five medium, and nine high (or use percentages, with one equal to a probability of 10%, five 50%, and nine 90%). Make sure the experts give their evaluations independently from each other.

Finally, analyze the average and spread of the expectational probabilities. Forecasts with an average score of seven or above can serve as the basis of a strategy. Of course, one should also prepare preventive and contingency strategies in case the forecasts with lower probabilities come about. The spread (standard deviation) is an indicator of reliability. Discuss answers with spreads of two and more with the experts. Remember to value the work of mavericks.

Benefits

A former CEO of Royal Dutch Shell once said, "It is impossible to predict the future, but it is dangerous not to try." Validating future assumptions facilitates analysis of the future. Assumptions provide analytical simplicity by reducing complexity. Future assumptions serve to reduce the number of possible futures that need to be considered—just as in a mathematical linear or nonlinear optimization, the constraints serve to reduce the number of possible solutions.

Assumptions also provide prerequisites for development and analysis of strategies. A strategic decision cannot be analyzed and evaluated before the future assumptions of the decision-maker are known. Every substantial human decision and action is to some extent based on assumptions about the future. The more uncertain the future is, the more necessary it is to clarify future assumptions (Dewar, 2002), and the more attention should be paid to their elaboration and formulation.

Future assumptions also facilitate communications about the future. As soon as assumptions are clearly stated (or perhaps documented in written form), potential misunderstandings can be identified and dealt with (Porter, 2004).

Finally, they act as frameworks for perceptions about the future. Future assumptions are heuristic. As soon as a future assumption is elaborated and documented, it creates a category for perception and observation of data. Thus, a future assumption is a starting point for monitoring any changes to the facts, trends, and issues related to the assumption.

Example

Between 1995 and 1998 two large competing airline companies, Boeing and Airbus, looked at the future of their market. Each company did everything it could to understand the future of air travel. They commissioned substantial studies and hired experts and futurists. Though their resulting quantitative forecasts about the growth of the air travel market were quite similar, each firm made different assumptions: Airbus assumed traffic between major hub cities served by large aircraft would continue to dominate intercontinental air traffic, while Boeing assumed direct flights to second-tier cities served by smaller aircraft would become more important. Airbus assumed cost would mean the most to passengers, so it reduced airfares by 20%. Boeing assumed time would mean the most, so it worked to bring passengers to their destinations 20% faster.

Consequently, Airbus developed its strategy based on the A380 while Boeing counted on its Sonic Cruiser. Both strategies appeared logical and valid. The outcomes are well-known: Airbus quickly got more than one hundred orders for its large craft, while Boeing had to abandon its new star of the skies. Boeing's billion-dollar bet affected more than 100,000 jobs. It had built its strategy on well-reasoned, yet ultimately intuitive, assumptions about the future which the market proved wrong.

Further reading

Dewar, J. (2002). *Assumption-Based Planning*. Cambridge, UK: Cambridge University Press.

Georgantzas, N. and Acar, W. (1995). *Scenario-Driven Planning*. Westport, CT: Quorum.

Micic, P. (2003). *Der ZukunftsManager*. Munich, Germany: Haufe.

Micic, P. and Marx, A. (2004). *Die Bank von Morgen denken und gestalten*. Eltville, Germany: ADG.

Porter, A. (2004). Technology Futures Analysis: Towards Integration of the Field and New Methods. *Technological Forecasting & Social Change, 71*, 287 - 303.

4.3 Think Visionary

4.3.1 Develop a Strategic Vision

A strategic vision is a lodestar—an image of the future that offers direction yet is never reached. Since the vision is a normative statement, it may also be considered a business philosophy, carried forward into the future. Peter Senge (1994) defines a vision as "a picture of the future you seek to create, described in the present tense as if it were happening now."

A strategic vision is aspired to throughout a strategic foresight activity, but emerges fully in the Visioning phase. It should be clearly formulated before proceeding to the construction of strategies and plans. This is the point in the activity where the learnings gained through Forecasting coalesce into a direction for the organization. However, visioning is an iterative process, as the formation of strategies and plans may raise questions that in turn make it sensible to revise the vision.

Key steps

Senge suggests there are five potential starting points for developing a vision. Organizations tend to be at one of these five points. His advice is to gradually shift the organization towards the most desirable of the five points: *co-creating*. The five stages are:

1. *Telling*—The boss decrees the vision and everyone else follows it.
2. *Selling*—The boss knows the vision, but needs to get the organization to buy in.
3. *Testing*—The boss has an idea or ideas about the vision and wants to know the organization's reaction before proceeding.
4. *Consulting*—The boss is putting together a vision and wants input from the organization.
5. *Co-creating*—The boss and the members of the organization build the vision together through a collaborative process.

While there are many different processes for constructing a vision, Senge suggests they should include the following questions:

- Who are the stakeholders? How do we work with them? How do we produce value for them?
- What are the most influential trends in our industry?
- What is our image in the marketplace? How do we compete?
- What is our unique contribution to the world around us? What is the impact of our work?
- How do we make money?
- What does our organization look like?

- How do we handle good or hard times?
- In what ways is our organization a great place to work?
- What are our values? How do people treat each other?
- How do we know that the future of our organization is secure?
- What is our organization's role in the community?

Benefits

A strategic vision can serve organizations as a template, model, or interpretive framework for making sense of the daily puzzle. It provides a rallying point for focusing the organization's work. In bad times, it can provide reassurance that current challenges will pass and are worth navigating through.

It aligns the organization and its stakeholders around a common purpose. Think of the power of FedEx's "Absolutely, Positively Overnight." This clearly communicates expectations to the workforce as well as to customers, and the outstanding performance of the company suggests these have indeed been aligned.

A caveat: A great vision statement does not guarantee great results. Unless the company and its stakeholders have bought into the vision, it is just words on paper. To be effective, the stakeholders must believe in the vision, and act accordingly.

Example

The renowned *Built to Last* study by Collins and Porras (1994) found that "visionary companies attain extraordinary long-term performance." Going back to 1926, such companies had average earnings more than fifteen times the general market. Similarly, Arie de Gues' *The Living Company* (1997) found evidence that companies striving to learn and grow outlast companies focused solely on economic returns. He cites the famed study by Royal Dutch/Shell that found the average life expectancy of Fortune 500 companies was under fifty years. The same study also found many companies that were over two hundred years old. The key difference between the short- and long-lived companies, de Gues found, was that the former focused on financial returns while the latter focused on the community of people comprising the organization. A key factor enabling the long-lived companies to maintain this focus on their people was a strong sense of identity and purpose. In each, a vision rallied the community to prosper during good times and persevere through the bad—and ultimately to outlive their economically focused competitors.

Further reading

Collins, J.C. and Porras, J.I. (1994). *Built to Last: Successful Habits of Visionary Companies*. New York: HarperCollins.

de Gues, A. (1997). *The Living Company: Habits for Survival in a Turbulent Business Environment*. Boston: Harvard Business School.

Senge, P., Kleiner, A., Roberts, C., Ross, R., and Smith, B. (1994). *The Fifth Discipline Fieldbook*. New York: Currency Doubleday.

4.3.2 Put the Strategic Vision in a Time Continuum

When an analyst links an organization's vision to a time continuum, he or she can help the organization track its progress towards the vision over time. First, however, the analyst should assess the organization's present situation as well as the potential futures for its operating environment (see *Section 3.0 Forecasting*).

Key steps

Start by analyzing the basic beliefs of the present: mission, business idea, operating environment. The idea is to increase the organization's self-understanding of "who we are." The next step is to formulate a *preferred direction of development* for the organization. This preferred direction can have several dimensions, such as spatial, quantitative, and qualitative. After defining the direction of development, the organization can choose specific years (2010, 2020...) for expressing its status relative to the preferred course of development—i.e., its progress towards the vision. For example:

- The present business idea: selling hammers and other tools for farmers at a single local shop
- Vision 2010: selling a wide range of construction instruments and tools for different customer segments at the state level, through fifteen stores
- Vision 2020: offering construction services (tools, consulting, designing, etc.) at the national level in eighty market centers, with five stores set to open in Canada within a couple more years

Benefits

Visions are used along with scenarios or other assessments of the future to formulate long-range strategic policies, typically with a time perspective of fifteen to twenty-five years. The purpose of these strategic policies is to guarantee as far as possible the realization of the organization's preferred direction under any scenario that could plausibly emerge. In principle, one set of strategic long-range policies is constructed per scenario.

On the basis of these strategic policies, medium- and short-range strategic development programs and proposals for strategies and plans can be defined. The idea is to gradually shorten the time perspective from fifteen or twenty-five years to five years, one year, and the immediate present.

The main benefit of linking a vision to a time continuum (the present, 2010, 2020...) is that it helps the organization construct a mental model along the lines of "This is how we proceed now, in the next year, within the next five years, and in the long run." Beyond one general vision, whose attainment may seem dauntingly distant, two or three sub-visions sequenced along a time continuum allow the organization to express its preferred long-range development in clear, achievable steps. Using specific points in time like 2010 and 2020 is symbolic, but helps to structure the future goals.

Example

About twenty years ago, a relatively large company in a smokestack industry was built on a very traditional business idea: it sold cement and lime powder mainly to other business customers. The company then undertook a strategic foresight activity using scenarios. During the study, visions were created and linked to a time continuum. One of the main insights that emerged was that the company should not only sell products at a low level of added value; it should aim at increasing its value-add by offering service elements along with its supply. This idea was implemented, and succeeded. Growth came as a byproduct of the visionary idea of moving a traditional smokestack company in the direction of a service business.

Further reading

Armstrong, J.S. (2001, May). *Principles of Forecasting: A Handbook for Researchers and Practitioners*. Hingham, MA: Kluwer Academic Publishers.

Millett, S. (2004, February). *Futuring and Visioning: Preparing for Success in the Future*. Viewed August 2005, www.battelle.org/dr-futuring/futuring-visioning.ppt.

4.3.3 Set Strategic Goals as Stretch Goals

A *stretch goal* sets an ambitious target to motivate an organization to aspire beyond its current comfort level. It should not be so ambitious as to be unrealistic, or so easily attainable that it fails to motivate. Stretch goals are typically set to achieve a major change rather than a routine one. Perhaps the most well-known expression of the stretch goal is the BHAG (big hairy audacious goal) popularized by Collins and Porras in *Built to Last* (1994).

Stretch goals are used as rallying points around which organizations garner support and motivation for the challenging activity of visioning. The stretch goal should be accompanied by shorter-term objectives that indicate progress towards the goal. Achieving a stretch goal can be intimidating, so having smaller-scale objectives along the way will enable a sense of progress that helps keep the team on track.

Key steps

Collins and Porras (1994) suggest four criteria for setting a good BHAG or stretch goal. These goals should:

- be set with understanding, not bravado
- have a long timeframe—ten to thirty years
- be clear, compelling, and easy to grasp
- directly reflect the organization's core values and core purpose

Collins uses Isaiah Berlin's parable of the fox and the hedgehog to develop the notion of a *hedgehog concept,* which simplifies "a complex world into a single organizing idea, a basic principle or concept that unifies and guides everything. It doesn't matter how complex the world is, a hedgehog reduces all challenges and dilemmas to simple—indeed almost simplistic—hedgehog ideas. For a hedgehog, anything that does not somehow relate to the hedgehog idea holds no relevance." Stretch goals, Collins suggests, should have the simple qualities of a hedgehog concept, committing the company uncompromisingly to one big idea.

Benefits

Stretch goals that are properly set can be wonderful motivators and rallying points for an organization. The longer-term timeframe and strategic nature of stretch goals require the approaches and tools of strategic foresight. At the same time, stretch goals should not be set or supported lightly. The analyst should be careful when designing an activity to avoid dubious stretch goals, which can frustrate and demoralize rather than motivate, and can taint the foresight work.

Example

Two classic examples of stretch goals from US history are the Manhattan Project and President Kennedy's challenge to put a man on the moon. The Manhattan Project to develop the atomic bomb mobilized the scientific community to develop breakthrough understanding in a very short timeframe, by defining the mission as critical to survival of the nation and even the free world. Similarly, Kennedy's man-on-the-moon project challenged the US spaceflight community to respond to the Soviet Union's lead in the space race. The community not only reached this objective but developed a lead in the space race, and never looked back.

Further reading

Collins, J. and Porras, J.I. (1994). *Built to Last: Successful Habits of Visionary Companies*. New York: HarperBusiness.

Collins, J. (2001). *Good to Great: Why Some Companies Make the Leap... and Others Don't*. New York: HarperBusiness.

McGarvey, R. (1997, February). Above and Beyond: Set Higher Goals for Your Employees—and They'll Excel. *Entrepreneur*.

4.3.4 You Get What You Think—Leverage the Positive

In many cases, organizations undertake visioning activities because they face a need for transformative change. They do not need to craft a vision if everything is going well and there are no big discontinuities on the horizon. Thus, most visioning is done under some form of duress—which can lead the organization to be overly focused on "the problems."

This guideline borrows from the *appreciative inquiry* approach in suggesting that even in the worst organizational crisis, there is much positive to build upon. Appreciative inquiry is based on Berger and Luckman's (1967) view that reality is socially constructed—in essence, what the organization thinks about and focuses on becomes its reality. If the organization focuses on the negative, it will tend to experience negative outcomes. If it focuses on the positive, it will tend to experience positive outcomes. Cooperrider (2005) suggests that "the single most prolific thing a group can do if its aims are to liberate the human spirit and consciously construct a better future is to make the positive-change core the common and explicit property of all."

Key steps

The appreciative inquiry approach begins with framing the visioning process. It puts a premium on the language used, suggesting this has a big influence on the mindset and tone of the activity. To begin with, rather than framing the visioning process as "problem solving," consider it "solution finding."

Cooperrider (2005) outlines four steps to appreciative inquiry. The first, discovery, involves exploring the organizational system for its positive change potential. This means scouring the organization for what is currently working, as well as what has worked in the past. This is carried out by an extensive interviewing process, following a script that is carefully crafted to embody the principles of remaining focused on the positive. Interviewing as many stakeholders as possible is encouraged. Some projects using appreciative inquiry interview hundreds of stakeholders.

The second and third steps are dreaming and designing. The approach to these steps is similar to that used in a Future Search process (Weisbord, 2000), referred to in *Guideline 3.4.1 Identify and Prioritize Areas of Common Ground*. Dreaming builds on the positive-change potential uncovered in discovery to create a clear, results-oriented vision. It seeks to uncover the organization's higher purpose. Design then translates that higher purpose into an organizational design that leverages this positive potential in pursuit of the vision.

The last step, destiny, is about institutionalizing the dream and design in the organization. It seeks to ensure that the positive momentum continues and becomes part of the way the organization operates in the future.

This guideline emphasizes focusing on the positive no matter which visioning process the analyst and organization decide to use. A caveat is that this approach can be challenging for organizations whose culture is more attuned to left-brain, bottom-line approaches emphasizing data and facts. While appreciative inquiry does build on positive examples and stories from the past and present, it is essentially a right-brain, highly intuitive approach. Be sure to diagnose the culture of the organization and modulate the degree to which this approach is applied.

Benefits

Leveraging the positive can benefit any organization going through a visioning process. It can be especially beneficial to organizations mired in "the problems." These organizations are overly focused on what is wrong, and fail to see that much is right. This guideline suggests systematically finding what is right and leveraging it in the visioning process.

Advocates of appreciative inquiry say this process can have an almost magical effect on an organization when it succeeds. The strategic conversation shifts from documenting problems and obstacles to exploring and finding solutions. Innovation, flexibility, integration, collaboration, affiliation, engagement, and coordination with the outside world flourish.

Like all methods, appreciative inquiry does not always work. It can fall flat in organizations not predisposed to this kind of approach. And its emphasis on the positive can discount some very real negatives that need to be addressed.

Example

Anderson et al. (2005) relate the story of Nutrimental Foods in Brazil applying appreciative inquiry: "The factory was closed for four days as they brought all 750 employees together, along with customers and suppliers, to create a new business vision. A year later profits were up 200%; absenteeism was lowered by 300%; and the company now does this kind of summit every year." (p. 40)

Further reading

Anderson, H., Cooperrider, D., Gergen, K., Gergen, M., McNamee, S. and Whitney, D. (2001). *The Appreciative Organization*. Chagrin Falls: Taos Institute Publications.

Berger, P. and Luckman, T. (1966). *The Social Construction of Reality*. New York: Doubleday.

Cooperrider, D. and Whitney, D. (2005). *A Positive Revolution in Change: Appreciative Inquiry*. San Francisco: Berrett-Koehler.

Weisbord, M. and Janoff, S. (2000). *Future Search: An Action Guide to Finding Common Ground in Organizations and Communities*. (2nd Ed.). San Francisco: Berrett-Koehler.

4.3.5 Remember Dator's Law: Any Useful Statement about the Future Should Appear to Be Ridiculous

Dare to be ridiculous and think surprising thoughts. Dator's Law states: "Any useful statement about the future should appear to be ridiculous." If a forecast sounds familiar, it probably relates to current events or the expected future. Dator adds, "The corollary is that when futurists make useful statements about the future, they should expect to be ridiculed and laughed at." (Dator, 1995)

Key steps

The mindset here is akin to Disney's concept, "the willing suspension of disbelief." This guideline emphasizes having the presence of mind to consider even the most off-the-wall solutions and search for the kernel of a useful idea within them. IDEO, the renowned design firm, has as one of its creative mantras, "Build upon wild ideas." As its former chief, Thomas Kelley, remarked in a 20-minute ABC-TV *Nightline* segment profiling IDEO's innovative work culture (available at www.abcnews.com), "If you didn't come up with any wild ideas, you wouldn't have any jumping-off points to come up with something really interesting." As both Dator and Kelley suggest, "really interesting" ideas are often accompanied by laughter—and these are the ideas to pay particular attention to, since laughter is often about connecting the expected to the unexpected, and therefore implies some degree of plausibility.

There are two types of futures—the expected (official future) and the unexpected. The expected future is hardly news. Where's the value in repeating what clients and audiences already expect? The foresight analyst has a higher purpose: to present futures that are both plausible and unexpected. Such futures may, at first glance, appear surprising or even ridiculous. It's the analyst's job to convince the organization that such futures are plausible and that, if they occur, they will have a big impact on the organization—which should therefore begin to understand and prepare for them.

This is one area where the analyst's mission carries some danger. The analyst must be prepared to appear ridiculous at first, stepping outside the organization's comfort zone and encouraging others to join in and contemplate the unexpected. Analysts need to be comfortable with seeming ridiculous in order to be provocative.

Benefits

The stronger the grip an official future has on an organization, the more ridiculous alternative futures may appear. But this makes alternatives all the more necessary, since an organization that believes only in its official future incurs great risk, and will be mightily surprised when that future does not come about. The analyst benefits the organization most when he or she is willing to go out on a limb to challenge the conventional thinking.

Example

Dator (1995) describes several examples of ideas that became foundational but seemed laughable when they first emerged:

- "Before 1776 (or so), the ridiculous ideas about the separation of Church and State espoused by a farmer known as Thomas Jefferson could be dismissed out of hand. Didn't he know that ALL nations (and England's colonies) had Established Religions? How in the world was he going to separate the church from the state, for heaven's sake?

- "Before 1819 (or so), the idea that a business organization could be considered a 'person' which should be accorded many of the rights that a live human being holds under the US Constitution must certainly have been laughable.

- "Before 1991 (or so), who would have dared believe the Mighty Evil Empire (the former Soviet Union) would crumble and fall with scarcely any bloodshed and without any foreign invasion?"

Further reading

Dator. J. (1995). Newt's Sweet Dreams. Hawaii Research Center for Futures Studies. Viewed June 2005, www.futures.hawaii.edu.

Hawken, P., Ogilvy, J., and Schwartz, P. (1982). *Seven Tomorrows: Towards a Voluntary History*. New York: Bantam Books.

Kelley, T. (2001). *The Art of Innovation: Lessons in Creativity from IDEO, America's Leading Design Firm*. New York: Currency Doubleday.

Koppel, T. (1999, July 13). The Deep Dive. *ABC News Nightline*. New York. ABC News.

4.3.6 Ask the "What If" Questions

Proponents of *systems thinking*, a key concept in strategic foresight, argue that for every intended consequence there is an unintended one. Asking "what if" explores the consequences of choosing one option over others. Organizations are too often surprised, even blindsided, because they have neglected to ask the "what if" questions that would have helped them anticipate a new competitor or product, a change in the market, etc.

Key steps

Asking "what if" questions during visioning is a useful way of assessing how important each proposed option is to the organization. For example, if the question "What if we choose not to adopt this idea?" is applied to a proposed option, and the answer comes back that it won't make much of a difference, the proposed option should be de-prioritized. If the answer is that it would make a huge difference, obviously the option should move up in priority.

Asking "what if" questions is not complicated. Analysts should build them into strategic foresight activities. For a proposed strategic direction, for instance, one might ask, "What if we implement this direction?" or "What if we don't?"

Benefits

The benefit of "what if" questions is that they can identify gaps in knowledge as well as potential opportunities and obstacles. Moreover, the practice creates a mindset of openness to possibilities, helping to avoid locking into a solution too early or failing to consider the full range of options (see *Guideline 3.3.10 Avoid Early Convergence of Ideas*). Asking "what if" thus improves the odds that the organization will avoid being victimized by a major surprise. Finally, the process of thinking through these questions prepares the organization to act when a big change does occur.

Example

Peter Schwartz (1991) elucidates the risk of not asking "what if" questions. In the mid-1970s, the US Census Bureau predicted births in the United States would remain at a steady three million per year. Administrators in educational institutions, relying on this information, decided to cut back on plans for new school buildings, and some even closed existing schools. By relying solely on an extrapolation of historical data and failing to ask "what if," both the Census Bureau and educational planners failed to consider what would happen if a majority of the baby boomers decided to have children. The boomers did produce an "echo boom," driving up the birthrate towards the end of the 1970s, and schools across the country had to construct modular classrooms as a stopgap measure until new buildings could be erected or existing ones expanded.

One organization that did apply the "what if" approach was the Berklee College of Music (Morrison and Wilson, 1997). As a relatively young school, Berklee decided to develop a strategic plan in order to carve out a preferred future for itself. The college asked questions such as: Will we attract sufficient numbers of students? What enrollment might be anticipated? Can we be financially stable? Will our students require financial aid? Who is likely to be our competition? Could there be relevant changes in music literacy, or in musical tastes?

By addressing issues like these upfront, Berklee was able to prepare for possible changes in its future—strong vs. modest enrollment, significant vs. minimal competition, etc. The exercise led to a shared vision for the college, and a sense of commitment among the staff.

Further reading

Morrison, J.L., and Wilson, I. (1997). Analyzing Environments and Developing Scenarios in Uncertain Times. In M.W. Peterson, D.D. Dill, L.A. Mets, and Associates, eds. *Planning and Management for a Changing Environment*. San Francisco: Jossey-Bass.

Schwartz, P. (1991). *The Art of the Long View: Planning for the Future in an Uncertain World*. New York: Currency Doubleday.

4.3.7 Sense and Enable the Emerging Future

Most visioning methods draw heavily on the past to inform the vision of the future. An alternative approach—*presencing*—advocated by Senge et al. (2004) is to work backward from the future and sense what "wants to emerge." Once the emergent future is sensed, it can be actualized or addressed in the present. The approach draws heavily upon intuitive techniques to help organizations visualize and realize the futures they would most like to see—acknowledging the past, but not being handcuffed by it.

Key steps

Presencing, as elaborated by Scharmer (2002), incorporates three distinct activities:

- sensing the external environment
- sensing the potential within oneself
- bringing this future potential into action

The first step is to sense emerging opportunities in the environment before they manifest as empirical data. This draws upon the various environmental-scanning techniques covered in *2.0 Scanning* for identifying weak signals of change.

Next is to sense the potential in oneself. Scharmer believes individuals can train themselves in various techniques for enhancing intuition, to bring forth insights that escape routine data-analysis techniques. It involves letting go of preconceived notions about the future and opening oneself up to alternative possibilities. While this is done at an individual level, the individual insights are brought to the group's attention using various dialoguing techniques. Markley (1998) has identified several techniques appropriate to this realm. In general, these techniques draw upon psychology and other fields to identify and sense individual potential.

Finally, the future potential is brought into reality by enacting emerging futures. Insights from scanning the environment are brought together with the insights from the intuitive techniques and subsequent dialogue, to identify a potential or emerging future for the organization. *Action research* (Stringer, 1996) provides techniques for bringing the emerging future to fruition.

Benefits

Scharmer suggests several benefits from moving through the presencing process. First, it inverts the organization's thinking from "being bound by judgmental reactions to opening up one's thoughts as a gateway to perception and apprehension." Put more simply, it gets individuals and organizations past the obvious and familiar objections to more creative possibilities regarding the future.

Second, it inverts the organization's feelings. It gets past the emotional reactions holding back the organization from trying something new, e.g., "We could never do that," or "That's not the way things are done around here." It goes beyond surface-level reactions to access deeper levels of perception and apprehension, accessing the organization's "emotional intelligence."

Third, it inverts the will of the organization, releasing it from the past. Many organizations are practically prisoners of their past. New ideas are shot down merely because they threaten an organizational identity that may have been built up over decades. With presencing, new ideas and potential identities are allowed to emerge.

Example

Chunghwa Post, a state-run communications agency in Taiwan with 30,000 employees, used presencing to transition from a government agency to a private corporation. The firm used a six-step presencing process:

1. Learning about presencing

2. Sharing stories of organizational learning and analysis of reality

3. Sharing knowledge

4. Team and leadership building

5. Undertaking the change process

6. Verification

Three years after the exercise, the organizers reported employee attitudes had changed "from being passive to active." The firm says it has received high rankings in customer satisfaction and that its overall operating performance has improved 12% annually, with additional increases in operational profits, profit contribution to the state, and employee performance. The benefits of employee learning have increased an estimated fivefold, as demonstrated by an increase in professional certifications and more than thirty new products and services.

Further reading

Markley, O.W. (1998, November/December). Visionary Futures: Guided Cognitive Imagery in Teaching and Learning about the Future. *American Behavioral Scientist, 42* (3), 522 - 530.

Scharmer, C.O. (2002, August). *Presencing: Illuminating the Blind Spot of Leadership*. Draft manuscript, viewed May 2005, www.ottoscharmer.com.

Senge, P., Scharmer, C.O., Jaworski, J. and Flowers, B.S. (2004). *Presence: Human Purpose and the Field of the Future*. Cambridge, MA: Society for Organizational Learning.

Shih, P.C. (2005). Creating a Government Organizational Learning Using the Presence Process. Presentation to Society for Organizational Learning, Global Forum 2005. Viewed May 2006, www.solonline.org/repository/download/CreatingaGovernmentPercy.ppt?item_id=8897432.

Stringer, E.T. (1996). *Action Research: A Handbook for Practitioners*. Thousand Oaks, CA: Sage Publications.

5 ▶ Planning

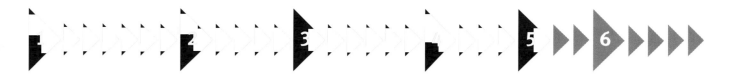

5.0 Planning

"Plan your work. Work your plan." —John Wooden

Planning is the bridge between the vision and action. The analysis team translates the vision into a strategy consisting of tactics leading directly to action. Thus the foresight activity returns from the realm of the long-term, big-picture future to the present, providing the organization with a roadmap of how it can get from where it currently is to where it would like to be in the future regarding the issue at hand.

The first set of Planning guidelines, *5.1 Think Strategically*, is about translating the vision and alternative future possibilities into strategy. The analyst's task here is to help the organization understand what could happen—the alternative futures—compared to what it would like to see happen—the vision—and show the difference between the two. How wide is the gap? The organization needs to recognize the degree of effort it is likely to face in realizing its preferred future, given the multiple potential futures. In some cases the gap will be manageable, while in others it may seem insurmountable. The analyst must keep the organization motivated when the odds of success look poor, for instance by pointing out the consequences of not acting. That said, the analyst should not always be an advocate for change, but rather an advocate for making the decision to act or not act in the full light of the likely alternative futures.

The second set, *5.2 Develop Strategic Options*, recognizes the uncertainty of the future and the need to develop contingency plans. The challenge here is to avoid the temptation to lock onto what the organization considers the best option—and ignore the rest. After spending time dealing in possibilities and uncertainties, there is a natural desire to want to "get down to business." The challenge is to demonstrate that considering a range of options does not mean inaction, but rather maintaining a robust, flexible approach.

5.1 Think Strategically

5.1.1 Enable Emergence

Emergence can occur when the parts of any system, interacting via simple rules, lead to surprising or unexpected results. It occurs in such diverse systems as stock markets, traffic patterns, and the human brain. Murray Gell-Mann in *The Quark and the Jaguar* (1994) characterizes the essence of emergence: "Structure arises without the imposition of special requirements from the outside. In an astonishing variety of contexts, apparently complex structures of behaviors emerge from systems characterized by simple rules."

Organizations that utilize emergence—and the management principles that encourage it—may be rewarded with more robust strategies as well as more innovation. Emergence depends on many of the same business practices that foster innovation, such as modular (rather than hierarchical) organization and a high level of interaction among business units. Strategic conversations, too, can be stronger thanks to a wide variety of grassroots inputs and a greater sense of investment by stakeholders.

Emergence can be cultivated, but not constructed as if from a recipe. No ten-step plan will automatically create emergence. Rather, it is based on a set of scientific metaphors, which can be kept in mind when crafting a strategic foresight activity. For instance, the way the components of an organization are structured can encourage emergent strategies. When developing a strategy, the analyst must think of how the strategy impacts the structure of the organization and vice versa. To attain the synergistic effects of emergence, strategy and organizational structure must evolve together.

Key steps

Analysts can take two actions to help an organization achieve emergence. The first is to identify the building blocks of the organization. These are the simplest unit of the business, whether individuals, workgroups, or project teams. By analogy, the simplest unit of the brain is a neuron; of an ant colony, an ant; of a stock market, a single trader or stock. If these basic units are not evident in the organizational structure, the organization might consider rearranging into a more modular structure. Rigid hierarchies and chains tend to be less conducive to the development of emergent strategies.

The second action is to map out and understand the rules that the organizational building blocks use to interact, collaborate, and communicate. Emergence comes from the pattern of interactions among the parts of a system, not from the sum of their individual achievements. If the organization is over-managed, emergence cannot occur. The goal for the analyst is to help foster and develop interaction, not dictate it. Let communication patterns evolve naturally. By having a modular organization, understanding the connections between the pieces, and encouraging lots of simple interactions, emergent strategies are more likely to occur within a business or organization.

Benefits

A number of benefits can be achieved by allowing business strategies to emerge from the interactions of various components in an organization, rather than dictating them top-down. It promotes more robust strategies, grassroots innovation, and a diversity of ideas.

What makes a strategy that emerges from the bottom up better than one from a specialized department, or from leadership? The first benefit of an "emergent organization" is the diversity of ideas that can be generated. Instead of assembling a team of stakeholders to devise a uniform strategy, this approach allows individual components of the organization to interact with as many other components as possible, creating dozens of possible strategies. While many will not succeed on their own, the organization is able to hedge its bets by examining as many strategies as possible and enabling the fittest one to survive. A side benefit of this is trust in the organization, since the individual parts now have a vested interest in the process.

The second benefit is more robust strategies. A business strategy needs to be successful in a number of potential business environments. Engineering a strategy from one individual's (or one group's) mental model yields a blueprint that can be successful in only a limited range of scenarios. By enabling multiple strategies to evolve across the organization, the organization as a whole is more likely to be viable across multiple possible business futures.

Example

An example of strategy emergence by the US Army in Iraq is chronicled by James Surowiecki (2004) in *The Wisdom of Crowds*. Every major military operation begins with a well-crafted, well-reviewed strategy. However, once war begins, the fog and friction of battle quickly create new conditions to which the forces must adapt. The US Army's strategy for Iraq was premised on encountering much greater resistance from the Iraqi forces during the initial invasion than it actually found. A new strategy had to be quickly developed. Since local commanders had more autonomy and responsibility than the Iraqi commanders did, as well as access to advanced communication systems, they were able to convey site-specific knowledge about the changing landscape throughout the personnel network. It was these interactions among the smaller units that created the new strategies for success during that phase of the operation.

Further reading

Gell-Mann, M. (1994). *The Quark and the Jaguar: Adventures in the Simple and the Complex*. New York: W.H. Freeman & Company.

Holland, J.H. (1998). *Emergence: From Chaos to Order*. New York: Perseus Books.

Johnson, S. (2001). *Emergence: The Connected Lives of Ants, Brains, Cities, and Software*. New York: Touchstone.

Surowiecki, J. (2004). *The Wisdom of Crowds: Why the Many Are Smarter than the Few and How Collective Wisdom Shapes Business, Economies, Societies, and Nations*. New York: Doubleday.

5.1.2 Make the Sociocultural Context Central

Make the human context central to any strategic foresight activity. Do not be overly enamored with industry analysis, technology, or business trends and forget or overlook the role of people. Many activities produce impressive reams of data but haven't thought through how the people affected would react or respond in the proposed future. Considering different sociocultural contexts can help the organization respond to a wider range of needs—be they demographic, sociological, ethnographic, physiological, psychological, etc.

Key steps

The analyst can help the organization see the importance of the sociocultural context and how it provides the baseline for understanding emerging needs and opportunities. Some leading organizations are forming Consumer or Customer Foresight/Insight programs. For example, Nokia has for about ten years been proactively using consumer foresight inputs in its development processes. These inputs are woven into the product development, design, and foresight/insight programs. This approach has been cited as one of the fundamental elements in Nokia's improved position in the mobile phone market in the 1990s. (Steinbock, 2001)

Consumer-centered programs start with identifying trends in the cultural, sociological, psychological, ethnographic, and demographic arenas and exploring their implications for various organizational activities. In other cases, organizations hire firms to help them get a feel for what is going on, ranging from very deep explorations of the cultural context, using tools such as Integral Futures (Slaughter, 2003) or Causal Layered Analysis (Inayatullah, 2004), to the more surface-level approaches epitomized by "cool hunting."

Several steps need to be followed in providing a cultural context for foresight work. A multidisciplinary "SWAT team" could be established with the skills to understand people, decision-making contexts, and the output context. The team collects trends either by searching themselves or working with one of the many capable brokers of trend information. Next, they analyze and prioritize the impacts of these trends. This information can then be communicated to the critical business processes where it is needed.

Benefits

Grounding the activity in an understanding of human behaviors and societal drivers is an underutilized approach. "Mainstream economics today views production as valuable primarily as a means to satisfy the needs and wants of consumers, but has taken a simple—some say, simplistic—approach to identifying those needs and wants." (Goodwin, Ackerman, and Kiron, 1995, p. 31). Or as Farrell (1998, p. 14) suggests, "In business, waves of demand must be actively surfed, with an acute knowledge of whether the wave is building up or moving into churning, energy-wasting whitewater. The essence of a good ride is knowing when to get in and out and maximizing one's advantage along the way."

Understanding emerging needs as an element of the organization's business system is crucial to right-timing its outputs and hence benefiting commercially. A challenge is that sociocultural inputs tend to be sourced with traditional market-research methods, which mostly highlight existing norms, values, and thoughts and overlook shifting contexts.

Example

The Beta vs. VHS competition among videotape manufacturers highlights the importance of correctly interpreting the sociocultural context. The Beta format focused on superior technical quality, while VHS focused on the usability of the technology in the broader context of the media industry and its customers. VHS won that battle. One fundamental problem with Beta was that it could not accommodate the length of a movie.

Another good example of inadequately considering sociocultural trends was the case of Nike and its production facilities in less-developed nations. After some of its contractors were found underpaying workers and using child labor, Nike suffered a media backlash and a slew of legal cases. The company's phenomenal growth in profits in the late 1990s took a hard hit. Consumer backlashes can have devastating consequences, as Nike found.

Further reading

Beyer, H. and Holtzblatt, K. (1998). *Contextual Design: Defining Customer-Centered Systems*. Oxford, UK: Morgan Kaufman.

Farrell, W. (1998). *How Hits Happen*. New York: HarperBusiness.

Goodwin, N., Ackerman, F., and Kiron, D. (1997). *The Consumer Society*. Chicago, IL: Island Press.

Inayatullah, S., ed. (2004). *The Causal Layered Analysis (CLA) Reader: Theory and Case Studies of an Integrative and Transformative Methodology*. Taipei: Tamkang University Press.

Marsh, N., McAllum, M., and Purcell, D. (2002). *Strategic Foresight: The Power of Standing in the Future*. Melbourne: Crown Content.

Slaughter, R. (2003). Integral Futures: A New Model for Futures Enquiry and Practice. In *Futures beyond Dystopia: Creating Social Foresight*. London: Routledge. (Available at www.foresightinternational.com.au)

Steinbock, D. (2001). *The Nokia Revolution: Success Factors of an Extraordinary Company*. New York: AMACOM.

5.1.3 Crafting Strategy Is About Stimulating Strategic Conversation

Strategic foresight is aimed at influencing an organization's strategy. Organizational theory, change management, and related disciplines suggest that changing strategy must be preceded by a change in the minds of decision-makers. Thus, *Guideline 1.3.2 Seek to Improve the Mental Model of Decision-makers* suggests that the fundamental purpose of strategic foresight is to influence the mental model of decision-makers. This guideline suggests that decision-makers' mental models are, in turn, influenced by the strategic conversations that take place in the organization. Therefore, a key objective of strategic foresight is to lay the groundwork for great strategic conversations.

A strategic foresight activity will uncover key issues concerning the organization's future that ought to enter the strategic conversation. The analyst should work to seed these conversations with important issues. Successful strategic foresight thus creates a buzz that is reflected not only in formal presentations, but also in the water-cooler discussions that are critical to shaping the organization's thinking.

Key steps

Kees van der Heijden (1996) suggests three steps for improving the strategic conversation. He advocates scenario planning as an excellent tool for framing this effort.

- First, the mental models of the organizations need to be surfaced through interviewing. These interviews will elicit the strategic agenda, as well as raising awareness that multiple views exist within the organization.
- These views can then be "scaffolded" by connecting and integrating them. Often, initial observations that appear

to have meaning and importance are not well-articulated or integrated; the analyst can help synthesize them into a wider body of codified knowledge that is clearly articulated, well-understood, and of direct use in decision-making. Accomplishing this requires good facilitation and process design.

- In particular, the facilitator needs to know how to employ the scaffolding process. The conversation should be facilitated—not chaired—and group dynamics optimized. In formal settings, the analyst needs either to be an experienced facilitator or to bring one in.

Van der Heijden offers several additional tips for guiding the strategic conversation. For instance, where the conversation ends up is important—but even more important is ensuring that views are expressed and ultimately converge. It is also recommended to avoid normative thinking (what an individual wants to happen) and instead focus on what might happen. At the same time, acknowledge personal vulnerabilities—be aware that some views may be seen as threatening by some people. The analyst should ensure the group acknowledges uncertainty and different worldviews, and that it explores possibilities by trying out new ideas and metaphors. Disasters and crises should be framed not as threats but as learning devices.

Benefits

Organizations tend to approach the future by relying on recipes that have worked well in the past. This biases their thinking towards the past and the tried-and-true. While this works well when the organizational context is stable and continuous with the past, it does not work well when the context is changing. And in the current global milieu, most organizations' contexts are characterized far more by turbulence and change than by stability and continuity. Emphasizing the importance of the strategic conversation enables organizations to engage critical issues, which in turn improves decision-making during strategy-making, as well as increasing the chances that the strategic foresight will be acted upon.

A caveat in crafting great conversations is suggested by Inayatullah (2000): "Attempts to create new futures can undermine current power structures. Administrators only agree to consider the future to gain new political alliances, to achieve modernity, [or] to gain funding or prestige, but rarely to make changes in institutional structure or consciousness." In other words, getting organizations to make fundamental changes is a very tricky business, unless they can be shown either that such changes are unavoidable or that the organizational profits will be boosted by implementing them.

Example

Arie de Gues (2002) recounts the story of his famous research project at Shell, which found that the average life expectancy of Fortune 500 firms was only forty to fifty years. The study also found many companies that were over two hundred years old. Three of the factors cited as instrumental to corporate longevity were related to excellent strategic conversations:

- Long-lived companies are sensitive to their environments, with the ability to learn and adapt.
- They are cohesive, with a strong sense of identity.
- They are tolerant, particularly of activities on the margins.

De Gues adds, "[learning's] essence was to change one's internal structure to remain in harmony with a changed environment." Organizations that are capable of learning are capable of changing their mental models in response to a changing environment.

Further reading

De Gues, A. (2002). *The Living Company*. Cambridge, MA: Harvard Business School.

Inayatullah, S. (2005). Methods and Epistemologies in Futures Studies. In *The Knowledge Base of Futures Studies, Vol. 2*. (R. Slaughter, ed.). (Professional Edition CD-ROM). Indooroopilly, Australia: Foresight International. (Available at www.foresightinternational.com.au)

Van der Heijden, K. (1996). *Scenarios: The Art of Strategic Conversations*. New York: Wiley.

Van der Heijden, K. (2002). *The Sixth Sense: Accelerating Organizational Learning with Scenarios*. New York: Wiley.

5.1.4 Know What to Change and What Not to Change

Strategic foresight is most interested in what will change. Analysts see change as part of progress, and expect and even want it to happen. On the downside, this can blind analysts to knowing what to conserve. But what is conserved determines what is free to be changed, and makes possible alternative futures.

The common phrase "Nothing stays the same" is a bit of hyperbole. Some things do stay the same for extended periods—e.g., language, beliefs, or values—although these too change over time. Likewise, "If it ain't broke, don't fix it," suggests that current success will continue unimpeded. This is equally exaggerated—and more pernicious, because it can lull an organization into complacency. Changes in the external environment mean that a strategy that worked years ago, and seems to be working still, is becoming increasingly obsolete with each passing year.

Key steps

This guideline is particularly relevant when an organization is overwhelmed by change. When an organization feels afflicted by change, or sees an urgent need to somehow "manage" it, taking a lateral step can help: flipping the thought process from a focus on change to a focus on conservation. By surrendering to what cannot be controlled, the organization can find new power in choosing what should be conserved.

The skill is in deciding what to keep and what to change. For that, knowledge of the emerging environment and its implications for the organization are required. While acknowledging that the environment is changing and the organization's strategy needs to be revised, the analyst first needs to see—and to help others see—that a preoccupation with "what will change" could lead to futures that nobody will want.

The second step is to ask, "What has been conserved that gives this organization its unique present?" The organization's history should be revisited (see *Guideline 2.2 Study History* for suggestions). Nearly always, employees will portray the organization's history as a series of events that led inexorably to this unique present; but in reality history is never predestined—it is a singular dynamic between transformation and conservation. When someone says their organization has existed since 1920, what they are really saying is that something has been conserved. That something could be purely the name, or it could be the technology, the culture, the market, etc. If nothing is conserved, then history and the future both disappear.

Thus, the question for the organization is, "What should we conserve so that our history continues into the future?" The critical choice is what should and should not be conserved, with the consequences of conserving or not conserving worked through for each element. The future, in this instance, is an image of what remains and what is absent from today's unique present.

Next, emphasize the "how" of conservation: by what means, and what are the obstacles and the opportunities?

Benefits

Focusing on what not to change is empowering. The future is unknowable and teams and individuals can feel impotent to affect it. This approach flips that dynamic: rather than focusing on something unknowable, it draws attention to what people do know—how they got here. They now have something that they can deal with.

Empowerment in turn generates a heightened sense of responsibility and investment. Choices about what should and should not be conserved in the present are now felt to be critical to the organization's future health and identity. There is also a sense of gratitude and collegiality for the predecessors who conserved certain things that today's stakeholders have stewardship of.

The most obvious pitfall of not following this process is a failure to conserve something fundamental to the organization's identity. The net effect is to wipe out that aspect in the minds of the people who now comprise the organization.

Example

Maintaining a viable organization requires a strategy that is in touch with the world as it is today, not as it was yesterday. According to Jack Welch, GE's former CEO, "We've long believed that when the rate of change inside an institution becomes slower than the rate of change outside, the end is in sight. The only question is when." Welch also observed: "After all the hype, it's really big old companies like GE that will reap the biggest benefits of the Internet." (McGinn, 2000) Other companies that have known what to change, and what not to, include: IBM, shifting from manufacturing to services; Kroger, moving ahead of A&P with the superstore; Wal-Mart, moving ahead of everyone with just-in-time inventory; and Microsoft, after Netscape.

Further reading

Beck, D. and Cowan, C. (1996). *Spiral Dynamics*. Oxford, UK: Blackwell.

Maturana, H. and Bunnell, P. (1999). The Biology of Business: Transformation through Conservation. *Reflections*, (1), 82 - 86.

McGinn, D. (2000, December). Jack Welch Goes Surfing. *Newsweek*.

Welch, J.F., Jr. et al. (2000). Letter to Share Owners. *GE 2000 Annual Report*. Viewed May 2005, www.ge.com/annual00/letter/page2.html.

5.1.5 Spot Areas of Strategic Choice by Identifying Critical Branching Points

A challenge for strategic foresight is to help organizations achieve or maintain a good fit with the strategic landscape—a key factor in how well they can anticipate and respond to transformational changes. Seen through an ecological lens, fitness entails searching an enormous landscape (or *possibility space*) to identify and respond to *branching points* quickly enough to avoid extinction. Branching points are especially useful to consider if an organization's strategic landscape is highly interconnected and erratic or volatile. All too often, organizations suffer by focusing on day-to-day problems while neglecting the larger landscape—i.e., clearing the rocks from the trail rather than turning off a trail that's about to peter out, onto the one that continues up the mountain.

In the early days of just-in-time manufacturing, experts could simply walk around a manufacturing facility and quickly identify areas where improvements could save millions of dollars in costs. A deep and broad understanding of the environment gave them an inherent gut feel for the critical influence points. Understanding the strategic landscape similarly enables identifying critical influence points.

Key steps

To identify critical branching points, one approach is to build a schematic of the evolving fitness environment. The map should identify pathways that include opposite possibilities, or branching points, in the evolution of impacts and outcomes. The pathways should offer a view of different ways the future may play out. Michel Godet notes, "If we think about it, identifying the range of possible futures... is also recognizing the diagram of bifurcations." Ilya Prigogine's work (1984) on dissipative structures found that when an open system reaches a point which is more complex than its own organizational capabilities, it reaches bifurcations—points at which a system can reorder itself to a new stability.

The Richardson model of international relations has found that in arms races, a point or set of points divides two very different sorts of behavior from each other. From any initial armament level, competing parties will either enter into a runaway arms race or disarm. At times it is clear which way the parties will go. However, very big differences in behavior can result depending on the degree of balance in the overall system. Likewise, a schematic of an organization's fitness environment will include pathways that show how a series of events can lead to a critical branching point. These events tell a story of how the organization gets from here to there, and provide a logic or foundation for setting basic strategic direction.

Branching points are often built around strategic uncertainties. Bear in mind that these alternative possibilities will in many cases contradict or exclude others. This allows consideration not only of likely outcomes, but also of unthinkable ones. Choosing only comfortable outcomes defeats the purpose of the activity.

Benefits

Mapping pathways and branching points that may lie ahead will not only suggest what the organization should do, it will define the things to watch. Branching points of particular strategic interest, i.e., that represent a critical pattern worth exploring, will suggest what matters.

Identifying branching points also aids in understanding the underlying logic that governs the organization's future, influencing its resource flows, employee relations, etc. It can help spot discontinuities that may already be in process— for example, a change in the rate of change, or inflection points that foreshadow significant discontinuities. It allows the organization to better identify choices, and particularly how the options open to it may be circumscribed or broadened.

Finally, this guideline offers another illustration of maps' usefulness for identifying key dimensions of choice. Impressionistic rather than crystalline, maps nonetheless provide enough clarity to be useful. They offer a context for exploring and informing executive debate and decision-making, and may contribute to a shared understanding of, and commitment to, actions.

Example

Andy Grove, former chair of Intel Corp., suggests that strategic inflection points mean full-scale changes in the way business is conducted. Thus, simply adopting new technology or fighting the competition with established methods may be insufficient. He recounts how in the 1980s, Intel's core business of memory chips was in disarray. The company was pouring 40% of its developmental capital spending into the memory-chip business, but it was producing only 3 - 4% of total revenues due to fierce Japanese competition. Intel had reached a strategic inflection point. Fortunately, it had investments in microprocessors, secondary though these were. Intel decided to give up the memory business and commit to micro-processors. Grove notes, "It was a very dramatic, complete shift of emphasis, and it entailed a very major retrenchment to resize the company; roughly speaking, one-third of the company was shut down and laid off, with factories closing and all of that. And then the PC really took off, and we were positioned to benefit from that, and the rest is history."

Further reading

Collins, J. (2001). *Good to Great*. New York: HarperCollins Publishers.

Godet, M. (2001). *Creating Futures: Scenario Planning as a Strategic Management Tool*. Plymouth, UK: Economica Ltd.

Grove, A.S. (1996). *Only the Paranoid Survive*. New York: Currency Doubleday.

Heilemann, J. (2001, June). Andy Grove's Rational Exuberance. *Wired*.

Mintzberg, H. (2003). Strategic Thinking as Seeing. In B. Garratt, ed. *Developing Strategic Thought: A Collection of the Best Thinking on Business Strategy*, London: Profile Books.

Prigogine, I. and Stenger, I. (1984). *Order Out of Chaos: Man's New Dialogue with Nature*. New York: Bantam.

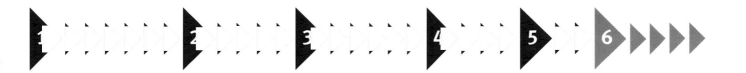

5.2 Develop Strategic Options

5.2.1 Base Strategic Recommendations on the Organization's Distinctive Attributes

While strategic foresight emphasizes the external environment, the analyst also needs to be aware of the organization's internal strengths. Strategy needs to be built on an organization's core resources and capabilities. It should be designed from the inside out. Every organization possesses unique qualities, which yield outcomes its customers value, and which cannot be economically imitated or effectively substituted by the competition. Analysts need to be constantly on the lookout for these unique qualities or resources when performing a strategic foresight activity. They may surface in analyses of operations, discussions with customers, partners, and suppliers, or even evaluations of units, departments, or individual employees.

Key steps

Determine how the organization is truly unique and try to connect that with something a customer wants. The differences can only be valuable in a competitive context if they are hard for rivals to imitate economically, and if customers are willing to pay something extra for them. Unique abilities can be surfaced in a number of ways. An analysis of the strengths and weaknesses of the competition can suggest how the organization stacks up—in client reactions, efficiency, renewal, industry best practices, unusual capabilities, etc. These analyses need to be performed on an ongoing basis.

But it is only by then looking inside, at the internal operations, that sources of potential greatness can be found. These may come from looking at units, operations, and product or service characteristics that outperform. But not necessarily. The most important information can often be had not by determining in what ways the organization is superior, but by finding out how it is inimitably unique and then turning that uniqueness into a source of something especially valuable for customers. One step in doing this is to identify the types of activities or outputs the uniqueness engenders, then exploring which kinds of clients would value that output.

Benefits

Imitating the best practices of others is notoriously difficult. First, a good deal of art, chance, rare resources, and uncertainty go into a competitor's success—often making imitation impossible. Even if imitation were possible, by the time the firm succeeded at it, the rival will often have progressed out of harm's way. Second, even if an activity can be easily imitated, its value will soon be competed away. Thus it is far better to look inside the organization for sources of inimitable uniqueness, figure out how to turn that uniqueness into something valuable for a viable market, and structure the organization's priorities and administrative systems to exploit that uniqueness and turn it into a core competency. This is the most important reason analysts should work with the organization's core capabilities.

Moreover, once the unique competency is built, it can be leveraged across different products and markets. This tends to allow that competency to reap greater rewards, which in turn can be used to further deepen and extend the competency. That keeps it relevant in a changing environment and forestalls imitation.

Example

Citibank owned a network of international banks which took many decades to build. No other banking company had that resource, nor could they create it within a reasonable time. But Citibank's international unit was losing a lot of money. It was unique but not valuable, in large part because the unit was not targeting the right clients nor organizing and rewarding its people appropriately for serving those clients. So CEO John Reed reorganized to go after the large, multinational cross-border clients that its international bank network was uniquely able to serve, and from whom it could make the most revenue. Then, it reorganized to favor those clients over the local clients by giving their account managers far more authority to cooperate with the bankers in the foreign offices. It also set up account teams for the cross-border clients that provided seamless service around the world—so Citibank could "deliver Citi to Coke in Khazakstan." Within eighteen months, the international division had turned enormous losses into an enormous profit.

Further reading

Miller, D., Eisenstat, R., and Foote, N. (2002, Spring). Strategy from the Inside Out. *California Management Review, 44,* 37 - 54. Reprinted in B. DeWit and R. Meyer, eds. (2004). *Strategy: Process, Content, and Context.* (3rd ed.)

Miller, D. (2003, October). An Asymmetry-Based View of Advantage. *Strategic Management Journal, 24,* 961 - 976.

5.2.2 Evaluate Proposed Strategy along Multiple Dimensions

Before implementing a strategy, it should first be evaluated among multiple dimensions. Strategy embodies a complex range of factors, and it may be inaccurately viewed as favorable or unfavorable if considered from a narrow perspective. Factors such as multiple performance measures, stakeholder perspectives, and timeframes need to be considered. For example, if a strategy is evaluated only on how well it performs after three years, its excellent performance after five years might be missed. Similarly, if one group of stakeholders is relied upon for its view of a strategy, favorable or unfavorable reactions from another stakeholder group are missed.

It is good practice to check up on the strategy as often as practical during its formulation, but the major work comes after it has been created and before it has been launched. After launch, fixing any mistakes will be much more costly.

Key steps

The evaluation criteria for a strategy are best set at the beginning of a strategic foresight activity, and designed to support the activity's objectives. This will help keep the eventual evaluation objective and provide the analyst and the organization with a framework for deciding whether to modify or move forward with the strategy that has subsequently been developed. If the evaluation criteria are not developed until the end of the activity, it might be tempting to tailor them to support the results—thus losing the value of doing the evaluation in the first place.

Each objective should have at least one criterion that suggests to the analyst whether an adjustment is necessary. In some cases, more than one criterion may be needed to capture the multiple dimensions of the strategy. The timeframe, for example, might include criteria that indicate how well the strategy is likely to do in the short, medium, and long term.

Although there are likely to be multiple criteria, each one should be as simple as possible. Organizations are prone to over-thinking the criteria and losing sight of their purpose, namely to provide useful feedback. Hours can be wasted quibbling over numbers or trying to attain precision, where a simple "high, medium, or low" may do. The goal is to be able to tell whether the strategy is likely to work as intended—not to create sophisticated evaluation criteria.

As the strategy is evaluated according to the criteria, it may be helpful to have outsiders participate to provide a more objective view. A challenge for the analysis team to be wary of here is becoming defensive about the results it has produced. In the long run, the team will be better served by listening open-mindedly to a difficult evaluation and giving due consideration to the suggested revisions. The team should then make any necessary adjustments before moving forward.

Benefits

Evaluating strategy along multiple dimensions will provide the most robust feedback and increase the odds of success. It counteracts the common tendency among organizations to define "sound strategy" too narrowly—seeing the landscape in conventional terms, as they have always seen things, and failing to consider potentially important new dimensions. It also helps to minimize the chances of being blindsided by an unexpected development in the future. Exploring multiple dimensions lends richness to the activity, helping to account for the widest range of possibilities and providing the most robust outcome.

Example

Long-distance phone companies failed to see beyond the industry price wars that commanded their attention in the 1990s, and missed the competitive implications of the rapid growth of the Internet. Trapped in one-upping their traditional competitors, they failed to perceive the Internet as an entirely new kind of competitor. A limited timeframe may have contributed to this oversight: strategic timeframes were compressed to focus on the short term, whereas the Internet represented a medium- or long-term threat. As a result, these former giants of industry are now either gone, bought out, or limping along as shells of their former selves.

Further reading

Amram, M. and Kulatilaka, N. (1999). *Real Options: Managing Strategic Investments in an Uncertain World*. Oxford, UK: Oxford University Press.

Miles, R.E. and Snow, C.C. (2003). *Organizational Strategy, Structure, and Process*. Palo Alto, CA: Stanford University Press.

Schoemaker, P. (1992, Fall). How to Link Strategic Vision to Core Capabilities. *Sloan Management Review*.

5.2.3 Include the "No-Go," the "Most Plausible," and the "Preferred" When Recommending Options

Most strategic foresight activities ultimately must provide guidance to decision-makers. What should be done as a result of the learning from the activity?

Recommendations should ideally include a no-go, most plausible, and preferred option. In other words, the analyst should advise what to avoid, what is most likely to happen, and what to work towards.

Key steps

A tool for helping delineate these kinds of options is the *Issues Paper*, developed by senior public policy analysts in Canada to provide top-level politicians, executives, and sector representatives with a succinct decision-making tool. It examines the strengths, weaknesses, opportunities, and threats relative to not doing anything, the preferred option, and at least one plausible preferred option.

The Issues Paper format is designed for easy skimming, usually no more than two pages long and with further detail included in attachments. The format includes:

- *Issue*: Succinctly describe the issue (two or three lines maximum).

- *Background*: Provide pertinent history on the past and present circumstances relative to the issue (e.g. stakeholders, goals and objectives, previous actions, lessons learned, and other relevant considerations). This should be in point form with bullets.

- *Options*: Describe three or four options (scenarios) that seem plausible and possible. Analyze the strengths, weaknesses, opportunities, and threats (SWOT) of each of the options. Include a:
  - "No Option"—What would happen if the organization stayed its present course?
  - "Preferred Option"—If considerations such as cost were not a big factor, what would be the best possible solution?
  - "Plausible Preferred Option"—Anticipating barriers to the preferred option, what might be good alternatives?
  - "Other Options"—Often, a solution proposed by a particular vested interest.

- *Recommendation*: Describe the preferred option for responsible action (a two- to three-line summary statement). A strong case for this option should have already been made in the Options section analysis.

- *Recommendation Rationale*: Utilize the six "W Questions." Why? (how this recommendation furthers the organization's vision, goals, objectives) What? (key elements) Who? (approvals, stakeholders, planners, implementers, evaluators) Where? (simulation, pilot test, general application). When? (implementation schedule) How? (Action Plan: Steps, Schedule, and Overcoming Barriers)

Benefits

The Issues Paper approach is useful in all situations where public, corporate, and NGO executives with limited time need to be able to make informed contributions to the debate and decisions relative to particular issues. A number of Issues Papers can be easily slipped into a briefcase for reading in a taxi or on a plane. One of the most important uses of the Issues Paper approach is to focus the issue and provide a context for the further development of policy options. It ensures a common basis of understanding for major sectoral discussions.

Example

The Issues Paper approach is now a widely used tool in public policy development in Canada, recognized as an effective instrument for analyses of context and development of policy options for both crisis management and ongoing policy development. In 1992, the once-abundant stocks of Northern codfish off the coast of Newfoundland collapsed from overfishing, and the Canadian government placed a moratorium on fishing them. Some 19,000 fishers and plant workers were directly affected and up to 20,000 other jobs were lost or harmed in the economic backwash (Steele, Andersen, and Green, 1992). For rural Newfoundland, this was especially devastating as cod-fishing had been the economic backbone of hundreds of communities. Numerous issues had to be considered, such as community adjustment, income maintenance, longer-term survival of the fishing industry, the reliability of the science, overfishing, international poaching, destructive fishing equipment, underutilized species, and even the impact of seals on the cod stocks. The Issues Paper approach proved handy to policymakers for quickly grasping both the issues and the options available.

Further reading

Burton, L.E. (1988, February). *Report of the Industry Committee of the National Advisory Board on Science and Technology to the Prime Minister*. (Fraser Mustard, Chair). Ottawa: Ministry of State for Science & Technology.

Burton, L.E. (1989, May 15). Report of the Private-Sector Challenge Committee of the National Advisory Board on Science and Technology to the Prime Minister (Robert Alexander, Chair). In *Keeping Canada Competitive: The Innovation Imperative*. Ottawa: Ministry of State for Science & Technology.

Burton, L.E. and Ferguson, J. (1991, April). Report of the Human Resource Development Committee of the National Advisory Board on Science and Technology to the Prime Minister (Hugh Wynne-Edwards, Chair). *In Learning to Win: Education, Training, and National Prosperity*. Ottawa: Ministry of State for Science & Technology.

Burton, L.E. (1999). *Guidelines for the Use of an Issues Paper Approach*. (Unpublished). Burnaby: Simon Fraser University.

Steele, D.H., Andersen, R., and Green, J.M. (1992). The Managed Commercial Annihilation of Northern Cod. *Newfoundland Studies, 8* (1), 34 - 68.

5.2.4 Have Contingency Plans for Surprises

"Probably something improbable will happen," said Aristotle. Similarly, a truism in strategic foresight is that "The surprise-free future is the most unlikely future." While surprises by definition cannot be foreseen, understanding that surprises are the norm rather than the exception can be extremely helpful. Thus, strategy recommendations need to be made robust by developing contingency plans for surprising events and developments.

Key steps

The first step in developing contingency plans is to identify possible surprising events. Think of any improbable event that could affect the organization or client. Consider strategic, technological, political, economic, social, and criminal events.

Second, go beyond isolated events to identify possible surprising developments and alternative futures. Scenario building is an excellent tool for imaging unexpected developments that could lead to alternative futures. One simple and effective method is to choose either two or three crucial questions about the future and allow these to function as intersecting axes, forming a simple matrix. For each question, define two extreme answers and place them at either end of that question's axis. Then consider how the extreme answers to one question interact with the extreme answers to the other(s), synthesizing the results into four scenarios of surprising futures (if two questions were used) or eight scenarios (if three questions were used).

Third, understand the vulnerabilities. Vulnerabilities are the parts of the strategy that cannot change quickly. While it is impossible to prepare for all possible surprises, understanding the vulnerable points is a good proxy. Also identify indicators that can provide early warning.

Lastly, for substantial threats, develop preventive and eventual strategies. Two practical ways to deal with contingencies include preventive strategies—i.e., strategies that minimize the probability of the contingency occurring; and eventual strategies—i.e., strategies that can be implemented if the contingency takes place.

When time is too short for a comprehensive analysis of possible surprises, vulnerabilities, and contingencies, ask some key questions: "What if we lose 30% of our revenues within four weeks? What can we do preventively? What can we do eventually when it really happens? Do we have the means to survive such a loss?"

Benefits

It is precisely their low probability that makes surprises and contingencies worth thinking about. Contingency plans boost the robustness of strategies and decisions. They ensure readiness for unexpected futures and help to safeguard against unexpected threats.

One purpose of developing contingency plans is to learn, a priori, to handle and manage situations which otherwise would be unmanageable because of lack of experience or lack of time, or both. Thinking in advance about the impacts and implications of surprises can help the organization respond quickly if a surprise does take place.

Thus, contingency planning can make uncertainty manageable. It enables and encourages decision-makers to identify what they do not know and make reflected judgments about it (Fahey and Randall, 1998). It can also reveal previously unconsidered strategic options and helps conceive of alternative strategies (Wack, 1986).

Example

Numerous organizations have successfully used contingency planning to survive collisions with shocking surprises, while others have foundered. In 1972 Royal Dutch/Shell imagined a scenario in which the price of oil rose to over $6, whereas the actual price was around $2.70. The scenario team analyzed the organization's resulting points of vulnerability and developed contingency plans that, when the oil crisis took place, helped Shell to become the most profitable of the "seven sisters" for more than a decade.

Gillette is known for its competence in razorblades. In some markets where its razors are sold, the word "Gillette" is used as a synonym for razorblade. Why is Gillette conducting research on lasers? Not because it is their core competency, but because it is pursuing a contingency strategy in case laser technology someday replaces conventional razorblades.

Inadequate contingency planning is exemplified by the Maginot Line. After World War I, France's minister of defense André Maginot insisted that France build a strong defense rampart to prevent Germany from attacking its borders again. Unfortunately Maginot, together with the rest of the cabinet, failed to imagine a scenario in which the Germans would invade France through Belgium, as they later did. The Maginot Line, a huge effort, is now regarded as one of the great failures of military planning.

Further reading

Fahey, L. and Randall, R. (1998). *Learning from the Future: Competitive Foresight Scenarios*. New York: Wiley.

Micic, P. (2003). *Der ZukunftsManager*. Munich, Germany: Haufe.

Micic, P. and Marx, A. (2004). *Die Bank von Morgen denken und gestalten*. Eltville, Germany: ADG.

Petersen, John L. (1999). *Out of the Blue: How to Anticipate Big Future Surprises*. Lanham, MD: Madison Books.

Wack, P. (1985, September/October). Scenarios: Uncharted Waters Ahead. *Harvard Business Review*, 73 - 89.

6 ▶ Acting

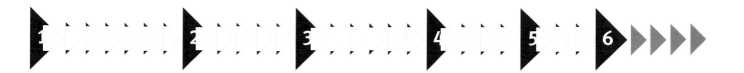

6.0 Acting

"Forewarned is forearmed."

The ultimate purpose of strategic foresight is to make better, more informed decisions in the present. Framing and Scanning establish the work context and knowledgebase to support this goal. Forecasting lays out a range of potential futures to consider. Visioning delineates the preferred future, and Planning lays out a path to that preferred future.

Ultimately, like any organizational activity, strategic foresight must demonstrate a link to the organization's mission, purpose, effectiveness, performance, and bottom line, or it will fall out of favor. Since the payoff for strategic foresight comes down the road, the analyst's challenge at this point is to convince the organization to devote precious resources to a payoff that may seem distant and uncertain. So Acting, the final phase, is largely about communication—making the abstract progressively more concrete. Assuming success and buy-in, the rest of the phase is about translating the plans into concrete actions.

This section also contains guidelines on how to institutionalize strategic foresight in the routines and processes of the organization. One of the traps of foresight is to do it only once, failing to leverage the learning and capabilities developed during earlier projects. An ongoing foresight capability can become an important asset for the organization. Strategic foresight can become a fundamental element of a learning organization, which is essential to success in today's fast-changing environment.

The first set of guidelines, *6.1 Communicate Results*, gets at the important yet often overlooked task of translating the forecast into terms the organization can understand and act upon. The message does not have to be favorable to the organization. In many cases, a challenging or threatening message is the best way to get attention. The key here, nevertheless, is for analysts to understand the organization so well that they can frame the message in terms its stakeholders understand.

The second set, *6.2 Create an Action Agenda*, lays out in concrete steps what the organization needs to do to avoid the undesirable futures and move towards its preferred one. The key here is mapping out plausible pathways so that the organization can see the way forward.

The third set, *6.3 Create an Intelligence System*, begins the process of weaving foresight into the fabric of the organization. The guidelines speak to the fundamental necessity of continually scanning the external environment for indicators of change. Developing an appreciation and capability for continuous and systematic scanning is the fundamental building block of an organizational foresight capability.

The fourth set, *6.4 Institutionalize Strategic Thinking*, extends the capability of building an intelligence system to a wider foresight capability. The analyst here needs to make the case for continuing beyond the present activity, and to convince the organization not only that it can but also that it should treat foresight as a required institutional capability—along with planning and even accounting and finance. A successful outcome to a specific foresight activity, of course, will speak for itself.

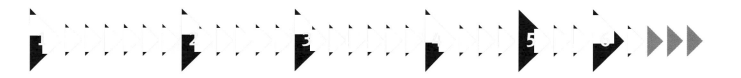

6.1 Communicate Results

6.1.1 Design Results for Communicability

The findings of a strategic foresight activity must be communicated in a way that the organization can understand and act on. Careful attention must be paid to designing a communication plan that meets the organization on its own terms, and in a way that gains the attention of time-strapped executives.

The most important point for communicating a project's results is the final presentation, which needs to be kept in mind from the beginning. A sound communications strategy will be designed in the early stages of the activity. In particular, gauge the organization's communication style—how its members prefer to process information—and provide frequent feedback sessions. This will enable the analyst to test and refine communication approaches.

Key steps

Begin with a formal or informal *chartering* meeting with sponsors and decision-makers to kick off an activity. Chartering (Rosenau et al., 2002) involves specifying and clarifying the expectations of the sponsors and the analysis team about the focus of the activity, how it will be carried out, and what the final deliverables should look like. Going through this process will provide important clues for designing the communication of the ultimate results.

Next, the analyst should plan as many feedback sessions as practical. These sessions will not only allow stakeholders to give feedback on the content, they will also provide further clues on how to design the communication of results in a way that ensures maximum effectiveness.

When the findings of the activity are in, it's important to develop a presentation strategy. The analyst should negotiate for as much—or as little—time as needed. While it will be typical to want more time to get across as much of the results as possible, it sometimes makes sense to tighten and sharpen the message in a shorter time period. Executives in time-stressed organizations will often be grateful for a shorter presentation.

When practical, negotiate the forum for the presentation. A typical boardroom presentation can limit the choices for communication formats, and sometimes it can be intimidating. Analysts who choose a more experiential means of communication, such as a group exercise or even a role-playing, should find more conducive settings that include tables for working, wall space for displays, or space to walk around.

Once the time and place for the presentation are set, spend time going over the communication style of the intended audience. Many analysts make the mistake of simply relying on the style they are most comfortable with, even if it is completely at odds with that of their audience. Analysts should seek to balance their personal style with that of their audience.

If PowerPoint is the required format for the deliverable, the presenter should try to enliven it. Sound or video clips might help bring it to life, for instance. Also, cutting down the number of slides by using handouts of particular details, or even wall posters, will help avoid the monotony of endless slides. Also look for alternative formats, which can help gain attention. Alternative formats could include storytelling, role-playing, workshop activities, videos, simulations, or gaming. Specific mechanisms might include provocative news headlines or broadcasts, or play-acting a situation that forces the decision-makers to grapple with the issues raised by the activity.

Benefits

While it may seem overly time-consuming to spend time upfront chartering the activity, this investment typically reaps dividends during the communication phase. It clarifies the expectations of sponsors and decision-makers and yields insights into how they prefer to process information. Likewise, frequent feedback sessions may seem to chew up time better spent on the activity itself. But these interactions can offer clues to preferred communication styles, and also contribute to buy-in as the organization becomes more and more involved with the activity.

Designing a creative presentation of the activity's results helps cut through the challenge of gaining attention. Far too many well-executed activities suffer from a failure to gain the attention they deserve because the results were not communicated in a way the decision-makers could relate to or act upon, so their minds wander and they start looking at their watches.

Example

An example of designing results for communicability comes from an analyst who participated in a strategic foresight activity for a large science and technology company. In the first presentation of the results of the study, the organization reported back that they preferred to see recommendations in the form of options to consider and choose from. They felt the consulting firm was being overly prescriptive as to what the organization should do. After a few more iterations, the clients set forth a "no solutions" mandate that effectively barred the analysis team from offering anything that even resembled a solution. While this initially proved difficult for the team members, they adjusted, and in subsequent projects sought to determine upfront if this was a "no-solutions" project. They used this approach successfully with other organizations as well.

Further reading

Davenport, T.H. and Beck, J.C. (2001). *The Attention Economy: Understanding the New Economy of Business*. Cambridge, MA: Harvard Business School.

Rosenau, M.D., Griffin, A., Castellion, G.A., and Anschuetz, N.F., eds. (2002). *The PDMA Handbook of New Product Development* (1st edition). New York: Wiley.

6.1.2 Tailor the Message to the Thinking Styles of the Audience

Strategic foresight typically involves complex analysis of complex issues, which presents a communications challenge that should not be underestimated. Very often the thinking style of the analyst and the team is different than that of the organization. Those drawn to strategic foresight and strategic thinking tend to have a mindset that embraces the complexity, ambiguity, and longer-term timeframe intrinsic to these fields. In most organizations, the prevalent thinking styles are concrete, detailed, here-and-now, and bottom-line, particularly among those in decision-making roles. This sets up an all-too-common mismatch between the analysis team and decision-maker.

Key steps

Begin considering the thinking styles of the organization when setting up and chartering an activity. While project negotiations can be very revealing about the organization's expectations, analysts should be careful not to take everything at face value. The organization is often not exactly sure what it wants, or may say it wants one thing when it really wants another. It might ask for the activity to be implemented in a particular format, but balk when it sees the results. It is up to analysts to do their best to understand what the organization really wants and anticipate the form of communication that will get the outcomes across most clearly. Understanding of the organization's thinking styles will evolve as the activity proceeds—it is especially helpful to interview the participants as part of the activity and look for style cues there.

The analysis team should start by analyzing its own thinking style (see *Guideline 1.1.2 Know Your Biases*). As team members become more comfortable and knowledgeable over time with their self-assessments, they can start to apply this learning in work with others, including in stakeholder interviews and interactions with the organization. It would be ideal to be able to assess the organization's thinking styles using a formal assessment tool, but this is rarely practical. More common is making a best approximation of the styles apparent. A lot can be learned by paying attention to style issues during interviews or updates, attending executive speeches, or analyzing organizational documents for clues.

However gleaned, this information is then used to tailor communications. Using the Kirton Adaptor-Innovator Assessment, for example, if it becomes apparent that the organization is on the Adaptor end of the innovation continuum, it would be unwise to recommend tearing down the existing system and building a new one. While the analysis team might prefer to recommend this, the advice would run counter to the preferences of the "adaptor." But even if the team felt compelled to tear down and rebuild, it could tailor the message along the lines of "an adaptive approach was considered, but rejected for the following reasons."

An emerging best practice is to combine a style assessment with Spiral Dynamics, an assessment tool that gets at thinking "content." Simply being aware of style differences does not bridge all communication gaps; people with diverse styles will still often have trouble communicating with one another. One way to help is to profile the team's color tier on the Spiral Dynamics assessment, which measures worldviews or belief systems. As with differences in thinking style, differences in worldview can manifest as communication gulfs that are not easily bridged without awareness of them. Someone with an "orange" preference for competition and victory may not understand someone with a "green" preference for participation and egalitarianism. The combination of understanding differences in both style and worldview suggests a powerful communication approach.

Benefits

Practitioners all too often bemoan the fact that a comprehensive and ultimately accurate analysis failed to influence decision-makers. Many times this is due to poor communication: excellent content delivered in a way that is either off-putting or misunderstood by the organization, thus limiting the influence of the study. The clear benefit is to avoid or at least lessen the chances of this occurring.

Example

Consider a hypothetical example based on a real-world experience of the author, and which will likely be familiar to many. A team of outside consultants arrives in the boardroom of a fairly straitlaced and conservative company, dressed in fashionable clothes and accessories and with a strut in their step. They are far younger than the client audience. Their presentation begins with a flashy and very loud video explaining what the organization needs to do. The subsequent presentation is almost pedagogical, with a tone of lecturing the organization about the mistakes they've been making, and beneath a thin veil implying that creative work is best left to creative types like themselves.

The somewhat stunned audience has little to say. They sit back in their chairs with pained expressions. They've been afraid to ask questions for fear of being made to look un-cool. They politely thank the presenting team for their efforts, and when the door closes after they leave, the real discussion begins. Unfortunately for the presenting team, it focuses far more on their obnoxious style than on the content, which is actually well thought-out and worthy of consideration. In this case and many others like it, however, the delivery undid the content and the proposal was rejected.

Further reading

Hermann, N. (1989). *The Creative Brain*. Lake Lurie, NC: Brain Books.

Janis, I. (1982). *Groupthink*. (2nd ed.). Boston: Houghton-Mifflin.

Kirton, M. (1994, revised). *Adaptors and Innovators: Styles of Creativity and Problem Solving*. London: Routledge.

6.1.3 Immerse Stakeholders and Decision-Makers in the Alternatives to Increase Buy-In

Many strategic foresight activities miss the mark in presenting results that surprise the organization. Organizations, and especially senior executives, do not enjoy being surprised or put on the spot. Asking for their input beforehand gives them a stake in the activity and eliminates the element of surprise.

Key steps

Stakeholders and decision-makers should be involved throughout the activity. A chartering process upfront can set expectations and begin the buy-in process. Interviews during data gathering are another point for immersion. Workshops to create alternatives or options are useful points to involve these groups, as are follow-up sessions to explore implications and potential actions. Throughout the process, frequent feedback sessions can be scheduled to keep the analyst in tune with the expectations of the stakeholders and decision-makers.

Numerous points in a foresight activity are well-suited to the involvement of stakeholders and decision-makers. The situation will dictate whether or when to use a particular opportunity. Some decision-makers, for example, prefer not to be involved much. In this case analysts must make judicious use of whatever time they can secure with the decision-makers, by emphasizing how important it is to the eventual outcome. In other situations, stakeholders and decision-makers can be overly intrusive. They may seek to dictate the course of the activity, and even the findings. Here the analyst will need to look for ways to regain control of the activity and reset the relationship. As both cases above suggest, the rule of thumb is to strive for a balance between involvement, which helps with buy-in, and maintaining the integrity of the activity and the analysis team.

Benefits

The benefits of buy-in are virtually self-explanatory. Stakeholders and decision-makers commission an activity to aid their work and decisions. An activity that fails to address these needs has missed its purpose. If time is invested in immersing stakeholders and decision-makers in the process, the ultimate findings are more likely to be useful to them and less subject to rejection. That said, however, involvement is not a panacea for winning buy-in. Sometimes stakeholder groups will participate and go along with the analyst, without being forthcoming about their objections since they do not want to be seen as intrusive. The best the analyst can do is to encourage frank and honest feedback. This includes not becoming defensive in response to critical feedback, but rather seeking ways to improve the activity. If the analyst genuinely accepts and deals with feedback it will tend to encourage more, and benefit everyone by increasing the odds that the activity's outcomes will meet expectations.

A caution about buy-in is not to win it at the cost of the activity's integrity. The analyst should not get caught up in telling the organization what it wants to hear. While this approach may work in the short term, most stakeholders and decision-makers will soon realize that such analyses produce little value since they are merely confirming predetermined conclusions. The analyst needs to be both tough and diplomatic. If stakeholders are resisting findings that the analyst strongly believes in, those concerns must be addressed and the rationales behind the findings explained. While this may be uncomfortable for the analyst at the time, the demonstration of independent thought and openness to contrary feedback will prove more useful to stakeholders and decision-makers, and make clear the analyst's value.

Example

A negative example of the failure to properly involve stakeholders comes from Shell's disposal of the Brent Spar floating oil-storage facility. Shell did obtain buy-in for its disposal strategy from the officials legally responsible for the disposal—which led it to ignore concerns from other stakeholders. Greenpeace, the environmental advocacy group, used the media to raise concerns and ultimately turn the public against the deep-sea disposal solution approved by authorities. (It is important to note that an organization cannot always choose its stakeholders). While involving activist groups in the problem-solving process would have been inconvenient and slowed things down, it would have brought their objections to light sooner, and provided more room for developing alternative options.

The good news is that more and more organizations have learned this lesson, and increasingly are involving potential opposition groups in strategic foresight activities and decision-making processes, including through mechanisms such as external advisory boards.

Further reading

Nutt, P. C. (2002). *Why Decisions Fail: Avoiding the Blunders and Traps That Lead to Debacles*. San Francisco: Berrett-Koehler.

Schrage, M. (2000). *Serious Play: How the World's Best Companies Simulate to Innovate*. Cambridge, MA: Harvard Business School Press.

Van Der Heijden, K. (2002). *The Sixth Sense: Accelerating Organizational Learning with Scenarios*. New York: Wiley.

6.1.4 Be Provocative

Part of the role of strategic foresight is to make organizations think about their changing situation. This is often quite challenging. Being provocative makes the organization confront internal and external change instead of sitting on its laurels, and offending it slightly can force it to think about its counterarguments. Both of these help the organization take personal responsibility for its future.

When the mandate is to make the organization think, or get it out of a rut, provoking and offending can work very well. This is often the role of an opening keynote speech at a conference, and can be equally effective in kicking off a strategic foresight activity. It is a good mechanism for engaging the organization in the rest of the activity.

Provoking and offending are better tools for limited time engagements, such as lectures or workshops, than for everyday use—one would eventually wear out one's welcome. But when an organization invests in an activity, it often expects to have its views challenged. In negotiating the activity, it's best to learn the organization's views regarding provocation. Some organizational cultures are uncomfortable with provocation, and it is best to know this beforehand.

Key steps

A tried-and-true formula is to first shock or frighten the organization about its current situation, even suggesting that it will go out of business if it doesn't change. Show in some depth why this could be the case, and describe the threats it faces. After establishing the threats, introduce the opportunities. Suggest that if the organization acts on its foresight, it will be able to avoid the threats and seize opportunities.

Provoking should be done on a regular basis. By contrast, offending should be used sparingly and cautiously. If offending remarks are chosen carefully and leavened with humor, people will laugh and actually enjoy them, and the offense will be short-lived. But they will also be forced to defend themselves and identify counterarguments—which can be a healthy process. Pointing out obvious inadequacies in an organization is worthwhile if it leads people to some guidance about how to solve the problems or live with them.

Benefits

Provoking and mildly offending essentially mean challenging the organization's existing mindsets and value sets, i.e., intellect and emotions. Putting people in an uncomfortable situation for a short while harnesses their energy to relieve the discomfort. Using humor helps to get through a listener's resistance to attack, but people can take the points on board. Organizations tending to complacency often get into trouble gradually, like frogs in a slowly heating pot. They can be very resistant to bland messages, which they get all the time, and let them slide off without impact. When the analyst says something provocative or offensive, they are forced to respond or engage in self-defense.

Example

BT's Ian Pearson is one foresight practitioner who has successfully played provocateur on innumerable occasions during his history of public presentations. Pearson promotes BT's vision of the future—which he and his team help develop—with a provocative multimedia presentation full of challenging forecasts. In so doing he spreads at least awareness of, if not adherence to, BT's visionary work. So tomorrow's developers of products and services will implicitly or explicitly be working towards a vision of the future put forth by BT.

Further reading

Hines, A. (2000, February). How Foresight Is Being Positioned Inside Today's Organization. *foresight: the journal of futures studies, strategic thinking, and policy, 2* (1).

Pearson, I., ed. (1998). *Atlas of the Future.* New York: John Wiley & Sons.

6.1.5 Modularize Outcomes—Keep the Good and Deal with the Bad

Throwing the baby out with the bathwater is a self-defeating reaction to negative outcomes. Organizations need to think in degrees of gray. They require an ability to sort thinking into modules, and know what to keep, what to get rid off, and what to deal with immediately. For example, when a product is launched and fails, the organization should aim to understand the components of this failure. When the root causes of a failure, or a success, are understood, it becomes clear that what actually failed or succeeded were discrete elements of the process. This learning enables the organization to preserve and build on valuable information or experience—which is present even in a disastrous initiative—not throw it away because it was part of a larger failure.

Key steps

When assessing an activity, the first step is to identify and assess modules in the larger activity. What were the key elements or actions? Next, interview the decision-makers and other active participants representing each of the modules. The analyst can help build a constructive culture into the interview process by making clear how the information will be used going forward.

Next focus on the modules that appear to contain the issues, and build a deeper understanding of what actually happened. For example, was the market not mature enough? Were the technologies not mature enough? Which ones? Was this offering too much, too soon? Was the organization unprepared to support it? Was the ecosystem not ready for it?

Analysis of the interview results can be sorted into the "good" and "bad" modules, and communicated to the organization. Thus, the entire activity will not be deemed a failure. Conversely, even successful activities will have their dysfunctional or "bad" elements that can provide opportunities for learning.

A better approach, of course, is to avoid getting into the situation in the first place through greater understanding of the market fundamentals of and organizational readiness. What is emerging in the organization's external context? What is shifting in the ecosystem? How are technologies shifting? What else is changing? It is not as simple as knowing it all and hence making all the right decisions. It is more about knowing more, and hence making wiser decisions, about the key alternative directions possible and their potential outcomes.

Benefits

The benefit of "keeping the baby" is preserving the good and learning from the bad, which can help the organization gain benefits from good modules sooner than others do and avoid pitfalls that others may experience. The downside of not doing this well is that the repercussions tend to be huge. Misunderstandings abound, and people draw all kinds of wrong conclusions and use those in their decision-making, to the detriment of activities to come. The activity is forever viewed through a myopic lens of failure/success, which can kill benefits that would be clear to those with a broader outlook.

Example

An example is the Apple Newton. The Newton was a pioneer of the "do-it-all" personal digital assistant (PDA), and defined many aspects of future PDAs. Yet Apple stopped its production in 1998. Post-mortem, the market's actions and numerous articles on the event suggested that Apple made a huge deal of the failure internally, burning many of the people involved. Once burned, twice shy: it became difficult for anyone at Apple to propose anything similar. The baby was tossed out with the bathwater!

What really happened? At Apple's core is a simple premise of user-friendly products, quality design (technical and industrial), and good purchasing experience. What was lacking in the organization's processes to enable it to understand the market better and handle the failure better? Judging by the "toss the baby out with the bathwater" framework, there was no module analysis designed to transparently keep the good from the experience and learn from the bad.

Now, the iPod brings new hope. The iPod represents many elements that could have been learned from the Newton project. Did Apple conclude that Newton was too much, too soon, not connected enough to the ecosystem providers, and based on immature technologies—and use that knowledge to strip the iPod down to a palm-size simple solution?

Further reading

Kahney, L. (2002, August 29). Apple's Newton Just Won't Drop. *Wired*.

Marsh, N., McAllum, M., and Purcell, D. (2002). *Strategic Foresight: The Power of Standing in the Future*. Melbourne: Crown Content.

6.1.6 Build Awareness of Change through Experience, Insight, and Reframing

Facts and ideas alone don't convince organizations to address change. The case for understanding and addressing important change may need to be made with a range of techniques, to get through to the organization on its own terms. Sometimes that means giving the organization a new experience. Often it means finding ways to restate or reframe the issue in a way that enables the organization to see the need to avoid a threat or take advantage of an opportunity.

Key steps

It is standard practice in foresight activities to immerse the organization in the issue at hand in order to help it think differently, freshen its perspective, and get it away from preconceptions and biases. To do this, it is crucial to bring in new ideas and connect them to the organization's interests. So the first step is to reach outside for new information and insights that the organization is not receiving through its usual channels. That means carefully selecting trends and insights that are relevant and impactful, while avoiding too much filtering, which may eliminate interesting ideas that could prove useful as more is learned about the situation.

With this pool of information, the analyst then needs to find ways to make the fresh insights relevant and meaningful to the organization. This is thoughtful, analytical work. Some people in the organization will be more naturally inclined to help with this activity than others. Find those people who think creatively and broadly, and tap their skills for these strategic conversations. Once the approach is decided, it is often useful to have organizational insiders themselves share the insights with the organization. The idea is to spread the ideas throughout the culture, so they will not seem shocking when they appear in the conclusions of the activity.

Finally, to get through to skeptics in the organization, here are some suggestions to make the insights compelling and memorable:

- Use images—The more powerful and colorful the presentation, the better. Photos, cartoons, and video may all be useful. A picture may be the most effective way to get some ideas through to the visually inclined.

- Use experiences—Where practical, experiential presentations are best: traveling to locations where relevant change is most visible, or where new opportunities may lie, such as in new markets. But relevant experiences can also be brought home, via multimedia or role-playing.

- Use tools that promote in-depth thinking—Creative problem-solving techniques, used in ideation sessions or scenario building, can open people to new perspectives.

Benefits

For most organizations, certain kinds of intelligence flow in regularly. Usually these are framed in the language of the organization's business or sector. And usually they originate within that sector. The organization has access to an ongoing stream of conventional wisdom and voices from that field or sector. Usually such information also has a short-term focus—the content in industry newsletters and emails is typically about the current year or even the current quarter.

The organization needs fresh insights from outside this stream of routine intelligence. The analyst can break through by highlighting new, or newly important, changes that may not be on the organization's radar, and make those new insights compelling and relevant.

Example

A select group of executives at a high-tech company needed to rethink their marketing and strategies to tap into new opportunities around the world. A futurist with whom they consulted raised their awareness of potentially huge opportunities for their business in emerging markets, even in resource-stressed poor countries. To convince their colleagues of the wider global market of opportunities, the team decided to stage an experiential event with colleagues and senior executives. They focused on water issues in the poorest parts of the world, assigning participants to role-play people from poor countries, emerging markets, and rich countries. The poorest got "dirty" water and plain rice for lunch. The experience was a hit, and effectively raised consciousness among the leaders of the organization about new challenges and opportunities in the global marketplace—including about water resources and water quality, a key area of opportunity identified by the analysis team.

Further reading

Kolb, D.A. (1984). *Experiential Learning: Experience as the Source of Learning and Development*. Englewood Cliffs, NJ: Prentice-Hall.

Markley, O.W. (1988). Using Depth Intuition in Creative Problem Solving and Strategic Innovation. *The Journal of Creative Behavior 22* (2), 65 - 100.

Shupp, L. (2004). Ethnofuturism. Viewed August 2005, www.cheskin.com/p/ar.asp?mlid=7&arid=13&art=1.

6.2 Create an Action Agenda

6.2.1 Create a Sense of Urgency

According to John Kotter (1995), successful change efforts begin with a leader communicating a sense of either crisis, potential crisis, or great opportunity. Kotter maintains that executives often underestimate how difficult it can be to move staff out of their comfort zones. He believes that in some instances, it may be necessary to generate an apparent crisis. However the sense of urgency is established, it needs to be felt throughout the organization. The majority of those in management—Kotter suggests 75%—need to be convinced that the organization can no longer operate as it has.

Key steps

How the analyst goes about creating a sense of urgency will vary by organization. Start by assessing the organization's culture: Is it very hierarchical? Is most communication formal or informal? Is there a feeling of pride? Do people seem to enjoy coming to work? Is there a willingness to try new ideas? Are people open and honest with one another, or are there constant turf battles and hidden agendas?

Knowing the culture of the organization will inform the decision of how to proceed. It may involve getting the attention of the CEO. It may be pulling together what Tom Peters has called a "skunk works"—an informal group of people who dare to dream, to confront the status quo, and to think outside normal constraints.

The analyst also needs to determine the best communication strategy to spread this sense of urgency. For an organization whose workforce is distributed geographically, the analyst may need to travel to various sites. Whatever approach is taken, it is essential that those viewed as leaders in the organization, whether by virtue of their position or their knowledge or achievements, come aboard early on.

Benefits

Evidence is ample that many change efforts fail—or at least fail to fully reach their goals. One study (Beer et al., 1990) of six large companies that undertook change initiatives found that only one of the six had substantial success, three made some progress, and two actually experienced decreased performance. Another study (Conference Board, 1994) of over 160 companies in the United States and Europe found that only a third were able to report success in their change efforts.

Failure to establish a sense of urgency is one of the four key reasons that change efforts fail, suggests Kotter (1996). Organizational cultures become complacent, mired in the "same old, same old." Creating a sense of urgency challenges complacency—and also helps to address the other key reasons for failure:

- Failure to establish a coalition of persons supporting the effort
- Under-communicating the vision
- Neglecting to connect changes to the organizational culture

In government, more than one president—for example, Jimmy Carter—has run on a platform of "cleaning house." But government employees are protected by civil service regulations. Many have seniority. Some are represented by powerful unions. During Carter's administration a prevalent attitude among bureaucrats was, "I was around before him, and I'll be around long after he's gone." What government leaders such as Carter failed to do was to put forth a compelling reason why the proposed changes were vital for the organization, thereby overcoming complacency, building support, and galvanizing people around a common vision. Carter never articulated a sense of urgency, and so his change efforts never materialized.

Example

Chrysler Corp.'s bailout by the US government in 1979, and subsequent revival, is an example of how creating a sense of urgency enabled a major change effort. CEO Lee Iacocca set an ambitious goal for Chrysler: not only to pay back the loans provided by the government and the banking industry, but also to reestablish Chrysler as an auto industry leader. Recognizing that some of his senior staff were part of the problem, Iacocca fired many executives. He also personally bargained with the union for cuts in wages and benefits. And he reduced his own salary to $1 per year, to model sacrifice in the name of worthwhile goals. Iacocca appreciated the importance of taking action. As he put it: "The trick is to make sure you don't die waiting for prosperity to come." He followed up his early steps by quickly introducing the enormously successful minivan. That success allowed him to garner support, attract financial backing, and build a climate of accomplishment.

Further reading

Bass, B.M. and Avolio, B.J. (1994). *Improving Organizational Effectiveness through Transformational Leadership*. Thousand Oaks, CA: Sage Publications.

Beer, M., Eisenstat, R.A., and Spector, B.A. (1990, November/December). Why Change Programs Don't Produce Change. *Harvard Business Review*.

Change Management: An Overview of Current Initiatives. (1994). New York: The Conference Board.

Kotter, J.P. (1995, March/April). Leading Change: Why Transformation Efforts Fail. *Harvard Business Review, 73* (2).

Kotter, J.P. (1996). *Leading Change*. Cambridge, MA: Harvard Business School Press.

Mische, M.A. (2000). *Strategic Renewal: Becoming a High-Performance Organization*. Upper Saddle River, NJ: Prentice Hall.

6.2.2 Reinforce What the Organization Is Already Doing and Build from There

Long-term, complex, contingent thinking is an acquired skill, one which few people have had the time or the need to practice consistently. Therefore, it is understandable that some analysts believe they have to start from scratch in explaining their approach or their deliverable. But that would be a mistake. People think about the future all the time, and sometimes in quite sophisticated ways.

Typical customers for strategic foresight plan their holidays, save money for their kids' college, buy insurance, change the oil in the car, bring an umbrella on a rainy day. While hardly unusual, all of these behaviors represent an understanding of a contingent future. The analyst, therefore, needs to simply move this thinking into the strategic environment of the organization in order to show it how to think about the future in a productive and systematic way.

Key steps

Most organizations have an almost automatic evaluation of whether a particular change is good or bad for it. Such evaluations, however, are based on underlying *values*—the root of *evaluation*. Identifying those values makes the basis of such judgments explicit and therefore more conscious and defensible. At the same time, the analyst can also point out other, sometimes competing, values that are not served by that change. Acknowledging those competing values usually does not alter the clients' evaluation of the change, but at least they now know that the change involves a tradeoff: some things get better, but others may not.

Begin by assessing what people in the organization already "know" about the future. Most are quite aware of the change going on around them. They have expectations about where that change is leading. And finally, they usually have an opinion or attitude about whether the change is good or not. The job of the analyst is to begin with this input and then expand it in particular directions. Identify changes the organization is not yet, or not fully, aware of. These newly identified changes don't replace or discount the ones the organization is already concerned with, but they add to the list. The analyst needs to be careful, however, to go beyond what the organization already knows without drowning it in an ocean of new information. Organizations can absorb and retain new knowledge, but the quantity of new knowledge and the rate of absorption are both limited.

Next, challenge the assumptions that underlie the organization's expectations. Most organizations expect the future to be like the present, only bigger and faster. That is real knowledge to build on, but the future can also be radically different from the present. As discussed in *Guideline 3.5.4 Emphasize Plausible Surprises*, change is rarely smooth and linear and some systems change radically, often with little notice. So taking into account the organization's expected or baseline future as one plausible scenario, the analyst shows how other futures are also plausible. For more on this, see *Guideline 1.3.2 Seek to Improve the Mental Model of Decision-makers*.

Benefits

This guideline reemphasizes the importance of understanding and starting with the organization's current mental model, recognizing its decision-makers' knowledge and experience in dealing with the future—and only then enhancing that knowledge and experience with the analyst's own knowledge about the future and how to deal with it. Introducing an organization to the future is a matter of persuasion: not only of the analyst's competence, but also of the reality of change and the need to do something about it now. Those experienced in persuasion always begin with the organization, where it is coming from, its knowledge, experience, values, and needs—an approach intrinsic to being able to influence the organization towards healthy change.

Working with the future is hard. People make short-sighted, wrong-headed decisions every day. It is easy, therefore, to fall into the misperception that most people are clueless when it comes to dealing with the future. This belief breeds a defensive and know-it-all attitude that turns people off. The antidote is to respect the organization, what it knows, and what it cares about. The analyst's job is to serve the organization, and this requires a baseline of empathy and humility. This approach not only prevents incorrect assumptions about the organization's knowledgebase and values—finding out what it does know and care about can provide valuable information in building the analyst's case for how to deal with the future, as described in *6.1.1 Design Results for Communicability*.

Example

Jack Welch, former CEO of GE, instituted an exercise called Destroy Your Business (DYB) in every GE business unit. DYB made unexpected futures palpable by having participants grapple with the possibility of going out of business. Each unit assembled a cross-functional team to benchmark competitors and examine the products and services they offered and how they operated.

In January 1999 Welch mandated that GE transform itself into an e-business, in response to the dot.com boom. The teams' goal was to present GE's top executives with a hypothetical Internet-based business plan that a competitor could use to erode GE's customer base. In addition, the teams proposed how they would change their existing business model in response to these threats. Today, GE is acknowledged as a leader in e-commerce.

Further reading

Ackoff, R.L. (n.d.). Controlling the Future: Forecasts, Assumptions, Scenarios, and Projections. *Presearch: Provoking Strategic Conversation*. Emeryville, CA: Global Business Network.

Levinson, M. (2000, July 15). Destructive Behavior. *CIO Magazine*.

Porter, M.E. (1996). What Is Strategy? *Harvard Business Review 74* (6), 61 - 74.

6.2.3 Aim the Activity at Helping to Make Better Decisions

Strategic foresight explores a wide range of trends that can affect an organization. At times, the activity may seem to raise a puzzling array of possibilities and options. Ultimately, however, to be useful it must help decision-makers make better decisions.

This guideline requires a shift of mindset from earlier phases, where keeping an open mind to the possibilities is paramount, to a "closing" mindset of prioritizing and making choices.

Key steps

A broad range of tools exists for making strategic choices, once the possibilities have been developed. First, however, ensure that the nature of the issue is fully understood.

Heifetz and Linsky (2002) make the important distinction between *adaptive challenges* and *technical challenges*. Adaptive challenges require new learning in order to be addressed, while technical challenges are those for which the necessary know-how already exists. The authors suggest that a key problem for organizations is confusing an adaptive challenge with a technical one—in other words, trying to solve a problem that requires new learning with existing know-how. The trick is that adaptive challenges can be very difficult to address, so organizations tend to have a strong bias towards technical approaches. The analyst, therefore, must first diagnose the nature of the challenge.

Once the challenge is identified, a number of tools are available for exploring options. The scenario-planning firm Global Business Network (www.gbn.com) has developed a useful framework for organizing options. Assuming there are four potential choices facing the team and clients, the options range as follows, from safest to riskiest:

- A *robust strategy* looks for elements common to all four options and focuses on these commonalities.
- A *hedge-your-bets strategy* gives equal weight to all four options; that is, it assumes all four are equally viable and divides the action equally across them.
- A *core-satellite strategy* emphasizes one option as the most likely and pays the most attention to it, but also pays lesser attention to the other options just in case.
- A *bet-the-farm strategy* selects one option as the best and invests all its energy in pursing that option.

One way to help make this concrete is to imagine you have $1 million and ten people to invest in your options. The robust strategy would first extract the common elements from each of the options, then allocate all the money and people to those. A hedge-your-bets strategy would allocate $250,000 and 2.5 people to each of the options. A core-satellite strategy would invest, say, $750,000 and seven people in the preferred option and spread the rest of the money and people across the others. A bet-the-farm strategy would invest all the money and people in the preferred option.

Benefits

Putting options in this format aids decision-making by making the future possibilities seem more real and concrete. It guides participants towards a preferred direction to embark on in the present.

This can sometimes be a difficult exercise for analysts, since by nature they will tend to want to develop more and more options and avoid committing to a single strategy and plan as long as possible. But delivering useful advice and options to decision-makers will make the analyst a vital partner for the organization. By using strategic foresight to solve real problems of concern, the analyst builds personal credibility as well as the credibility of strategic foresight in general.

Example

A classic example of a bet-the-farm strategy—and the risks it entails—comes from the former chemical company Monsanto. In the early 1990s, Monsanto made the tough strategic choice to sell off its chemicals businesses and focus exclusively on biotechnology. Unanticipated resistance to genetically modified foods, primarily in Europe, had disastrous consequences for the company. It was acquired by the pharmaceutical company Upjohn, and pretty much lost its identity for several years, until being cut loose by Upjohn and reemerging as a company specializing in agricultural products and solutions.

Further reading

Heifetz, R.A. and Linsky, M. (2002). *Leadership on the Line: Staying Alive through the Dangers of Leading*. Boston: Harvard Business School Press.

Hoyt, B. (2001, June - July). Beyond Scenarios: Strategy Alternatives Using Strategy Options. The Williams Inference Center.

Ogilvy, J., Gregory, E., and Harris, G. (n.d.). After the Scenarios, Then What? Strategic Conversation, Early Indicators, and the Art of Communicating Scenarios. *Presearch: Provoking Strategic Conversation 2* (1).

6.2.4 Make Decisions Without All the Desired Data

No matter how hard one tries, no matter how many resources are deployed, no matter how deep the research—all of the information necessary to make perfect decisions is never present. At some point, long before all the facts are in, decisions must be made.

Like most processes, information gathering adheres to the law of diminishing returns. At some point the amount and value of information generated begins to diminish. The right point to stop gathering information varies from activity to activity, and depends on the value of the information and its related cost. Ultimately, however, deciding when to stop depends primarily on how much ambiguity and risk the organization is willing to accept. Being willing to make decisions without all the data has a major upside: it avoids "analysis-paralysis"—the habit of continually delaying a decision in pursuit of more information.

Of course, situations do exist in which it is possible to know "everything," but these are rare and typically artificial in nature. In the game of chess, for example, it is theoretically possible to consider every possible move and countermove. However, even in a simple game the computing power needed to evaluate every possible move is beyond the capabilities of either chess grandmasters or the world's most powerful computers. Rather than examining all possible moves, both human and computer players reduce the complexity by considering only a partial set of strategies and moves. In order to make the game playable, they cut short the search for all available information.

In an ideal world, decisions would never be made without all relevant data. But as in professional chess, not only are key facts perpetually out of reach; it is impossible to know in advance with certainty which information is relevant to decision-making and which is simply noise. This revelation may frustrate the analyst—or offer some small comfort.

Key steps

A rule of thumb in making the decision about when to stop gathering information is to ask how much it would cost to acquire the next "important" bit of information. Would that information significantly increase the likelihood of arriving at the desired answer and is that increase in certainty worth the cost? If it would, then by all means make the additional investment. Otherwise work with what is available, and suggest moving to a decision.

To appreciate how important, or unimportant, increased amounts of information are to decision-making, it's instructive to start keeping track of how you would decide to resolve an issue during the various stages of data collection. At what point did the final decision lock in? Fifty percent of the way through data gathering? Seventy-five percent? Ninety percent? At what point did the organization become comfortable with its decision?

The biggest obstacle to this guideline is the illusion that the decision-making process is perfect and rational and the only right way to decide something is to gather all the facts. Another obstacle is that information is often gathered simply to "check a box" without any real intent of using it.

Benefits

While curtailing data-gathering may seem almost negligent, the reality is that decisions are typically made under the naïve belief that all the facts are in, when what's really happening is that preferred information-gathering resources have been exhausted or time has run out and expediency forces a decision.

Being conscious of the inability to gather and integrate all the facts helps to optimize decision-making. It also curbs spending before the costs of information retrieval and analysis outweigh the benefits.

Example

In the early 1980s, IBM would curtail its information-gathering and reporting processes via a very simple tactic. Each year at a certain point, the Information Technology department would stop distributing its management reports to all internal departments. The department would restart distribution of a particular report only if it received a complaint about its absence. While the percentage of reports that were permanently stopped varied from year to year, one account suggested that roughly 25% of monthly reports were no longer produced.

Further reading

Gladwell, M. (2005). Blink: *The Power of Thinking without Thinking*. New York: Little, Brown & Co.

Klein, G. (2004). *The Power of Intuition: How to Use Your Gut Feelings to Make Better Decisions at Work*. New York: Currency Doubleday.

6.2.5 Create Milestones Along the Path to the Preferred Future, and Celebrate Small Successes Along the Way

It is important to plant milestones throughout a strategic foresight activity. These not only keep an activity on track, they can also provide occasion to celebrate small successes along the way.

Analysts should seek out small "wins" early on to build momentum for the activity. John Kotter (1996) suggests that effective change requires "short-term wins." Organizations are more likely to remain interested and supportive of a foresight activity if they can see clear progress that is unmistakably related to the goals. Failure to highlight such progress is among the key reasons why change efforts fail; see *Guideline 6.2.1 Create a Sense of Urgency* for others.

Key steps

Several steps will help establish milestones and small successes.

- First, define the milestones. Be sure they are realistic and doable.
- Next, ask those involved in the implementation to be on the lookout for indicators that the plan is working effectively, however small these might be. Be sure to reward the change agents—those who are helping to make the plan a reality.
- Also be ready to make mid-course adjustments. If it becomes clear that a milestone is not going to be met, adjust the timeline well before it comes due.
- Finally, keep an eye out for naysayers. Where possible, meet with them to persuade them that: (a) the project is in fact moving ahead; or (b) their attitude is counterproductive to the goals of the organization.

Benefits

As Rosabeth Moss Kanter (1992) and others have observed, progress is often made in incremental steps that together result in major change. Analysts interested in achieving change need to be cognizant of the fact that many people resist change, especially large change. But those same resistors are less likely to hold back or thwart the effort if the change comes in small doses.

Establishing and reaching milestones, and celebrating successes, helps guard against complacency, one of the key reasons change initiatives fail. Moreover, individuals who are contributing to the goal are rewarded, which motivates them to help build a coalition of supporters.

Another reason it is important to establish milestones and celebrate small victories is that big change efforts, such as those aiming to change an organizational culture, take a long time. There is evidence that it requires up to seven years to effect a meaningful change in organizational culture. Setting and reaching milestones, celebrating small (and then hopefully larger) successes are critical to sustaining a commitment to an improved culture.

Example

Bell Atlantic demonstrated the effectiveness of celebrating small successes under CEO Raymond Smith, who launched a change initiative by meeting with over 1,400 managers in small seminars in order to articulate corporate values. Smith made sure the managers were actively engaged in editing the values statement word by word. He recognized that in a large organization, the most important factor for success was the myriad day-to-day interactions among the workforce. If those contacts were argumentative, with people defending their turf, the organization would suffer, bureaucracies would develop, and internal competition will be rife. So Smith used these small, frequent interactions as a way of building coalitions, engendering support, finding common ground, and celebrating the small victories along the way.

Further reading

Kanter, R.M., Stein, B.A., and Jick, T.D. (1992). *The Challenge of Organizational Change: How Companies Experience It and Leaders Guide It*. New York: Free Press.

Kotter, J. (1996). *Leading Change*. Cambridge, MA: Harvard Business School Press.

Rogers, E.M. (2003). *Diffusion of Innovations*. (5th Edition). New York: Free Press.

6.2.6 Recommend Investing in at Least One Unlikely Idea

One dimension of strategic foresight is challenging mainstream ideas and developing alternatives. Analysts should actively stimulate the exploration of unlikely or even seemingly impossible ideas. Going one step further, they should invest in at least one of them. This signals to the organization that considering and preparing for alternative futures is important enough to merit investment.

Key steps

Three steps will facilitate successful recommendation of unlikely ideas.

- First, the need for at least one unlikely idea should be actively promoted by making this explicit in the design of the foresight activity.

- Second, it is important to find one or more *relevant* unlikely ideas (not all unlikely ideas qualify for further analysis). After compiling this short list of unlikely ideas, the organization needs to make a selection.

- Third, since the analyst is dealing with an unlikely idea, sufficient time and effort must be spent developing it in order to make it credible. Furthermore, the potential consequences of the idea need to be explored and developed.

An unlikely idea can be addressed in different ways, but the following questions will help elaborate it:

- Why is the idea unlikely or impossible today?
- What changes are required in order to make the idea likely?
- How might this idea come to fruition?
- What would be the consequences if this idea did come to life?

It is important to present an unlikely idea in such a way that it may be seen as a serious alternative. If an unlikely idea is ridiculed, it will be counterproductive, strengthening conventional thinking instead of challenging it.

Benefits

One of the original aspects of exploratory strategic thinking is the emphasis it places on *alternative ideas, weak signals* (small developments with potentially high impact), *counterfactuals* (things that could have happened), and *counterintuitive* ideas (unlikely ideas). The task of the analyst is to make sure these types of ideas can be developed within the activity itself, in order to avoid the final strategy becoming just "today x 2."

Although some people are naturally talented for this type of unconventional thinking, most people need some encouragement to move beyond what they hold possible. Therefore, analysts may include an explicit task in the process to develop at least one unlikely idea.

A common attitude towards the future is one of regret: "If we had known earlier, then we could have..." This guidelines helps minimize the likelihood of this statement—even though it will never be possible to avoid missing some opportunities.

Example

An important example again comes from Shell, which once considered the fall of the Berlin Wall during a strategic activity. Although the idea was highly unlikely (even impossible, at that moment in time), it would have had important consequences for Shell's investment decisions since major Soviet oil and gas reserves could have become accessible on the world market, threatening profit margins. Although this option was finally abandoned in the strategic decision process, its inclusion helped widen the decision-makers' scope of what was possible. The fact that the Berlin Wall did fall is in that respect only an encouragement to continue developing unlikely ideas—they may be far more likely than they appear.

Further reading

Amram, M. and Kulatilaka, N. (1999). *Real Options: Managing Strategic Investments in an Uncertain World*. Oxford, UK: Oxford University Press.

Christensen, C.M. and Raynor, M. (2003). *The Innovator's Solution: Creating and Sustaining Successful Growth*. Cambridge, MA: Harvard Business School Press.

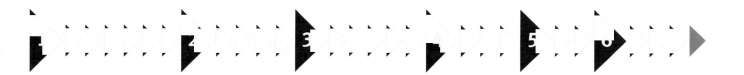

6.3 Create an Intelligence System

6.3.1 Create an Intelligence System Aligned by Strategic Foresight and Linked to the Planning Process

Organizations should develop a formal, customized system for developing business intelligence. This system should be concerned with monitoring and reporting on the external business environment. It should take its tasking from key decision-makers and be designed to feed the formal planning process. Organizations large enough to require a formal planning process deserve to have an appropriately modeled intelligence system for providing relevant and actionable information to the planning process and its actors.

Key steps

Analysts should first identify the key intelligence consumers. Typically these are senior executives, but they could easily be critical staff deep within the organization. Analysts should determine how these consumers prefer to receive and digest information used for making decisions. These preferences should inform the timing and format of the intelligence products.

This prescription contains a key assumption: that the organizational decision-makers are themselves in line with the formal planning process. If the planning process is nonexistent, or if decision-makers find it irrelevant, then this prescription must be tabled until a working planning process is put in place.

Analysts should then examine the organization's formal planning process. Critical points to look for include: official trends lists, data and information pertaining to strategic goals (which themselves often revolve around customers, markets, and products), and environmental situations important for major initiatives and activities. Process and scheduling are also important: at what points during the year will decision-makers, planners, and other staff need timely and updated information? At what points in the annual process is intelligence most useful?

Once these needs are identified, the means for fulfilling them must be identified. Large organizations can afford entire units devoted to the production of business intelligence, while small organizations may need to create temporary or ad hoc assignments or outsource the intelligence function altogether. Whatever the situation, an explicit system or schedule for developing intelligence should be established.

Benefits

An intelligence system aligned with the formal planning process can provide not merely more information, but better and timelier information. Alignment with planning ensures that scarce internal resources are used to answer appropriate strategic and tactical questions—questions directly linked to official goals and interests.

An aligned intelligence system also directly informs planning. Strategic planners, and planning taskforces, receive relevant and timely information almost without asking. They will come rely on the intelligence providers who anticipate their information needs. An intelligence system ensures that planning does not take place in an information vacuum, and that there is a standing, stable process for providing information.

A formal intelligence system also provides a common process for asking questions and receiving answers. Dedicated research staff, subject-matter experts, and other key analysts are known and available to produce actionable information. Planners and decision-makers know whom to contact to obtain actionable information. In turn, analysts and research staff have a shared understanding about standing information needs and priorities, relying on the planning process and its goals to prioritize requests and needs.

Example

A healthcare organization was experiencing significant internal growth and rising complexity. With the explosion of staff and information technology within a relatively short period, the amount of information and communications exploded, resulting in information overload and narrowed perspectives or attention deficit. As the company confronted the situation, contemplating issues such as organizational change, succession planning, and performance management, it was suggested that a formal intelligence process linked to the strategic planning process might improve the information flowing to senior decision-makers. This, however, would require dedicated staff time and the reorganization of a small corporate unit. Senior decision-makers declined to green-light the idea.

As a result, the amount of information flowing to decision-makers kept growing, with only a small percent related to corporate strategies and goals. Decision-makers experienced greater difficulty in processing and prioritizing the mass of information presented to them. The organization also failed to rationalize its internal research resources, which were seldom employed to provide intelligence on issues decision-makers recognized as truly strategic, instead focusing on operational and tactical questions.

Further reading

Hines, A. (2003). An Audit for Organizational Futurists: Ten Questions Every Organizational Futurist Should Be Able to Answer. *foresight, 5* (1), 20 - 33.

Kaplan, R.S. and Norton, D.P. (1996). *The Balanced Scorecard: Translating Strategy into Action*. Cambridge, MA: Harvard Business School Press.

Lum, R. (2002, June 1). When in Doubt, Vision Your Way Out. *Futures*.

6.3.2 Establish an Early Warning System to Detect Weak Signals

Establish a system that scans for possible changes in the context of the organization. The relevant fields of observation need to be defined, as do the questions that need to be answered and the people who will be the sources of information. An early warning system should be established when an organization is operating in a turbulent environment (which applies to most organizations today), and when seeking to detect early signals as precursors of opportunities and threats.

Key steps

First, identify the most important fields of observation. Find factors like organizational needs, competition, technological advances, legal issues, and the like.

Second, determine the pivotal questions about the future. These will be questions such as: How will the needs of the organization change substantially? What technologies will gain most in importance? How will the business or organizational models change?

Third, determine pivotal questions about strategic opportunities. Strategic radar should not only look into the future of the organization's contextual environment; it should also detect early signals for new or different ways to design strategy. Hence, define pivotal strategy questions such as: How can products, services, and solutions like ours be sold? How might the effects of our products, services, and solutions be achieved in different ways using substitute technologies? How can people be led to excellence? How can the efficiency of internal systems and processes be increased?

Fourth, determine your sensors. People are the sensors in your strategic radar system—automated search systems can provide raw material, but not analysis. Distribute questions about strategy to team members, asking them to focus on just one. This is a good way to calibrate the strategic attention of the organization. By specializing on just one pivotal question, the sensors will be able to see more of the future than colleagues with scattered attention.

Finally, pick appropriate sources. Reading and watching all the relevant sources for radar questions is one way, but a time-consuming one. It is much more efficient when sensors network with experts, in effect recruiting them as second-tier sensors outside the organization. These external sensors round out the worldview of the internals, who lack the time to keep up with the myriad trends and signals on the outer circles of their radar.

Benefits

The abilities to anticipate changes and developments, and to perceive and understand the resulting threats and opportunities, before competitors do—and before these changes have substantial impact on the organization—are key success factors. In turbulent environments, strategic radar systems help the organization see more of the future than their competitors—because in turbulent markets, there is already competition for foresight. Everybody is looking into the future, but those who do it more professionally, by delineating what strategic knowledge is most valuable and defining pivotal questions and establishing internal and external "sensors," have the capacity to be much more successful.

An early-warning system also buys time. Threats tend to grow and opportunities tend to shrink over the course of time; that is, failing to address a threat will magnify its consequences, while failing to address an opportunity will allow someone else to step into the gap. Organizations that have the tools in place to detect weak signals are more likely to benefit from the threats and opportunities they herald, because these organizations have more time to think, to develop, and to act. A strategic radar system can also develop and update strategies in real-time. It keeps the organization informed about important future changes and developments at a very early stage of their emergence. This is a necessary prerequisite for developing a strategy and keeping it up-to-date.

Lastly, it makes much more efficient use of organizational attention. Environmental scanning can be very time-consuming, cost-intensive, and ineffective when carried out with the usual, informal approach of "I heard someone say…" or "I read somewhere…." When formalized and streamlined, it can substantially increase the efficiency and the benefits of corporate attention and intelligence.

Example

BASF uses a system called BASIKS to monitor and track information about key questions. BASIKS continuously scans about 60,000 internal and external sources and monitors some 100 subjects. It has some 2,500 users, and can be adapted to the individual information needs of researchers or branch managers. Hewlett-Packard uses a similar system, called ELMI-B.

BASIKS and ELMI-B are software systems that gather data about key indicators—but analysts are required to analyze the data to detect real threats and opportunities. Detecting the signals of the future is a necessary but not sufficient prerequisite. Many times relevant information was already available, even within the organization, but either nobody was aware of it or nobody understood what it meant, so no action was taken. Therefore many companies have implemented simple radar systems that use human abilities to complement software support.

Further reading

Albrecht, K. (2000). *Corporate Radar*. New York: AMACOM.

Micic, P. (2003). *Der ZukunftsManager*. Munich, Germany: Haufe.

Micic, P. and Marx, A. (2004). *Die Bank von Morgen denken und gestalten*. Eltville, Germany: ADG.

Krystek, U. and Müller-Stewens, G. (1993). *Frühaufklärung für Unternehmen*. Stuttgart, Germany: Schäffer-Poeschel.

6.3.3 Look for Sources of Turbulence in the System

Strategic foresight is often called up in response to turbulence. Systems research shows that rising environmental turbulence can stimulate higher-level failures in large systems, such as ecosystems, businesses, and other organizations. A lack of flexibility or preparedness can lead to a failure to accommodate the disruptions, which in turn can lead to serious problems. Environmental scanning for emerging sources of turbulence can be quite productive in avoiding these problems. As the old adage says, "It isn't the rattlesnake you see that bites you."

Key steps

Scanning for turbulence overlaps with trend tracking and environmental scanning. Each seeks to identify emerging environmental patterns in order to encourage consideration of the broadest possible influences. While a combination of tracking emerging turbulence along with more solid trend extrapolation can identify potential sources of turbulence, scanning for turbulence shifts the focus to invite consideration of disruptive events and peripheral elements and issues that either exhibit, or seem vulnerable to exhibiting, turbulent behavior.

The analyst needs to identify agitating trends and events before these become a problem, so that alternative coping strategies can be identified and possibly developed before the turbulence becomes a significant problem. More complex systems or organizations that have higher levels of interdependence are more turbulent, because increased interdependency suggests the system is subject to disruption from more sources, which in turn suggests more disruptions. In scanning for sources of turbulence, consider not only trends but also sectors viewed with uncertainty, as they may be sources of potentially disruptive events.

Areas of increasing interdependence also serve as likely sources of turbulence, according to research by Stuart Kauffman (1996) into the evolution of binary networks and fitness landscapes. Recognizing potential sources of disruption stimulates the generation of alternative strategies and mechanisms for avoiding the impact of the disruption. From a practical viewpoint, the systemic response to increasing turbulence is to diversify sourcing in order to reduce vulnerability on single sources of information, energy, feedstock, etc.

Benefits

Turbulence can be disruptive at any phase of a system's maturation, but is particularly troublesome for mature systems and organizations that have optimized and streamlined operations for less turbulent conditions. Environmental scanning should be an ongoing process for all organizations seeking to avoid surprises. Expanding scanning to include potential sources of turbulence or disruption is always appropriate, but is particularly important for more mature organizations.

There is a balance between the level of redundancy needed in an organization and the level of turbulence in its environment. One of the key characteristics of a mature organization is that it has pared away inefficient pathways and locked into efficient ones. This increased efficiency, however, comes at the expense of flexibility. The lack of flexibility causes mature organizations to become "brittle"—more vulnerable to failure under changing conditions. Perspectives tend to narrow, which can lead to pervasive denial of the pertinence of external events and trends. Getting organizations to consider factors beyond their normal horizons is often difficult, for doing so not only defies their sense of what is pertinent, but it also diminishes the efficiency that they have grown comfortable with and value.

Even when mature organizations are severely struggling, they often retain a strong tendency to look deeper inside themselves, rather than more broadly outside—to be reductive rather than holistic. The application of critical thinking, causal mapping, and scenario-style developmental logic to the sources and impacts of turbulence offers opportunities for the organization to recognize areas of strain, as well as possible strategies for avoiding traumatic impacts.

Experience with mature organizations is likely to reinforce the claim that they frequently deny the pertinence or significance of events or influences outside their traditional and artificially narrow scope of influence. A narrow, selective scope of awareness blinds the organization to pending disruption.

Example

IBM's failure to recognize the potential of small personal computers to totally redefine and reorganize the computer industry is a classic example of this problem. This guideline suggests something further—the anticipation of turbulence from a more generic perspective, with the associated implication of deliberately sacrificing some efficiency to establish more diversity of critical supplies, sources, and structures and gain increased flexibility and robustness for accommodating expected turbulence.

Further reading

Forrest, C.J. (2001). *Time Related Sources of Model Failure*. Paper Presented at the 19th International Conference of the System Dynamics Society, Atlanta, Georgia.

Forrest, C.J. (2004). *Evolution and Behavior of System Structure: Eight Perspectives for Examining Complex Issues*. Paper Presented at the 22nd International Conference of the System Dynamics Society, Oxford, England.

Kauffman, S. (1996). *At Home in the Universe: The Search for the Laws of Self-Organization and Complexity*. New York: Oxford USA.

Voros, J. (2001). Reframing Environmental Scanning: An Integral Approach. *foresight: the journal of futures studies, strategic thinking, and policy, 3* (6).

6.3.4 Look for Indicators That Suggest a Crisis May Be Pending

Most of the important changes an analyst has to deal with will come suddenly and, to most, unexpectedly. But must organizations simply accept being victims of sudden change? Is there no way to receive indications of when such change might occur? It's common to go back over the record after the crisis and find the signs. This guideline suggests identifying those signs before the crisis occurs.

Key steps

Each crisis is unique; and the more severe it is, the harder it is to predict because it is so unusual. On the other hand, systems theory gives a clue to one type of crisis—a system break due to "far-from-equilibrium" conditions. Most system variables operate in range around some relatively stable equilibrium point. When the range increases (turbulence or volatility) or the equilibrium point shifts, the system can approach some boundary beyond which it moves to a completely different structure and equilibrium point. Moving to the new structure creates a crisis, because the organization is not used to working in that new territory.

Beware, therefore, of far-from-equilibrium conditions. They may indicate a crisis is more likely. Far-from-equilibrium conditions are not hard to detect. They exist whenever system variables exceed their historical range of variation. What is hard to tell is how far from the boundary the system is. The system might be able to sustain the unusual conditions for a long time, or it might be on the verge of crisis. Being aware of the far-from-equilibrium conditions is better than not, and building contingencies against the potential crisis is better yet.

Maintaining the historical record of key variables is the basis for noting far-from-equilibrium conditions. That much is mathematical. Judgment comes in when deciding how far "far-from-equilibrium" needs to be in order to start mentioning the possibility of a crisis. Analysts will do well to treat all major system transitions as a crisis, even the beneficial ones, because they all entail a new perspective and a new way of being successful.

Benefits

The Corporate Strategy Board (2000) found that "identifying discontinuous change" was one of the five most important skills their member analysts needed to be successful in their positions. Furthermore, this skill was one of three that entry-level analysts did not bring from their educational training into the workplace.

Analysts need to be on the lookout for discontinuous change more than anyone else in the organization. It is a tough position to maintain because most of the crises they forecast will not occur, or will be averted before they occur. The analyst's credibility therefore rests on the support for the alert, not on whether the crisis actually develops. It is easy to see the signs of crisis in hindsight as well as the reasons that those signs are generally ignored.

Example

Much is written about major discontinuities after the fact, particularly about the signs that preceded the events. Nevertheless, these disruptions were a surprise to most people. For example, the Soviet Union had been the Western world's archenemy for so long that US intelligence agencies could not believe that its internal reforms in the late 1980s were anything but a ruse to lull the United States into complacency. And, perhaps more importantly, the intel agencies and the US military were reluctant to admit the defeat of their longstanding foe, because they did not know what their role would be after that.

Another example is the Arpanet (predecessor to the Internet), created in 1969. Thanks to Arpanet, email was common in scientific and academic circles by the 1980s. Therefore, why did it take so long for two of the world's leading businessmen (Bill Gates in 1995 and Jack Welch in 1998) to recognize the discontinuity represented by the Internet? The simple answers are (a) Gates already owned the desktop (his goal) and didn't want to relinquish that territory, and (b) Welch said he didn't want to learn to type!

One last example involves the dot-com bubble in the 1990s. Many, if not most, people thought the run-up of tech stocks with no profits was unsustainable, but they told themselves that perhaps the "new economy" talk was actually true and a radically new level of productivity was driving the stock prices. They also didn't want to get out too early and miss the last phase of the boom.

Further reading

Corporate Strategy Board. (2000). *State of the Union: 2000 Member Survey*. Washington, DC: Corporate Strategy Board.

Keeling, C.D. and Whorf, T.P. (1998). *Atmospheric CO2 Concentrations (Ppmv) Derived from in situ Air Samples Collected at Mauna Loa Observatory, Hawaii*. San Diego CA: Scripps Institute of Oceanography. See http://Cdiac.Esd.Ornl.Gov/Trends/Co2/Contents.Htm.

Neftel, A. et al. (1994). *Historical CO2 Record from the Siple Station Ice Core*. University of Bern, Switzerland, Physics Institute. See http://Cdiac.Esd.Ornl.Gov/Trends/Co2/Contents.Htm.

Ophart, C. (2003). "Evidence for Global Warming." *Virtual Chembook*. Elmhurst, IL: Elmhurst College. Viewed May 2005, http://Chemistry.Beloit.Edu/Warming/Pdf/Vostok.Pdf.

The National Commission on Terrorist Attacks on the United States. (2004). *The 9-11 Commission Report*. Washington, DC: Government Printing Office. Viewed May 2005, www.9-11commission.gov/report/911Report_Ch1.htm.

6.3.5 Choose Indicators That Are Easy to Understand and Collect

"Once the different scenarios have been fleshed out and their implications for the focal issue determined, then it's worth spending time and imagination on identifying a few indicators to monitor in an ongoing way." (Schwartz, 2001: 246 - 247)

Leading indicators are observable quantities or events that indicate whether the future is moving in one direction or another. But monitoring leading indicators is not a central task in most organizations. Therefore a monitoring program needs to be simple and easy to maintain. In fact, the best monitoring program uses indicators that are obvious, or at least so easy to understand and collect that it is obvious what is occurring as soon as the data appears. Otherwise the activity might be judged superfluous and will not—and should not—be continued.

The term "leading indicators" comes from economics, which monitors dozens of economic statistics to forecast the short-term (six- to ten-month) future of the economy. Economists use leading indicators the same way that foresight analysts do, but in the narrower context of monitoring basic, implicit scenarios: whether the economy will continue on its present course or not. Foresight analysts use leading indicators to monitor the occurrence of any alternative future, economic or otherwise.

Key steps

The first question is, "How will the organization know when one or another alternative is actually happening?" In other words, "What would happen first, second, and third were this alternative to actually unfold?" The answers are the raw material for leading indicators.

Leading indicators come in two types: *events* and *variables*. Events are discrete occurrences, the stuff of headlines and news items. Elections, legislation and court cases are political events. Announcements of breakthroughs are scientific or technological events. New products or services are economic events, and so on. Variables, on the other hand, are continuous quantities that vary over time, the stuff of trends and long-term changes. Population size and birthrate are demographic variables; economic growth and trade deficits are economic variables.

Events either happen or they don't—pretty simple. But variables can act in a number of ways. Variables that have been constant over the recent past can begin to change. Variables that have been changing over the recent past can level off and become constant, or their rate of change can change (speeding up or slowing down). And even more dramatically, variables that have been changing in one direction can reverse and start changing in a different direction. Any one of those movements could be an indicator that one or another scenario is developing.

The next step after identifying the events and variables is to identify where the information about the events and variables will come from. Events are reported in some sort of media outlet (broadcast, print, Web, etc.). If the event is important, it will appear in the daily news, but some type of clipping service might be required for more obscure events.

Variables appear differently. Sometimes a report about the change in a variable will appear in the media, but these reports are unreliable because studies may go unreported or the news reports do not contain the exact values of the variable. Instead, one must go to the source of the variables—either government outlets or proprietary services. The latter can be expensive, but if it is important to know the future as soon as possible, the cost of the information is small compared to the financial consequences of not knowing the future soon enough.

The final step is to establish a regular monitoring program with defined responsibilities, such as who is responsible for monitoring each event or variable; the source of the information for each; how the information will be stored; and to whom will the information be reported?

Benefits

Getting an early warning about which alternatives are actually emerging can be extremely valuable, since they can point to the emergence of one or another scenario and allow decisions to be affirmed or revised depending on how the future is developing. Leading indicators, carefully chosen after the formation of alternative futures, are the means to monitor the future as it comes more clearly into view.

Another advantage of a leading indicators program is that it can focus data collection on the few indicators that are important for the development of one or another alternative. Monitoring leading indicators leverages the value of the scenarios by keeping them alive within the organization's strategic conversations and by providing the earliest possible information on how to influence the future in a timely fashion.

Example

Leading indicators were used in a study for a government agency on the long-term (30-year) impact of new technologies. The analysis team wrote nine scenarios based on technologies that they believed would significantly change the agency's operations in the future. Backcasting from those scenarios, the team identified three to eight scientific, technological, political, or commercial events (leading indicators) for each scenario that would indicate that the technology was developing faster than trends would indicate. The team then made recommendations on what the organization should do if and when any of these events occurred. The recommendations ranged from increased frequency of monitoring to full-scale deployment of the new technology.

Further reading

Coates, J.F., Coates, V., Jarratt, J., and Heinz, L. (1986). *Issues Management: How You Can Plan, Manage for the Future.* Bethesda, MD: Lomond Publications.

Schwartz, P. (1991). *The Art of the Long View.* New York: Currency Doubleday.

6.4 Institutionalize Strategic Thinking

6.4.1 Choose, Design, and Make Explicit a Conceptual Framework

Conceptual frameworks define terms, relationships, and a rationale for systems or processes. These assumptions also define the structure and process of the planning system. A well-developed and articulated framework provides a coherent structure and logic for aligning the elements of a planning process. Any organization that cannot quickly and clearly explain how and why its planning process works needs to assess its basic framework. New organizations in particular would do well to start off by defining an explicit planning framework.

Key steps

Most organizations have either an articulated planning process or an informal one. Rarely, they have none at all. Begin by articulating the planning framework as it currently exists. Review planning documents and the "calendar of events," and talk with any units or individuals officially tasked with planning. Identify the number and type of management meetings that occur and help determine where the locus of decision-making resides for various issues.

Once the existing process is delineated, the next step for an articulated planning process is to compare it with the literature and make appropriate recommendations for change. For an informal one, make it formal by writing it down and then following the same procedure for the articulated process. In the case of no planning at all, it is best to do the necessary research, recommend a process, and then do the comparison suggested for articulated processes.

The second step is to conduct research. The point is to identify and become familiar with different planning frameworks, such as those of Collins and Porras (2002) and Kaplan and Norton (2000). This allows the analyst to find a framework that best fits the organization, rather than trying to fit the organization into a particular framework.

The third step is to determine how closely the organization's current approach aligns with established frameworks. If the current approach resembles an established framework, then the analyst should modify it to take account of a variety of internal characteristics, including organizational structure, decision-making customs, existing plans, and day-to-day operations.

Benefits

The main benefit of making a conceptual framework explicit is effectiveness. Making something explicit allows its assumptions to be tested and improved upon. When organizations fail to make important processes such as planning explicit, decision-makers and staff will have a variety of interpretations of what is important and what needs to be done.

It is also difficult to bring order and consistency to decision-making itself when there is no explicit framework for planning.

An explicit and coherent planning framework improves the organization's ability to align staff actions with organizational priorities and provide an appropriate system of compensation and incentives. Everyone knows what the goals are, what methods for achieving the goals are acceptable, and why they are being pursued. It is simply easier to consistently communicate something that is written down and well-thought-out than something that remains tacit.

That said, a smaller literature (Mintzberg, 1994) suggests that formal planning is not only useless, but might be harmful because it takes time away from actually learning what the truly effective strategies are. The main antidote to this claim is to be wary of making the planning process something that becomes an end in itself, rather than a means to an end. The planning process is a tool for better understanding, not a set of forms to be filled out or a list of boxes to be checked. If it starts to feel like the latter, reassess the conceptual framework.

Example

A healthcare organization with a successful history as a relatively small company experienced a period of fairly rapid growth, and was quickly seen by its competitors as the new 800-pound gorilla. The organization outgrew many of its internal processes, systems, and customs. Corporate planning was one of the organizational processes that showed its age, requiring considerable amounts of time to produce plans that were seldom read or used.

This explicit process fell by the wayside, until it became clear that the organization once again needed a formal planning process. The planning unit eventually adopted the Balanced Scorecard from Kaplan and Norton. Over the course of a couple of years, the terminology and construct of the new framework became well-known and accepted. A key measure of the success of the effort was the commentary by management that for the first time in a long time, official planning-related meetings (now quarterly rather than annual) were productive and informative. Senior managers were enlisted to lead and take ownership of these meetings, and their interest and involvement in the progress towards the company's goals was key to the process' success, as well as a key indicator of its success.

Further reading

Ackoff, R.L. (1999). *Recreating the Corporation: A Design of Organizations for the 21st Century*. Oxford, UK: Oxford University Press.

Collins, J. and Porras, J. (2002). *Built to Last: Successful Habits of Visionary Companies*. New York: Harperbusiness Essentials.

Kaplan, R. and Norton, D. (2000). *The Strategy-Focused Organization: How Balanced Scorecard Companies Thrive in the New Business Environment*. Cambridge, MA: Harvard Business School.

Mintzberg, H. (1994). *The Rise and Fall of Strategic Planning*. New York: Free Press.

6.4.2 Develop Future Cadence

Future cadence refers to a balanced, rhythmic flow in studying the future. It applies both to the analyst and the organization. For the analyst, studying trends and issues on a regular basis is a way to develop a gut feel for how the future is unfolding and changing. Regular study develops a discipline of understanding change, which over time fosters an intuitive sense for how the environment is changing. Beyond the individual, persuading organizations to pay attention to the future on a regular basis will help them build a culture that is more attuned to change. Establishing a foresight system will likely be more successful after doing a strategic foresight activity that has turned out well for the organization, as it will be more inclined to follow the analyst's advice after experiencing success firsthand.

Key steps

While scanning for trends and issues is part of daily practice, analysts can also benefit from setting aside time on a weekly basis to reflect on insights garnered during the week. Setting aside a regular time will establish a discipline to ensure that this important activity does not get lost in the daily shuffle. This dedicated time can be used to incorporate the results of studying trends and issues into a framework (see *Guideline 2.3.1 Scan the Environment for Awareness of How the Context Is Changing*). An upfront time investment is required to build this framework, but once it is established, the ongoing study serves to reinforce and enhance the mental model of the analyst. Eventually, the framework will be incorporated into the mental model, and lead to the intuitive sense of change that analysts develop over time.

While it is unnecessary, and can be counterproductive, to seek to make clients into foresight professionals (as *Guideline 1.2.3 Don't Try to Make Clients into Foresight Professionals* advises), encouraging the organization to pay regular attention to the future is valuable. Its study of the future need not be as deep as that of the foresight analyst, but some form of attention is useful in building a culture more comfortable with change. It could take the form of a monthly trends brown-bag luncheon, or some other mechanism for keeping the future alive between focused strategic-foresight activities.

The cadence or regularity of this study is important. Periodic explorations of the future followed by distractions elsewhere will not accumulate the knowledge and wisdom that regular study produces. An on-again, off-again approach creates a situation of continually getting-up-to-speed and relearning—increasing the organization's risk of being blindsided by unexpected events, a contingency that is avoided with regular study.

Benefits

Studying the future on a regular basis develops a robust mental model and intuition—valuable assets for the foresight analyst. These will come in handy during projects or conversations with the organization, when a problem or issue emerges and the analyst has a strong mental model or intuition to draw upon. Analysts will grow increasingly confident about their ability to think on their feet and handle situations that confound the less-experienced.

Similarly, the organization will develop increased confidence to deal with the future, as it studies trends and issues on a regular basis. Developments that once inspired fear or confusion will be met with a calm sense of understanding and an ability to respond positively.

Experienced foresight analysts commonly report developing an intuitive feel for dealing with the future as they gain experience from extended study. One of the somewhat unfortunate byproducts of this intuition is that, if it is not accompanied by "showing your work," the organization may have difficulty following along. It can also lead to a perception that foresight is some sort of wizardry rather than based on sound methodology. Methods too can become second nature, to the extent that they may be obscure to the client. It is important, therefore, for analysts to support their intuition by outlining to the organization how their conclusions were reached and provide the supporting methodology and data.

Example

Kees van der Heijden (2002) emphasizes how important intuition is to "get to scenarios that truly challenge the mindsets of the decision-makers." Collyns and Tibbs (1998) recount the extraordinary intuition of the great scenario planner Pierre Wack, who actively cultivated this faculty throughout his career. Wack had been strongly influenced during his teen years by the philosopher Georges Gurdjieff, one of the 20th century's preeminent mystics and spiritual teachers. Wack participated in a variety of rigorous, demanding spiritual exercises, including practice in "seeing the future" as clairvoyants do. This immersion enabled him to complement his own highly rational, logical style of thinking with an expanded sense of perception. The hallmark of his approach to scenarios was a unique blend of deep perception and intellectual rigor. Wack later explained that scenario work was his special personal challenge of perception and mental acuity.

Further reading

Collyns, N. and Tibbs, H. (1998). In Memory of Pierre Wack. *Global Business Network News, 9* (1), 2 - 10.

Hines, A. (2000, October). Where Do Your Trends Come From? *foresight: the journal of futures studies, strategic thinking, and policy, 2* (5).

Senge, P., Scharmer, C.O., Jaworski, J., and Flowers, B.S. (2005). *Presence: An Exploration of Profound Change in People, Organizations, and Society*. New York: Currency.

Van der Heijden, K. et al. (2002). *The Sixth Sense: Accelerating Organizational Learning with Scenarios*. New York: Wiley.

6.4.3 Repeat Strategic Foresight Activities on a Regular Basis

While many strategic foresight activities are one-off, the quality of the process and outcomes—and the value-add—will grow when they are conducted more regularly. However, this repetition should not turn them into mechanical exercises, since the basis of an activity is to deal creatively with uncertain developments and events, and creativity is not a mechanical skill.

Key steps

An analyst challenged to move beyond a single strategy has two major concerns to deal with. On the one hand, every activity has to be sufficiently unique to attract participants and to challenge them by placing them in a non-routine setting. On the other hand, repetition of activities may lead to a more experienced approach. In the most ideal situation an analyst is asked to design a repetitive process. More often, foresight activities are repeated for contingent reasons—mostly because an earlier approach was a success. In that case, analysts need to study carefully why the earlier activity was a success. Furthermore, during the design and implementation of any activity, it is important that the analyst keep track of its evolution—perhaps through a personal journal—so the details of the experience will be available for later activities.

Benefits

There are three important reasons why foresight activities need to be repeated. First, like any skill, thinking about the future is something one has to learn, both individually and in group settings. Especially in a group learning process, it is very unlikely that the first activity will be flawless. Thus it is important to underscore the possibilities for improvement at the end of a process.

Second, repetition teaches the analyst to recognize earlier in the process which variables and trends are to be watched or worked out. Although one has to remain vigilant for new or unexpected variables, experience shows which variables are undoubtedly to be included—and this also allows more sophisticated kinds of preparation.

Third, the value of a strategic claim is time-bound. External and internal events and trends will impact the ideas explored in an activity. As a consequence, merely updating an earlier strategy is rarely effective, as if there were flaws in yesterday's strategy that could be repaired with today's knowledge. A strategy is not a bicycle tire that can be patched. Every strategy reflects the strategic balance of the moment of its creation. Evolution and time will necessitate new strategies, which can only be developed through new foresight activities.

Although repetition is needed, foresight should never become a mechanical activity. Each activity should bring sufficient surprise in its architecture to trigger creative thinking. In practice, foresight activities are often standalone. Practitioners will find it much harder to arrange the right setting more than once than to avoid structural repetition. Since people and issues change, strategic activities are likely to be different anyway.

Example

Several approaches have benefited from repetition over time. The first and most important example is undoubtedly Shell's experience and the many generations of scenario methods that have flowed from it and been applied in boardrooms around the world. Another example can be found in the UK's technology foresight programs, which have evolved through three generations to meet changing requirements and growing experience (Miles and Keenan, 2003).

In May 1993 the UK government launched the Technology Foresight Program to foster closer interaction among scientists, industry, and government through a program to identify future opportunities and threats for science, technology, and engineering. Three rounds of foresight studies were launched, each lasting three to five years. The first two took slightly different approaches to identifying likely social, economic, and market trends over a future timeframe of one to two decades, and the developments in science, engineering, technology, and infrastructure that would be required to best address these future needs. The third reviewed the first two and shifted the program to refocus on science and technology. In this round, the analysts sought to be more flexible to take account of emerging developments and to focus resources more clearly on where they could add the most value. Instead of the longer three- to five-year study period, a more fluid, rolling program of projects was established in 2002 in order to target emerging issues more quickly. This program has become well-regarded as an excellent example of government foresight.

Further reading

Miles, I. and Keenan, M. (2003). Two and a Half Cycles of Foresight in the UK. Technikfolgenabschätzung: Theorie und Praxis. *ITAS Journal on Technology Assessment, 12* (2), 41 - 49.

The Previous Foresight Rounds: A Brief History. (n.d.). *Foresight: Making the Future Work for You*. Viewed August 2005, www.foresight.gov.uk.

Van der Heijden, K. (1996). *Scenarios: The Art of Strategic Conservation*. New York: Wiley.

6.4.4 Develop Training Programs to Institutionalize Strategic Foresight

Unfortunately, simply performing a successful strategic foresight activity is rarely enough to inspire an organization to embrace foresight. The analyst needs to follow up on activities with dedicated training programs and other efforts to instill strategic thinking and foresight into the organization's culture. Proposing a foresight training immediately after a successful activity is a good idea. In fact, if several projects are successful the organization is likely to ask for training. Nothing inspires interest in new ways of doing things like successful results. It will also strengthen the training if examples are drawn from the organization's own practical experience.

Key steps

A common mistake is to seek to educate first, then do project work. While education is a sensible and even noble goal, new training programs tend to be met with skepticism. People in today's lean organizations are time-pressed and reluctant to dedicate time to any activity unless it can clearly be shown to benefit their personal bottom line.

Prepare for such requests in advance. Have the program developed, or at least outlined, in order to be ready when the opportunity arises. If the program is not ready, interest may fade or someone else will be asked to do it—even if they are less qualified. And if this happens, it could lead to a case where someone else introduces approaches or tools that run counter to best practices, thus creating the potential for damaging the credibility of foresight or creating confusion about the best ways to do it.

During a foresight activity, begin sketching out ideas on how to teach others to do it. Keep notes during project work and observe what works and what doesn't. Debriefing and making these notes after each activity is a good practice.

An interesting dilemma in thinking through the purposes of a training program is whether it should be designed to teach others how to do the work themselves, or should simply train them to apply foresight in their daily work. In most cases, opportunities for many people in the organization to become foresight analysts themselves are limited. But opportunities to apply the principles behind strategic foresight are abundant. Thus, the recommendation of this guideline is to focus the training program on teaching the organization when to use strategic foresight and how to apply it, and to teach the underlying principles in ways that can be useful in daily practice.

When developing the program, illustrate the ideas with real-life examples from work with the organization, wherever possible. This establishes credibility. Bringing in outside examples also helps. Organizations often recognize their own tendencies to become inbred, and analysts can boost their own credibility by showing how other organizations have successfully applied the principles and tools being taught. Also show examples of failure: in organizations, fear is often a greater motivator than success.

The training program itself should follow standard best practices for designing learning experiences, such as employing multiple learning styles. It is particularly important in teaching strategic foresight to have participants work with the ideas themselves as much as possible. Since strategic foresight is highly conceptual and often abstract, it can be easy to get overly theoretical and lose sight of the practical. Look for opportunities to quickly demonstrate how to apply the ideas in practice. Design lots of exercises and activities. It is also an excellent idea, where practical, to have the participants bring a real-life work problem with them to work on as an example throughout the training.

Benefits

Developing training programs is a key step in institutionalizing strategic foresight in the organizations you work with. Project work is valuable, but typically will not be enough to influence and ultimately change the culture. Training programs instill the principles in the organization and build a wider audience, in essence creating a positive feedback loop, where successful projects generate demand for training which in turn generates demand for more projects. Eventually, critical mass builds such that strategic foresight becomes a routine process and is embedded in key work processes throughout the organization.

Example

An analyst at a Fortune 500 company described how his initial work in strategic foresight inspired demand for two different kinds of training. The first centered on teaching participants how to be more creative and innovative in their work. He developed a day-long training course that provided an overview of key concepts and tools, and also introduced an external trainer who provided instruction in a specific technique. Later in his work, demand emerged for a more practical, "how-to" workshop aimed at applying the practices of strategic foresight to new business development. This led him to create a two-day workshop which became a standard part of the training curriculum for new business development. In both cases, the training was requested as a result of word-of-mouth that the techniques provided useful results in the day-to-day work of employees.

Further reading

Hamel, G. (2001, April 2). Inside the Revolution: Innovation's New Math. *Fortune*.

Hines, A., Kelly, K., and Noesen, S. (2001, Fall). Viral Futures at Dow. *Futures Research Quarterly*.

Senge, P.M. (1990). *The Fifth Discipline: The Art and Practice of the Learning Organization*. London: Random House.

6.4.5 Reinforce that Learning Is the Best Approach for Organizations in Complex and Unpredictable Environments

Alongside the specific tasks and goals of a strategic foresight activity is the long-term goal of promoting learning and helping the organization to become a learning organization. Learning organizations, according to Peter Senge, are "organizations where people continually expand their capacity to create the results they truly desire, where new and expansive patterns of thinking are nurtured, where collective aspiration is set free, and where people are continually learning to see the whole together." Incorporating opportunities for learning not only improves the prospects for the task at hand, but stimulates interest in learning and foresight.

Key steps

The design of an activity should incorporate opportunities for learning, such as interviews, workshops, and frequent feedback and review sessions. The analyst should aim for an iterative relationship with the organization, continually sharing information back and forth, thus stimulating interest in the learning from the activity as well as in the activity itself.

Senge et al. describe five disciplines of organizational learning in *the Dance of Change* (1991, 32). The first, *personal mastery*, involves formulating a coherent picture of the results people most desire to gain as individuals (their personal vision), alongside a realistic assessment of the current state of their lives today (their current reality). Learning to cultivate the tension between vision and reality (represented by the icon of a rubber band) can expand people's capacity to make better choices, and to achieve more of the results that they have chosen.

The second, *mental models*, is the discipline of reflection and inquiry. Skills are focused on developing awareness of the attitudes and perceptions that influence thought and interaction. By continually reflecting upon, talking about, and reconsidering these internal pictures of the world, people can gain more capability in governing their actions and decisions. The icon here portrays one of the more powerful principles of this discipline, the "ladder of inference"—depicting how people leap instantly to counterproductive conclusions and assumptions.

The third discipline, *shared vision*, establishes a focus on mutual purpose. People learn to nourish a sense of commitment in a group or organization by developing shared images of the future they seek to create (symbolized by the eye), and the principles and guiding practices by which they hope to get there.

The fourth discipline, *team learning*, is about group interaction. Through techniques like dialogue and skillful discussion, teams transform their collective thinking, learning to mobilize their energies and abilities to achieve results greater than the sum of the individual members' talents. The icon symbolizes the natural alignment of a learning-oriented team as a flock of birds in flight.

In the fifth, *systems thinking*, people learn to better understand interdependency and change, and thereby to deal more effectively with the forces that shape the consequences of our actions.

Throughout any foresight activity, the analyst should continually search for ways to promote the value of strategic foresight as a tool for learning about how the world outside the organization is changing, and how that will in turn influence what happens inside.

Benefits

Management guru Donald Schon (1973) notes, "The loss of the stable state means that our society and all of its institutions are in *continuous* processes of transformation. We cannot expect new stable states that will endure for our own lifetimes. We must learn to understand, guide, influence, and manage these transformations. We must make the capacity for undertaking them integral to ourselves and to our institutions. We must, in other words, become adept at learning. We must become able not only to transform our institutions, in response to changing situations and requirements; we must invent and develop institutions which are 'learning systems,' that is to say, systems capable of bringing about their own continuing transformation."

Example

Hanover Insurance was widely regarded as a paramount example of a learning organization. Between 1969 and 1991, when Bill O'Brien was vice president of marketing and then CEO, Hanover went from the bottom of the property and liability insurance business to the top quartile. Senge (1994) described O'Brien's work as "the most dramatic, sustained corporate renewal I know of." O'Brien himself spoke of a twenty-two year transformational journey and was proud that "our people had an opportunity to learn and mature." He focused his attention first and foremost on helping people grow, and sought to support and foster that growth.

Further reading

De Geus, A. (1988). Planning as Learning. *Harvard Business Review 66*(2), 70 - 74.

O'Brien, W.J. *Character and the Corporation*. (2002). Review by Adam Kahane. Cambridge, MA: Society for Organizational Learning.

Schon, D.A. (1973). *Beyond the Stable State: Public and Private Learning in a Changing Society*. Harmondsworth: Penguin.

Senge, P., Kleiner, A., Roberts, C., Ross, R., and Smith, B. (1994). *The Fifth Discipline Fieldbook*. New York: Currency Doubleday.

Senge, P., Roberts, C., Ross, R., Roth, G., Smith, B., and Kleiner, A. (1999). *The Dance of Change: The Challenges of Sustaining Momentum in Learning Organizations*. New York: Currency Doubleday.

6.4.6 Shift Attitudes towards Receptiveness to Change

George Bernard Shaw said, "You see things and say 'Why?' But I dream things that never were and I say 'Why not?'"

It is important to cultivate receptiveness to the new: "Let's try and understand this better." The new disturbs existing comfort zones and positions and as a consequence is often dismissed or challenged—it just does not fit with the established order. It is important to recognize this behavior and to educate the organization on its potential consequences, and to give specific ideas for better ways to deal with the new and surprising. In an organization this requires some investment in thinking. If the organization is in a hurry to get results, encourage it to invest twice as much—this is the wisest investment it can make.

Key steps

Executives who have grown up in one kind of organization or in one industry are often firmly invested in their opinions. Eventually many of their views become hard-wired into the organization as conventional wisdom. The more firmly invested in these views an organization is, the harder it is for the analyst to help it let go and explore new ideas.

A simple starting point and approach is to gain agreement that it is important to the organization to improve its receptivity to the new. Model the causes and consequences of behavioral differences towards new information and ideas.

Next, research and understand the key areas where the organization is concerned with the new. These might be about industry growth or decline, as an example of areas where blinders are the most expensive to the organization.

Armed with this knowledge, create a few workshops specifically about highlighting the meaning of the program and the methods to get to some change—focusing on the behavior and the selected content elements. If possible, connect this goal into a leadership development program or other similar programs. Push participants to "lead by example," and model it yourself.

Be sure to connect the behavior-oriented push to a programmatic approach to foresight. Make a concerted effort to show the value. Measure the impacts of these programs through employee interviews, such as a 360-degree assessment specifically on how the key areas of the business are being improved by this.

Benefits

Encouraging receptiveness to the new is a good practice in general, but will likely "stick" better in an organization when change is imminent or taking place. Many organizations recognize the value of strategic programs, which aim to sensitize their people and approaches to the shifts in markets and industries and to better understand the meaning of those shifts. In periods of growth, organizations may try to build innovation programs, strategic foresight programs, or ideation programs, or at minimum try scenario planning. Often the early attempts are sub-optimal in that they lack a programmatic follow-through activity, and thus fall short of the broad impact they could have.

Also, many organizations have established some means to track trends in their environment. If these rely on classical market-research methods alone, the foresight generated tends to be a linear extrapolation of today's impacts—and hence will most likely miss the opportunities and risks that a strategic foresight program would be able to identify.

'e

ane (2002) tells a remarkable story of transformation in Guatemala. The country has the dubious distinc-
g had one of the longest-running and most brutal civil wars in Latin America, from 1992 - 1996. More than

out the Future

200,000 people were killed or "disappeared." After a truce, the Vision Guatemala project was formed to help vision a new future for the country. A team of forty-four—including political leaders, academics, business and community leaders, former guerillas and military officers, government officials, human rights activists, journalists, indigenous people, national and local politicians, clergy, trade unionists, and young people—were led through a scenario process by Kahane. The key attraction of the exercise was the process of deep dialogue among people who had previously never spoken with each other. It led to the team enrolling sixty "multipliers," or grassroots leaders, who worked not to disseminate the scenarios but to replicate the dialogue process in local initiatives. This process of dialogue was instrumental in producing the visioning effort's successful results.

Further reading

De Geus, A. (1997). *The Living Company: Habits for Survival in a Turbulent Business Environment*. Cambridge, MA: Harvard Business School Press.

Kahane, A. (2002). *Changing the World by How We Talk and Listen*. Unpublished manuscript. Beverly, MA: Generon Consulting.

Kleiner, A. (1996). *The Age of Heretics*. New York: Currency Doubleday.

Marsh, N., McAllum, M., and Purcell, D. (2002). *Strategic Foresight: The Power of Standing in the Future*. Melbourne: Crown Content.

Ohmae, K. (1982). *The Mind of the Strategist: The Art of Japanese Business*. New York: McGraw-Hill.

ng   ut the Future

Afterword

This book is for the analyst seeking guidance on strategic foresight. It not intended to "convert" anyone into becoming a strategic foresight professional. On the other hand, the lure of long-term change can be compelling. Many who get bitten by the foresight bug want to learn more.

A good place to start is the World Future Society (www.wfs.org), a clearinghouse of information about studying the future. The WFS was formed in 1967, publishes a popular magazine (*The Futurist*), a scholarly journal (*Futures Research Quarterly*), and a practically indispensable review of publications relevant to the future (*Future Survey*). The society also runs an annual conference which each summer brings together a wide range of practitioners and others with diverse views about the future. Finally, it hosts a book service that lists most of the futures books now in print.

In 1971, a parallel organization, the World Futures Studies Federation (www.wfsf.org), formed in Europe. The Federation is a more global and academically oriented association for those seeking to delve deeper into the scholarship of foresight. It hosts different thematic conferences at various locations across the globe.

The Association of Professional Futurists (www.profuturists.org) is a smaller, newer community of foresight professionals that comes together for networking and professional development. Readers of this book may be interested in its student or provisional member category for those seeking to become professionals, since it provides an opportunity to learn about foresight within a community of professional practitioners.

Another option for those interested in learning more about strategic foresight is to enroll in one of the handful of dedicated higher-education programs across the globe. In the United States, the University of Houston and the University of Hawaii have longstanding programs dedicated to foresight. The Houston program is a freestanding Master's Degree in Futures Studies aimed at preparing students in professional foresight, and the Hawaii program offers a concentration in Futures within a Master's or Doctorate in Political Science degree. Across the Pacific Ocean, the Australian Foresight Institute at Swinburne Technological University in Melbourne also offers a Master's degree in Strategic Foresight. Several other programs and courses exist in spots across the globe.

Whichever option the analyst pursues, we authors offer our thanks and support, and suspect that our paths will cross some time in the future. We look forward to it.